A Time Traveller' Challenge t

Harnessing the Soul

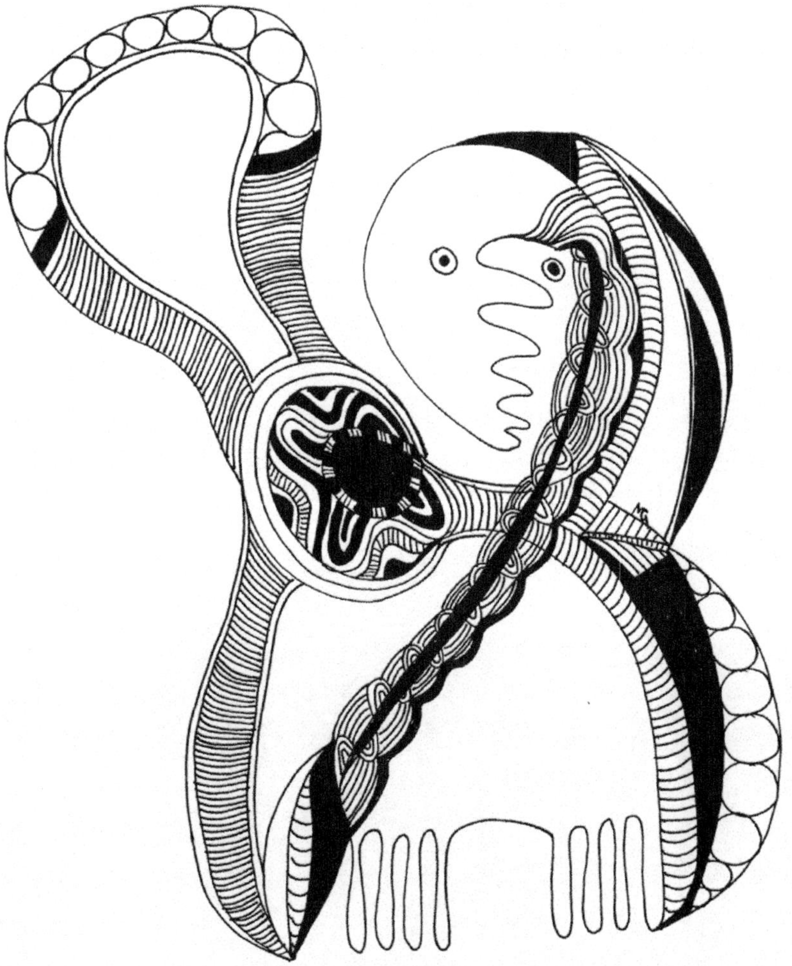

By
MARTINA GRUBMUELLER

Other books by the author:
Syncholistic - Exploring Consciousness

Copyright 2023 ©Martina Grubmueller. All rights reserved. No part of this publication, text or illustrations, may be reproduced, stored in a retrieval system or transmitted, in any form or by any means, without the prior written consent of the publisher or a license from the author.

Illustrations Copyright 2023 ©Martina Grubmueller

In loving memory of Angelika Spranger.

May your travels have been peaceful.

Photography Angelika Spranger

CONTENTS

THE SOLILOQUY OF AN 'I AM' - 5 -

MY NAME IS MG; ETERNAL TRAVELLER (ET012) - 11 -

BITS ABOUT ME - 19 -

CHAPTER I: RELATIONSHIPS & SEXUALNESS - 27 -

PART ONE: The Mirror of Relationships - 27 -
PART TWO: The Value of Relationships - 31 -
PART THREE: A Bridge to Higher Consciousness - 44 -

CHAPTER II: EMBODIMENT & ABUSE - 53 -

PART ONE: Pain Body & Buddy - 53 -
PART TWO: Abuse & Karmic Hairball - 74 -

CHAPTER III: EMOTIONS & SELF-KNOWLEDGE - 89 -

PART ONE: Emotional Purification & Action - 89 -
PART TWO: Clearing & Healing Marbles - 99 -
PART THREE: Emotional Renaissance - 114 -

CHAPTER IV: GROUNDING & MASTERY - 127 -

PART ONE: Sat Nam Presence - 127 -
PART TWO: Mastery – The Work - 139 -

CHAPTER V: LEADERSHIP & TIME - 160 -

PART ONE: I AM Choices & Mediumship - 161 -
PART TWO: Pioneering Leaders in Action - 167 -
THE FOUR C's OF EQUINE LEADERSHIP - 170 -
PART THREE: Time – Social Agreement - 177 -

CHAPTER VI: PURPOSE & AVATAR EMERGENCE - 185 -

PART ONE: Man & His Tools - 185 -
PART TWO: The Avatar Emergence - 191 -

CHAPTER VII: WALK-INS & DREAMTIME - 203 -

PART I: Walk-ins - 203 -
PART TWO: Dreamtime Shenanigans - 209 -

CHAPTER VIII: DRAGON, EARTH - 219 -

PART ONE: Consciousness Explorers - 221 -
PART TWO: Interspecies Collaboration - 232 -
PART THREE: One Look Back, Two Steps Forward - 240 -

THE SOLILOQUY OF AN 'I AM'

A Journey Through Consciousness Evolution

She asks about the journey of the I AM, for she knows it will reveal new states of awareness. It's been a long time of curious seeking, of stumbling over arduous challenges and endless streams of ancient memories along the spirals of creation. Some experimentations lead her astray, whilst others point and direct her towards purity and purpose. She knows coming home to herself is an art she wants to master, a possibility within this lifetime that awaits to be claimed. Divine Source cheers on the cosmic creator as she collects precious gifts during her travels within the earthly realm and beyond. 'Home' is not a hidden place open to a chosen few, but anyone's choice of becoming joyfully embodied and spiritually aware. She awakens her spirit to engage with life in all its glory, discovers the wonders of living in a body, and endeavours to understand her experiences to turn the gained knowledge into her soul's wisdom. Whatever form she takes, she remains a spark of spirit in the eternal now.

"What am I?"

Before 'she' can even ask that question; she is pure boundless light, a luminous intensity about to be married off to matter and start her individualisation journey as a unique soul. This omnipresent lifeforce is an ineffable mind pondering expression, a marvellous idea of an epic adventure seeking to engage and understand the intricacies of consciousness through human qualities that allow for introspection. It is a divine intelligence that employs sacred geometry to construct both macro and microscopic holograms, shapes, and portals, connecting the above with the below. A splendid tree of life, fashioned in the divine image, that reunites soul families and dreamtime societies, awakening the universal dreamer from an eternal slumber.

"Who am I?"

She asks and shall receive. Decisions are made, contracts are drawn up, cells are divided, and the one becomes the many. Then, with a final push, a slap, a breath, a cry, and the severing of the umbilical cord, she enters this world to grow and learn without a clear set of instructions! As a physical being calibrated into time and space, secretly chaperoned by her soul, she perfects her senses to exist within this strange world of duality. She eagerly embraces her destiny, determined to improve her life's quality, whilst her body at times struggles to find its footing. Moved by desire and divinely guided by Source, she throws herself into chaos, promising to bring back memories that log the story of her adventurous travels through all levels of creation, preservation, and destruction.

"How am I?" She wonders and curiously enquires about her state of being.

Where do these restrictions come from that define my world? Countless thoughts are roaming through her mind, keeping her awake, and yet, she feels so dreadfully asleep. Who do they belong to? Why all this conflict, so much pain? Polarised within herself and controlled by her circumstances, she wanders through the halls of ignorance and tacit consent. During rare moments of inner contemplation and self-reflection, she manages to identify less with the world around her and experiences fleeting moments of spiritual inspiration and glimpses of other realms of existence. She fights, loves, laughs, and cries... she learns to play and gets played by her emotions but she keeps going. Her inner fire continues to shine brightly, and she never gives up, never gives in, or ever stands still, even in times of contrast and polarity, revealing her passion and happiness amidst her sorrow and distress.

"When am I?"

She asks for her internal time keeper to appear. He tells her all is well and the time is always 'now' to deal with the feelings and sensations that blur the vision of her true mission.

Occasionally, she experiences moments of grace where she is able to set aside the emotions that pull at her heartstrings, as she tumbles through life, choosing between A and B and slowly learning to ask for C, D or E. Still torn between the social programs and her inner knowingness, she goes off track attending to the wounds of others. Her heart is filled with love and wisdom. She remains committed to helping others, even if it means neglecting her own needs. Her throat reminds her to speak objectively, and to equally honour and balance oppositional forces both earthly and spiritual. The resolution of karma continues, and she begins to rely more on her inner voice, which reassuringly guides her along her path.

"Why am I?" She asks out loud with evident impatience.

Spirit gently nudges her to embrace her truth and enforce her will, and yet, she finds herself repeatedly frustrated as she struggles to recognise her true self. Relentlessly, she perseveres in seeking clarity of purpose and calls out to likeminded companions to join her on the journey of self-discovery. As her internal teacher awakens and her thirst for wisdom and understanding grows, she finds herself drawn in new directions. Gradually, she heals old hurts and hauntings, nurturing the flame of renewal and new beginnings as she moves towards a more boundless and timeless way of being.

"Where am I?"

She asks and the map starts to reveal itself, true transformation begins to happen. As the shadows get less frightening, the reflections turn into joyful contemplation. There is no place to go, no time to waste or gain, no self or other to judge. Home is ancient wisdom now, ready to be taught by the scholars of man's cosmic story. Home is love, pulsating with a harmonious frequency that arises from an innate understanding of one's own authenticity. She now knows that she is in the right place, always has been, and ever will be. Her trinity of eyes well up with tears of recognition of a growing oneness among families of cosmic consciousness explorers. Her heart, bathed in soothing and liberating waves of light, keeps reminding her of why she came to Earth.

"*I am who I am.*"

Standing tall in her vibrant rainbow coat, she repeats her motto, grounded in the wisdom of who she is and has become. A new galactic passport signifies her return to the universal network of divine co-creators, and she joins her fellow galactic travellers as she takes her place on the multidimensional stage as a representative and guide of the 5th world of peace. Her sovereignty blossoms with the self-respect and recognition she earned through blood and sweat, experienced through trial and error, and fortified through commitment to self-love. Duality and polarity are the playgrounds she heeds for reaching this level of self-realisation, and her spiritual perception and multidimensional reception expand to new horizons. Unified with her merging soul, she serves and celebrates with her soul connections in near and distant places.

"*We are.*"

She speaks with conviction, drawing from the depths of her soul's wisdom. As a celestial alchemist, she greets her fellow travellers with gratitude, mutual respect, and honour, recognising their shared cosmic purpose. The archetypal network of group consciousness, both on and off world, has revealed itself to the humble mediator, on her long journey to higher wisdom and heartfelt compassion. Her body has been a trusted instrument of mediation and revelation, and she will treasure its gifts forever, marvelling in the oneness of the self with all selves. She acknowledges her soul's many travels as an essential contribution to the transformation of the universe's fabric before she continues along the Rainbow Bridge she has built on her way to higher evolution. Eventually, she surrenders all her bodies and merges with the One Mind, free from pain or fear and filled with eternal bliss.

"*Who am I?*"

As she struggles to catch her breath in a new and unfamiliar world, she reflects on the endless cycle of existence. From formlessness to various forms, from source connection to disconnection, from unity to division, and back again. The divine circles continue to spiral in and out of spacetime, as spirit progresses in wisdom through the choices of its everchanging soul vehicles. With each lifetime, she refines her travelling consciousness, recollects her extensive past, and her sense of self as she acknowledges the illusory nature of it all. With tremendous gratitude for the gift of this divine magic, she commends all her soul aspects for their contribution during the colourful journeys to the great spirit awakening to ETERNAL LIFE. She now knows in the heart of all her hearts:

A TRUE TIME TRAVELLER ....SHE IS, WAS, AND EVER WILL BE.

My name is MG; Eternal Traveller (ET012)

We are all adventurous, eternal explorers on a journey of self-discovery towards higher purpose, unconditional love, and universal wisdom. Like a windy river making its way back to the ocean, we splash and stumble over and around the rocks on our path from challenge to infinite choice. We are guided by an unseen and mysterious intelligence; its supreme sustenance greater than our conscious minds can yet comprehend. Through the fabric of space-time continuum, our animated spirit brings forth and cultivates unique soul perspectives. Based on our state of mind and the fluctuations in our brainwaves, we travel inter-dimensionally. This can be as simple as reaching a highly relaxed theta state in meditation that creates a greater level of awareness, giving us access to other dimensional data such as visions and visitations by beings from other realms. Our job is to get out of our own way. As we demolish the dams that obstruct free energy flow and dismantle old structures of our conditioned psyche, we liberate a vitality that restores our inherent capacities of fully functioning on multiple planes of existence and supports the unveiling of our divine origins.

"Eternity is in love with the creations of time." - William Blake.

What if we, too, can greatly relish our perennial existence and focus on happily creating with our intuitive genius, whilst inhabiting this remarkable planetary ship that we call home? As we are going through the great dreamtime awakening, we all have an opportunity to gain more conscious awareness on our endless travels through time and space. During both dream and waking states, we simultaneously experience a multitude of infinitely intelligent dimensions, some with life forms and others without. All stages of consciousness are a force in nature that we can safely harness through a focused process of purification, concentration, and meditation.

How much dedication and enthusiasm we put into self-reflection and self- healing will determine the level of our spiritual empowerment and how much of our true celestial potential we can eventually tap into.

We refer to ourselves as Homo sapiens; 'modern and wise man.' Yet, so much wisdom has been, and still is, kept from us. Our embodied species is here to remedy and resolve all dramas and traumas from the past that keeps us endlessly looping around linear and non-linear realities. We are faced with the mammoth task of disentangling from the manipulated narrative and expanding our degree of awakened influence. Resistance to this old operating system is futile. The wise sage knows how to transmute chaos into order and prepares for a new world. He does not succumb to a despairing herd mentality, but instead shines through when leading by example.

Freewill is our birth right in this Milky Way galaxy and we claim our legacy through exercising a multitude of choices. Any respectable scholar of worldly wisdom will agree that this reality we are experiencing appears very real in the here and now, notwithstanding the scientific evidence arriving at its holographic nature. Our job is not to condemn or prove the illusory make up of this reality, but to revel in its infinite possibilities and to perpetually out-create it. We are to circumvent algorithmic predictability and add our individual soul-stamps to eventually move beyond a limited causal reality into full universal awareness. Time travel, itself, is an integral and multifaceted part of our experience that has been witnessed and claimed on many personal accounts throughout history. We are not going to discuss the mechanical ways of time travel here but will exclusively consider travelling through the different layers of consciousness, for the purpose of healing the many levels of our persona and the forging of our multi-dimensionally aware avatars. It is remarkably effortless to abandon our physical vehicles without consciously being aware of it.

In all likelihood, less exciting than operating a time machine out of a science fiction movie, until we have a better and more appreciative grasp on our incarnating soul and body dynamics. Understanding the basics of your travelling consciousness is an essential step towards expanding your awareness and contributing to human power shifts, the global unification and galactic recalibration. Our body is a conscious and sophisticated suit; a full-on spiritual, time travelling technology that is able to self-repair, record and integrate all the experiences from the various worlds you have ever travelled to and lived in. In order to prevent overwhelm, physical discomfort, and spiritual disconnection, it is vital to establish rapport and reconcile with our material and immaterial environment. An overburdened nervous system goes hand in hand with an elusive existence and a lack of soul presence. This may cause attention deficit that impacts our daily interactions and intimate relationships. We've all had conversations with preoccupied and absentminded people – it's like speaking to an automaton body, right?

How much does your soul, truly, inhabit your physical body? And if you are not present in the body, where are you? And how does this affect your life?

In the amateur state of beingness, we are not fully conscious and are less aware of the various ranges of energy exchange. We get triggered by other people's pains and responses and are easily pulled into their agendas. Through a lack of appreciation for our psychic abilities, we pick up on emotional imbalances and take on psychological burdens, as well as give others access to our core energy, ending up depleted and drained ourselves. My time as a natural healer, prior to developing more awareness, affirmed the importance of energy cleanliness. By taking on harmful energies from family, friends, and clients, I experienced emotional and physical distress... and yes, by all means, we can reclaim our power by releasing those energies without causing harm.

The same applies to when we obliviously tune into unhealed wounds of our own soul aspects, or other versions of ourselves that are functioning inside linear time, or in other dimensional realities all-together. Drawing from personal experience, it is crucial for individuals with traits of enablers and martyrs to take personal responsibility in healing their personality. They can greatly benefit from prioritising self-sovereignty before resuming their service to others. The immensity of our soul is vast and split into different shards, of which many require healing and re-integration, dating back to the early days of Lemuria when we did not live as solid physical entities but rather as etheric bodies. As true time travellers, we simultaneously occupy a multitude of time streams to varying degrees of awareness. Until we identify and recover our soul essence in its entirety, we keep looping and reliving dramas and traumas from past and future realities. The more awareness we have around our multi-layered existence, the more accountable to living a well synchronised life we have to become. This is an important part of the I AM fortification process that eventually leads to an unconditional loving understanding and a strong unified vibratory signature. You are in possession of a full arsenal of innate healing skills to harness your potential and this book will serve you to unearth, dust and polish them, as some of us are already experiencing a merging of the realms and are willing to lift the veil to take a peek into their multidimensional existence.

Did you know that when you remember emotionally-polarised events in the past or the future, more often than not, you abandon your body?

Whilst putting up the Christmas tree one year, I found myself contemplating my days back in Austria in the first flat that I shared with my older sister, after my parents had asked me to leave home. We had a disastrous Christmas where the roof above the flat burnt down and we had to move out until it was restored. Some of the blue baubles that I was decorating the tree with were dating back to around that time.

My mind started to wander and within a split second, I found myself entangled with the challenges from thirty years ago. Charged memories are crafty... hiding in the background, eager to leap forward when least expected. This kind of emotional recall is a form of bilocation, which is a component of consciousness time travel. The Christmas decoration triggered old, unresolved pain and created an emotional response. The use of the word 'travel' is almost misleading, as all our memories are overlayed on top of each other – simultaneously and instantly available, without us having to physically revisit past or future events. It's quite possible that some of my soul's fractals were still energetically frozen in the old timeframe, or perhaps I picked up on the sadness of any family members or friends that I shared my life with then and had since left behind. Precious moments like these can serve as a strong catalyst for change. Don't give into the need for external validation, as it can hinder the healing process and lead you astray from the magic at hand. At that moment in front of the tree, I chose to trust the impulse and clear the emotional layer, welcoming the trigger as an opportunity to manifest more presence into my life. Do you see how healing through time travel can be that simple?

Consciousness manifests dually and singularly, both through us and because of us. The perception of both states of being is in our mental and experiential grasp as we learn to think inclusively and suspend all indoctrinated separation. Human beings play a significant and transformational role as implicate and explicate observers, perceivers and conceptual thinkers in service to the evolution of consciousness. The essence of spirit is expressed through the self-sustained act of reflective thinking, our capacity to cognise, remember, and heal our personal experiences across time and space. As natural receivers of cosmic energy, we conduct and transduce energy to our fellow man, the other three kingdoms, and our planet Earth itself. Our bodies are highly developed grounding instruments, thus playing an essential role in the interconnected web of life.

Every one of our atoms possesses an innate intelligence that has a discriminative quality, a selective power and ability to repel and attract. As a species we experience, enjoy, or suffer as a result of our formed inner landscape of beliefs when interpreting and defining these inflowing energies.

Next time you drive your car, cycle or take a walk, instead of focusing on your destination, perceive yourself being still and allow everything that you encounter to move through you without leaving a trace behind. Get a sense of what being a conduit feels like with a safe practice. By doing so, you can begin to comprehend the astral realms and understand your proficiency as a sacred, neutral, channel of energy. All adaptations of the material world involve some form of energetic transmutation and constructions. Time and space travel is how we create and perceive as human beings. To facilitate this process, ensure that your mind is sufficiently clear and receptive, and pay attention to how such interaction influences you and what lessons you can draw from the experience.

Heightened states of awareness allow us to see and feel the many layers of the seen and unseen spiritual realms that interact with us to a considerably greater extent than what is commonly acknowledged. We would all have easy, unlimited access to divine universal wisdom if we were not empowering the forced belief system that creates convoluted, labyrinthine webs of harmful entanglement. In essence, the power of time travel through consciousness lies in our ability to retrieve and disentangle from these webs, heal the wounds of the past so we can understand the present, and create a better future for ourselves and others. Through conscious time travel, we can instantly experience time in all of its diverse colours and frequencies within and outside the shared collective reality rules. An expanded understanding of the nature of time and reality opens up a multifaceted playground for humanity to explore. As we begin to piece together a more comprehensive version of history and the evolution of man, we gain a greater appreciation for the unlimited domain of truth.

The influence of a time traveller's entangled observation extends far beyond the confines of our physical reality and affects our story on all levels of existence. The repercussions of quantum entanglements pierce through the holographic veils. As a result of a conditioned mind that has forgotten its spiritual origin and its multidimensional influence, we consider ourselves at the mercy of a limited physical and perishable body. The goal for this life is the realisation that our form may not be permanent, but yet infinitely evolving. With that said, we are to joyfully master every moment and exercise our freewill cautiously, responsibly, without wasting life's invitation to euphorically create. A human mind that is clear places importance on maintaining an active and healthy body and understands its role in the cosmic order.

This may seem like a big undertaking and responsibility because it is. Step one is to acknowledge our shortcomings and entertain the idea of restoring ourselves physically, mentally, and emotionally through the synthesis of our fragmented soul and the unifications of timelines. The next step is to assess, review, and evaluate our current state of being in order to take appropriate action towards gradual transformation into wholeness. Step three involves appreciating that there are no hard or fast rules to achieve self-realisation, and it's best to begin by seeking freedom from the need to control outcomes. Adaptability, flexibility, and a good sense of humour serve us well, as we continue to shatter the old ways and roll with the punches. Freedom from control does not mean lacking control, but to consciously apply our steady energy towards a focused intention, with the aim for higher expansion. Accessing and healing our memories in the DNA, along with learning how to function on multiple frequencies, will assist us in rebuilding our body and in turn, expand our spectrum of experiences. Our choices open doors to the unlimited point of view but just as easily, if we should abuse them as a means to an end, can lead to us wallowing in opposition and resistance.

The art of choosing is not forcing or controlling a universal match, but continuously offsetting conflicting tendencies, leading to a more coherent personal ambition. The more joy and practice we put behind our choices, the greater the impact they will have.

Try on the following three values that I like to summarise as the PAW.

P for PERSEVERANCE: Be tenaciously dedicated in making choices without pre-emptying the probabilities by concluding a specific outcome and keep choosing. Choice does not give up.

A for ALLOWANCE: Everyone's experience is valid, and so is every choice. If we make choices from a place of true allowance, they will give rise to new levels of understanding irrespective of the outcome. We are here to transcend the 'rights and wrongs' of this world. Choice does not judge.

W for WONDER: Remain curious and full of wonderment as choices often have a mind of their own. Trust that they intrinsically carry a willingness to be of service to your divinely purposeful unfolding. Choice does not control.

Failure and triumph teach us to embrace the fullness of our ephemeral rendezvous with this empirical world. From lifetime to lifetime, we engage in a short-lived romance between spirit and matter to develop our personality and claim higher levels of consciousness. We carry within multiple perspectives of a paradoxical, yet all-encompassing truth as a result of our extensive travels. Consciousness is an intelligent and pliable framework that governs the building of concepts and forms. Travelling through that consciousness is not too different to browsing data streams on the internet; think of surfing the waves of consciousness and adding your personal search history.

We can log in and out of different spacetime frequencies to neutrally observe, heal or co-create with past and future emanations. No doubt, this process demands caution and a full range of responsibilities on our part. My intention for this book is to trigger memories on your soul's journey towards healing and introspection, permitting greater pattern recognition, and offering practical methods for personal salvation and self-realisation on your designated path. Without turning a blind eye to this world's perversion of human virtues, I would like to stress the importance of healing and adjusting our individual karma and to focus on the way forward, to ultimately join the group of embodied masters on their way to galactic citizenship. Snippets of my personal story from *Challenge to Choice* subtly weave through the following pages to accompany your personal exploration. Simply allow yourself to surrender to the presented flow that deliberately takes you on a ride, alternating between a focus on the physical, disciplined self-empowerment work and a more spiritually expanded ambition. Each chapter stands on its own for you to focus on specific areas of interest. As a well-practiced traveller, you can surf in and out of the book in a non-linear fashion; reading, recording and practicing what resonates in the moment.

Bits About Me

I was born in Austria, in a town just outside of Vienna - the legendary 'City of Music & Dreams,' branded through the likes of Mozart, Falco and Freud. During my younger years, I cannot recall having any momentous dreams or specific expectations for my life, aside from a desire for emotional and financial independence. I have always had a passion for music and dancing. Growing up in a resilient yet creative family unit, I learned to be innovative out of necessity and accustomed to always being on-the-job.

As a young girl, I enjoyed spending days on end playing in the Danube woods with my younger brother. We pretended to hunt for wild boar, developed unique recipes for boar sausages and sold them in our very own butchery shop to imaginary customers. Creativity is often epitomised by the arts and music; a somewhat narrow view of life's creative treasures indeed. The innocent and childlike muse naturally exudes this magical vibration that resides deeply within our hearts and if nurtured, often well into adolescence. We must reclaim this magic at all cost!

With no regrets and genuine gratitude towards my birth family for imparting their hard-earned survival skills to me, I cherish the valuable lessons gained from all the challenging lifetimes spent in this Earth school. These experiences motivated me to recalibrate emotionally and become the person that I am today. My persistent keen interest in studying other people's behaviours and actions opened up many doors to screwed up realities throughout my life. I gained profound insights that kept me inquisitive amidst conflicting and contrasting experiences, but at the time, I was oblivious to the toll it took on my physical body. Whilst many of us have individually endured or inflicted massive treachery throughout our journeys, it is the seemingly insignificant incidents that hold a lot of collective wisdom as they happen to all of us in one form or another.

During my first corporate employment as an accountant, I learned about the unique little perks of retributive justice when a vindictive supervisor attempted to get me fired at the start of my career. Fortunately, the manager recognized the injustice and instead offered me an autonomous role that was equal to hers. Success is not only achieved through knowledge and determination and but also through the ability to embrace change and overcome obstacles. Many of us fail to acknowledge their powerful soul's energy and the catalytic force that attracts people who are stuck in superiority or control loops, and falsely accuse or take advantage of others.

Our unclaimed innate potency, veiled by innocence and a lack of self-awareness, can serve as a trigger for emotional dominance by those who are not willing to own their disempowered state of being. It is important to not internalize the belief that you are the source of all evil or to take on the responsibility for the wrongdoings of others, despite any messages or projections that may have been directed towards you.

My early enquiry into human primal and societal interaction started to make sense much later in life, when I understood it to be an essential part of my vocation. As I navigated through the complexities of the business world, I began to recognize the value of adaptability, perseverance, and a positive mindset. At the age of twenty-three, I began working internationally at a privately owned metal trading company in Vienna. This was the beginning of being exposed to a life very different to what I had known before. I worked ludicrously long hours in a multicultural environment with a contrasting bunch of people from very eclectic walks of life. Some of them were staggeringly affluent and functioned outside of conventional constraints. What initially felt like being thrown into the cold water at the deep end, turned into an extraordinary opportunity for personal growth and professional development that I will eternally treasure. Our paths are paved with synchronistic meetings and events and it often takes time and retrospection for us to see the beauty in this invisible guiding force. With my limited school English at the time, I would have likely declined the job offer if it hadn't been for one person – the sole Austrian member among a panel of American interviewers who challenged me to take a leap of faith and step out of my comfort zone. He encouraged me to stop playing small. I have a great deal of appreciation for that man who briefly entered my life at just the right time.

Take a moment to reflect on your own life – can you recall any situation or people that played a significant role in your personal growth? There are multiple potential futures that we can select from to actively shape and create the reality we desire.

On our journey of awakening to our spiritual self, we continuously break away or build upon our destined foundations. Abrupt and unforeseen changes to our familiar circumstances are only natural and often what it takes to fully animate one's spirit. Seek and inquisitively follow the serendipitous breadcrumbs that guide the way and reinforce your calling. In aid of our personal growth, life has a subtle way of repeating challenges to help us see our limitations and to snap out of the false comfort of engrained resistance. A universal intelligence keeps nudging us towards karmic resolution and our ever-evolving purpose... not so gently at times.

The confrontational conversations and the discord that I observed privately and in the corporate arena were a mixture of control, jealousy, and supremacy to ignorantly fill the holes of one's own preconceived inadequacy. Although we had lots of fun times, most individuals in this business were still in 'money making me' mode. Between witnessing frequent personality clashes and competitive business rivalries, I thoroughly enjoyed the international interaction that expanded my horizon beyond my smalltown upbringing. During those days, I didn't have much time to ponder on emotional healing or the purpose of life. However, I focused on excelling in my career and was able to achieve financial independence at an early stage. We were all perfect examples of how prevalent ideologies and our upbringing shape our adult expectations and impact our actions, until we begin to question them.

When viewing the world through the eyes of others, we can learn many valuable lessons and yet we often remain blind to our own truth or potential. During these early corporate years, I found myself naturally taking on the roles of coordinator and harmoniser in addition to my official duties. I was dealing with cosmopolitan nationalities along with challenging responsibilities and hierarchies. It helped me develop assertiveness and resilience in the face of adversity. I discovered my gift for peacekeeping and my commitment to a cause that I had otherwise not given myself credit for.

Self-nurture and energy cleanliness are most valuable teachings that I only adapted later in life. However, I did learn a great deal about choosing and the importance of trusting to take the first step without knowing where it would lead. In retrospect, my life was like speed dating then; a year would feel like a mere five minutes before I had to move on to the next challenge and opportunity. My successful and corporate journey lasted for over twenty years and led me to work in Vienna, London, New York, Isle of Man, and Cape Town until later returning to London in 2001, where I now live with my partner and daughter.

Let's keep fast forwarding to the year 2005, where I was gifted a Bowen treatment that profoundly impacted my health and well-being. It had a remarkable effect on some of my longstanding physical ailments after just one treatment and I decided to learn the technique, whilst still working full time. A year's worth of extensive training to become a Bowen practitioner kicked off a chain of highly unanticipated events. By the end of 2008, I had left the corporate world and started on a path of studying the complexity of the body, mind, and soul through a variety of multifaceted practices such as NLP, Hypnotherapy, Time Line Therapy, Reiki, Kinesiology, and many more. The same year, I formed 'Syncholistic' - a self-development company, as a result of my holistic healing approach along with my new interest in synchronicities.

For the many years that followed after my corporate departure, I worked as a therapist and yoga teacher certified in a multitude of modalities, which allowed me to collect and apply a prolific range of healing tools. In the early days, I felt naturally drawn to techniques that assisted physical ailments and particularly the deprogramming of the subconscious mind and nervous system. I turned what had assisted my own personal progression and healing into a business opportunity, in service to others. Whilst I always felt naturally guided by some innate intelligence, I neither questioned nor particularly acknowledged it.

Only as I increasingly pursued higher levels of awareness, did I become more conscious of the synchronicities that have always guided me along the way.

I remember March of 2014 in London. At an Access Consciousness class with Gary Douglas, a workshop participant took to the microphone to share her walk-in experience. As she was talking my body had an intense and baffling reaction. Tears were streaming down my face and my heart was racing... leading me to question if I was a walk-in also? During a reading in May of the same year with Andrew Bartzis, the *Galactic Historian*, he confirmed that I had, in fact, experienced a soul walk-in during puberty. My foetal soul walked out a few years later, during adolescence. The mechanics of soul exchanges are rather complex and I will cover more of my explorations on this subject with Andrew later in the book. Whilst a walk-in experience can be a result of an accident, mine was not a straight-forward exchange of souls but rather a soul faction that had entered the body within dreamtime. I had many nightmares during my childhood and puberty years and can't place the incident with any certainty.

After years of spiritual exploration and self-mastery I have become more aligned with my soul's expression and find it easier to surrender into trusting my inner compass and appreciate the wide, wonderful net of divine support. A more intellectual understanding of the unfoldment of soul and purpose allows us to become magical practitioners of life. One of my contributions in this lifetime is to create a unity field for people to experience greater awareness. This has fuelled my continuous interest in the reconciliation of opposing tendencies, conflict resolution and pattern recognition. As a catalyst for the transformation of human and galactic potential, I enjoy assisting individuals identify their self-sabotaging behavioural patterns and emotional triggers, so they can overcome their self-imposed limitations and tap into the limitless possibilities of multidimensional existence.

We can all heal the disconnect of our body-soul relationship and reclaim our emotional and mental power, as well as deepen our understanding of our place in the intricate web of Earth's existence in this solar system. During our current incarnation on Earth, we have the chance to live in bodies that are lighter and more integrated, paving the way for a new era of interstellar connections, should we decide to embrace it.

I am eternally grateful for the presence of my signature frequency matches in all degrees of separation; the many contributors and relevant sources of information, some mentioned in these pages, that have accompanied and guided me along my path to perpetual self- mastery. It is my sincere honour to continue this cycle of inspiration with this book offering to you.

MG; Magic&Gratitude

CHAPTER I: RELATIONSHIPS & SEXUALNESS

PART ONE: The Mirror of Relationships

It's never too late to relate.

Self-reliance is a sacred neutral alliance between our many selves. We are not one but many, reflected in this world of endless mirrors. Only through relationships can we experience and try to understand this reality. Once we have embraced and integrated all levels of awareness equally, we can whole-heartedly trust in the relationship of our unified aspects, no longer feeling that we are at the mercy of outside circumstances and open-mindedly expand our field of influence and collaboration.   In the beginning of my healing exploration, I worked a lot with the basic mirror principle for the purpose of becoming more aware of my hurt, repressed and denied 'I's that had been running this and other lifetimes. The idea is to look for unacknowledged programming reflected in the behaviour of those we surround ourselves with. It is probably more correct to say that we unconsciously project our unhealed parts onto others and they too, in unawareness, reflect them back at us. Being attracted or repelled by people who show us qualities in ourselves that we are oblivious to, or are not willing to embrace, helps us unearth limiting or destructive beliefs that are deeply buried in our DNA. All relationships, inclusive but not limited to human ones, are magical tools for self-reflection as nothing and no one in this reality has a truly isolated existence. During the planning phase of our character-building years, we don't acknowledge the adversarial grip between attraction and repulsion and often fall prey to one side or the other. Exaggerated bravery or rebel tendencies are a smoke screen for someone who is trying to cover up old hurt and insecurities. Paradoxical indeed and yet, if undetected, this blind spot can endlessly fuel relationship disputes and social dissonance along the entire spectrum of existence.

Our masked 'I's expertly keep us arguing for our shortcomings and outsmart each other's limitations instead of promoting cocreation and shared victories. This grave disparity plays well into how we still, inadvertently, separate the light from the dark and the soul from the body. We are either obsessed with our physicality and material possessions or with life's meaning and spiritual attainment. In doing so, we literally force one to triumph over the other instead of preserving the integrity of spirit with matter and their equal union within every expression. The majority of people still conform to social conventions. They do not question the generally accepted rules and hierarchies of our institutions, marriage or family structure, and fail to recognise the fundamental interconnectedness of humanity and its spiritual roots. This can lead to a sense of alienation from others, as well as lack of purpose or meaning in one's life. Irrespective of background, race, denomination and gender, as an embodied human being we hold within ourselves the metaphorical sperm and egg of our spirit and matter attributes, prodding us to be carried to full term throughout all stages of life. Our alliances may still be influenced by the reality we inhabit, but ultimately, they have the potential to contribute to the greater good of humanity by promoting unity and spiritual growth.

Every relationship is a response to our level of awareness and personal choice that expresses itself within this causal reality, ultimately serving the expansion of consciousness. Our personality's maturation process is all about learning to actively balance our internal and external relationships and become fiercely free of the grip of overidentification and ownership. One way of conceptualizing this is by using the analogy of a project, such as a book. We initiate the process of writing a book by creating a mental stimulus and concept, and forming a connection or relationship with it. As we proceed writing, the book takes on momentum through the written words and the layout of its chapters. It begins to develop its own consciousness and contributes to the planning of its content. In order for the book to be fully realised and successfully brought into existence, the author must appreciate its active role in the creative process.

This requires a willingness to step back and allow the book's guidance to freely emerge, so that the final product becomes a mutual co-creation. In a similar way, this concept applies to all forms of interaction, including human relationships which require mutual support, effective communication and individual self-awareness.

Our soul desires to be fully and freely embodied and authentically represented by its agent – the ego. Abundance and success come when we channel a balanced focus towards all of our plans, goals and ideas and cyclically surrender them to the primary and supreme guidance – *the divine lifeforce*. We ARE the psychic welders that can fuse the shadow and the light, the body and soul.

Our relationships are light reflections; an appropriation of the whole. With a regular healing practice, you will arrive at a point where you can simply notice incoherent patterns in your environment, no longer relating them to yourself. As you ease into not getting triggered by adverse vibrations, you learn to keep them at a distance without having to excessively shield, separate or protect yourself from them. We can direct and reverse energy and lessen the impact or even transduce energetic frequencies as we move into higher levels of mastery. A benevolent command of energy is important in order to maintain healthy interrelations and to build new alliances within and beyond this earthly realm.

Great Mystery works with and through us, and its mirrors can safely guide us towards deeper insights, penetrating into past life and future relations. The mirrors of relationship will reflect new visions and images and remind us to discern all reflections equally with compassion and gratitude. With every breath we take, every wound we heal, we serve our own spiritual unfolding and affect our brothers and sisters as well as consciousness at large. In a mastered state of awareness, we can use the mirror principle and consciously expand our investigation into the immaterial realms and multiple planes of existence.

Carl Jung introduced the notion that perception is projection; presupposing that we can only perceive what is already in our awareness. As we continue to confidently cross the threshold from the known into the unknown, we enter the depths of our unconscious and come to realise that the entire empirical world is interrelated and a reflection of the One Mind, God Source, Spirit or whatever you prefer to call it.

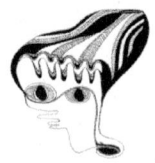

A Simple Mirror Reflection Exercise

The next time you are drawn to someone, ask yourself *what attracted you? Is it their beauty, their sense of freedom, or confidence that keeps you enthralled?* On the other hand, look out for unpleasant qualities that might catch your attention. Until we heal our ancient wounds of separation, we will seek whatever remains fragmented within the self and try to combat it externally. Our relationships, whether they are friendships to romantic partnerships, at any level of intimacy, aid us in becoming more integrated and whole as individuals.

1. Think of an individual you are fond of:
   - *What trait or energy do you most like about that person?*
   - *Are you missing this trait in yourself?*
   - *How would it benefit you?*
   - *What can you be, do to acknowledge this energy in yourself?*
   - *Where in your body can you feel this exploration?*
   Confirm, claim, and release it.

2. Now, think of an individual that triggers you:
   - *What trait or energy do you dislike most about that person?*
   - *Where do you see this energy in yourself?*
   - *What if you'd stop denying this energy in yourself?*
   - *What can you be and do to heal this energy in yourself?*
   - *Where in your body can you feel this exploration?*
   Confirm, claim, and release it.

The search of who we are is never complete. As we keep adding new perspectives and insights, our perception will soar well beyond the old levels of projection.

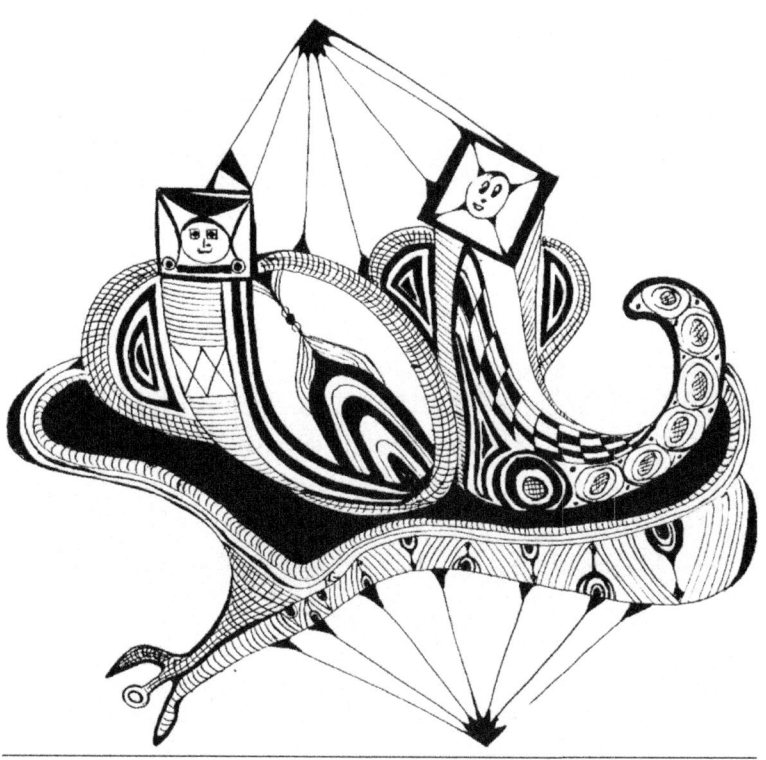

PART TWO: The Value of Relationships

Opport-Unity

Our actions and choices play a significant role in shaping not only our own lives but the lives of those around us. Our behaviours can influence others, and the patterns that emerge from these interactions create a ripple effect that impacts the world around us. Open opponent or familiar pal – our search for recognition and external validation often elicits criticism in relationships. It is important to be mindful of people's needs and wants when sharing information and offering assistance.

Unsolicited advice can come across as intrusive and belligerent. By compulsively obliging others either through our own neediness or fear of conflict, we may encounter strong resistance and cause more harm than good. Upon facing such a situation, it's best to just pause, take a breath, and change the narrative. You can easily shift the energy by expanding yourself out beyond your perceived identity and your body... house... city... country... galaxy... all the way into the universal you. Expanding your perspective in this way can help you approach the situation with greater compassion and without compromising your own growth. Blame, shame and guilt arise when we identify too closely with our stories and allow them to define us. Such an association cannot exist in an expanded space of beingness. As long as we hold onto our unhealed stories, we remain trapped, and cut off parts of ourselves which, in turn, will criticise and attack us internally. This is often the pain that gets projected onto others by means of futile assistance. Self-help is true caring.

The struggle between genuine giving and receiving will persist until everyone has embraced their divinity and claimed the god spark within themselves. At the basis of humanity is a mystical yearning to be whole that keeps us in constant rapport and discord with all vital lifeforces. All is energy in its purest form of communication, inextricably and infinitely interconnected. Our bodies are not separate from all the awareness within and around us, even though it appears so. This illusory separation creates the ultimate limitation. Not only are we the spider weaving its web but the web itself, and the fly that gets entangled in it. Unlike in shape or form, kind or character, everything and everyone adds to the kaleidoscope of colour and celestial design. Once people begin to recognise the importance of this truth, we can unite our species and build a legacy for the new Earth. Humans are known to alternate between periods of stagnation and high levels of effort and achievement as we naturally follow the rhythmic cycles of perpetual out-creation.

As an example, consumerism and sociability have undergone significant changes over the last couple of years due to social media, technological advancements, and the pandemic. As technology companies inundate the market with electronic communication tools, online shopping, and artificially intelligent support devices, fewer and fewer people are engaging in traditional face-to-face interactions and socialising methods. We spend more time at home. If we view the trajectory and broaden our area of focus, we can see how our personal interactions are profoundly impacted by the altered state of collective consciousness, and not all of it is bad. Some people may feel isolated, but many have turned inwards and used this time to revitalise, advance spiritually, and change their careers and lives all-together.

We are in a massive window of opportunity with the objective of humanity's welfare and reunification. Need and opportunity shake hands, extended in service to humankind. Our primary goal should be to aid individuals in overcoming their fear and apprehension towards the unsettling and unpredictable circumstances that are emerging, and support them in establishing a sense of self-sustaining stability. Furthermore, we must initiate the process of bringing together people who share similar thoughts and ideas on a broader and international level. Many of us have already started to offer support and inspiration through the formation of educational groups and philanthropic organisations in service of this world's grand restoration. Our individual soul qualities set us apart. Let's not deny or fight over them but embrace and foster our unique contributions that ultimately define the oneness we are striving for. We are to acknowledge and remedy our weaknesses whilst cultivating our strengths that have been buried in the shadows of servitude to a system gone awry and freshly engage them in reconciling humanity. The entire world is in unrest and upheaval.

Every one of us must take full ownership of our place in transmuting corrupt, wicked and vile emanations, and redefine harm-less-ness. How? By healing thyself and reuniting.

By connecting with people and places, we activate our contractual soul and destiny dynamics and awaken dormant, hidden aspects of the self. The process of conscious creation involves learning how to focus in coherent and perceptive alignment with our soul's purpose and making more civilised and joyful choices to achieve this. This can instantly attract new relationships and create new manifestations, as originally intended by spirit. The great remembering has begun and we are being called to act as an inspired group of masters in the making. Living without harm to any sentient kind are no longer just words.

Passion Sparks Healing

Let's look at the passionate spark between two people who are destined to meet, like two ships accidentally colliding in the dark. Our DNA radios incessantly broadcast our frequency and genetic memory throughout the quantum field. Fated encounters are being orchestrated as an opportune moment for two souls to embark on a joint voyage of karmic resolution. The critical thinking faculty often steps back when two people meet in such a manner. The emotional body takes over and dominates the feelings and regular daily activities in the early stages... we don't feel like eating, can't sleep, and call it falling in love. In doing so, we subconsciously download and check through each other's ancient memory files, whilst pondering the voices of passion and desire urging us to courageously ride the waves of consciousness. By following the call to action, we must helm the wheel of karma and navigate an innovative narrative towards the emergence of new soul qualities. Such synchronistic 'collisions' often pave the way to not only rekindle old soul relations, but also to release old bondage.

Whilst working in the oil industry, I met my partner during one business phone call from oceans apart. After a brief conversation, we both knew a meeting was inevitable. An emergence of such deep sense of certainty is not necessarily driven by physical appearance. I had no idea what he looked like until we met. The connection between our souls had been instantly revealed through the psychic pheromones expressed in our voices.

Passion comes from the Latin word 'PATI' – to suffer, referring to the suffering of Jesus Christ. Is the purpose of our passionate reunions to ignite emotional suffering, or is it the first step to freedom from the rising waves of relenting emotions and desires? Maybe the passion of Christ is inviting us to transmute emotions into a more intelligent and elevated form of love. The interaction that follows an instant attraction, regardless of duration and circumstance, usually provides evidence to this enquiry. *How is passionate desire linked to suffering?*

With our consciousness fractured over eons of time we have lost faith in love, abused our power, and now we have to earn it back. As a spirited team of path-finders and truth-seekers, we have a strong sense of a common motive and reason for embodiment that reunites us as couples and communities. Due to race amnesia, we forget about our pre-arranged soul contracts and the mission we came to fulfill, instead, we may become enamoured with the familiar, comfortable, and safe. Most of us are old warrior souls pioneering the new paradigm and with this admirable cause in mind, we are to keep our eyes fixed on seeking remedy and resolve for the pains inflicted upon each other during our ancient ancestral battles. Intimate relationships provide a platform for us to reconcile our innate divine masculine and feminine energies and enhance our receptivity to soul reunions. However, the nature of relationships can vary greatly. Some may feel overwhelming and endless, much like pouring resources into a never-ending pit while others are like indulging in a box of delightful chocolates.

Both dynamics offer an opportunity to heal old wounds and restore equilibrium between giving and receiving within oneself and others. As a relationship matures, and the partners become more comfortable with one another, passion often declines - the suffering lessens. When passion fades, greater prospects begin to surface. The scarcity spell attached to passion is being lifted and the energy behind it reveals itself as something grander in scope than it might have appeared at first glance. Spirit uniquely invokes passion to dig deeper into the motive of love. Under the false premise 'no lust no love,' couples often start to separate at the stage where lustful passion diminishes without ever having claimed its most precious gift. Typically, we find another partner to continue on the addictive path of the passionate thrill-seeker, repeating the cycles of physical instant gratification, without ever promoting a sense of love for the self.

Unclaimed love seeks to be conquered!

If lust is not harnessed as love in the context of a divine union between two people, the mind keeps creating desire. Neither lust nor pleasure can satisfy desire. Desire does not seek happiness. Desire is a habit that continuously attracts attention in anticipation of being resolved. Attention satiates desire's cravings but does not bid to fully quench its flames. With no result, the habit remains and feeds on another subject or object of desire. For those who are caught in this exhausting triangle of passion, lust, and desire, it might be useful to take some time out and contemplate all those unfulfilled claims within yourself. The renunciation of desire, in general, can help to break free from the cycle of habit and attachment, allowing us to turn passion into love. In the presence of true love, there is no need for desire; a happy ending after all! This emphasises the rudimentary idea of a relationship, which is self-interest; a quality and service to one another for individual and spiritual completeness. As healed and self- assured masters, we can come to appreciate passion as an important step on the stairway of illumination to true generosity of spirit, which fertilises life on the physical and spiritual planes.

Not all couples are destined to remain together and ultimately share the fruits of their karmic-resolution-labour. Some may stay in different capacities, and others may be finally released. As free-willed beings, we learn to appreciate all peak moments of contrast and polarity as valuable anchor points. Times of upheaval or pleasure put us in touch with our purpose and teach us to embrace reason and freedom instead of personal conflict. Irrespective of outcome, any relationship serves to heal the long-suffered separation from eternal source.

Love is immortal and infinitely inclusive.

Committed minds will continue to share common reality bubbles in search of their ultimate purpose, forever changing the micro and macrocosm. A mutually beneficial partnership with a spiritually common goal can be rekindled at all times and transformed into something greater. The way ahead is mapped by new levels of love, compassion, and a mature witnessing of each other's personal journeys.

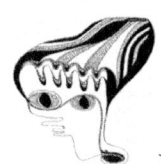

Inner Relationship Dialogue

Take a few minutes to notice how far you have come on your journey of relating. Find a moment of stillness to reflect and ponder the following questions:

Q: What are the three most significant lessons you have learned through the relationships in your life?

Q: Who or what are you still holding onto in the physical reality that is no longer serving you in your pursuit of joy and liberation?

Q: How much time do you spend distracting yourself from committing to your body and soul?

Q: Do you seek out relations that truly inspire your soul spark?

Q: Are you willing to give true love a chance??

Q: Do you spend enough time in silence to hear the whispers of your divine guidance?

Q: Are you still judging your insights and awareness to fit in and not stand out?

Q: How much of your energy is being misplaced and needs re-routing?

Q: What relationships are possible that you haven't allowed yet?

Q: Is it time to stop focusing on your deficiencies and remember your individual assets?

Q: What is it going to take to stop sacrificing your body and honour its need for stability and balance?

Dharmic Relationship

We are approaching the end of an era of co-dependency characterised by excessive sharing and compulsive caring. The outdated hero's myth of death and sacrifice is losing power, as the disciplined student awakens to universal love instead of internecine war. Our soul's frequency transcends matter and extends throughout time and space, resonating with the cosmic sea of love calling on all dharmic warriors to reclaim their power. We are moving into a new stage of conscious and interdependent living, engaging in sacred co-creating with all realms of existence, including the mineral, plant, animal, and spiritual kingdoms, not just the human realm. As we shift away from mutual dependence and the need to be completed by another, we step on the dharmic pathway to spiritual integrity. This new stage of life emphasises mutual contribution, divine purpose, and bridging of the lower and the higher mind. It is often experienced later in life, when the mental faculty has been sufficiently developed, and we begin to live in fuller awareness of our soul.

This deeper love is no more or less desirable than the passionate initial spark experienced in the elementary stage of two people lusting after each other; every phase serves the individual. The period of detachment experienced by a seasoned couple can be the temporary phase that reflects emotional maturity and marks the beginning of growing telepathy between them. It can be initially challenging and perplexing if this phase is not understood as a generous silence, a sign of respect and personal integrity. It marks the ending of an old way of engagement; a reorientation of how they identify with each other, and making way for new beginnings and horizons to be explored together. Creating on the dharmic path has a different feel to it. The short-sighted pursuit of momentary pleasure becomes less important as we have outlived the standards set by the collective narrative and take refuge in our own knowingness.

When we remain steadfast in our authentic truth and cultivate the level of allowance that is required to create beyond mediocrity, we find joy and happiness in sharing ordinary moments of togetherness. This has nothing to do with what people often call having to compromise to make a relationship work. The word 'compromise' entails the idea of having to accept standards that are lower than desirable. In my world, there no longer is a value in claiming less than what I know is possible in order to accommodate someone else's model of the world, as it does not serve either one in the long run. This does not mean that we won't get caught up in old habitual patterns of doubt and hesitation, that occasionally resurface and trigger a lack of trust on our probationary dharmic path, so easily projected onto others. Instead of reverting back to condemning the world around us, we have to honour the growing pains of our soul and the many shifts and changes that it takes to train the human to function well in this spacetime continuum. The solution for any nagging and prolonged difficulties is often just a choice away. The more conscious we can be at those choice points, the more we claim our authority as an embodied avatar.

The path to intelligent love is learning to abide by our choices and their respective consequences without trepidation or regrets. Never stop demanding more of yourself and allow the mystery that is encrypted in your soul's blueprint to emerge with a sense of direction. Many couples have contracted to come here during this time of self-remembering to assist each other with disentangling the sticky timeline paradox. That doesn't necessarily mean they are going to awaken together or at equal measure during this lifetime. Some relationships are bound to end for the individuals to empower themselves and strengthen their conviction to follow their divine guidance. Alternatively, one spouse may be holding space for the other to evolve with ease, which can benefit both. My personal relationship choices have allowed me to limit outside distractions so I can explore and heal my inner relationship and cultivate a responsiveness within the higher planes.

This has guided me to work together with innovative and progressive people in exchange of an expanded vision with a view to build a new world. Relationships are potent facilitators, helping us become more fluent and congruent with a wider range of vibrations. In the surrender of any preconceived ideas, criticisms, prides, or prejudices, we open ourselves up to work in a higher field of service. For everything we hate there is something to love, and all that remains is simply breathing. Life is an open-ended invitation to retrieve and awaken dormant capacities within each other through boundless interactions, including but not limited to fatal attractions. Ditch whatever you have learned about good or bad relationships and you may be surprised what is waiting for you beyond conclusion and certainty.

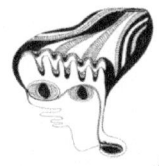

An Expanded Relationship 'Imagitation'

This story is based on a dream I once had that wanted to be told within the context of this chapter, for it speaks of oneness and the relationship with everything around and within ourselves. Feel free to continue the story using your imagination.

A Dreamtime Story

The desert was his home. Ahmed grew up in Alexandria as the son of a gemstone merchant. Helping his dad out with the shipments and getting to know the magical powers of the semi-precious and precious stones was one of his favourite occupations growing up. His father was proud of his trade and took the healing properties of the stones very serious. For hours they would sit together in the sun, polishing and admiring the stones. His dad loved talking about his passion and Ahmed enjoyed listening. The warm sun rays brought those stones to life and purified their crystalline structure until they sparkled in remarkable colours and shades.

They would often cleanse them with salt before wrapping them up, ready for dispatch to their clientele. These precious times of bonding and learning from his dad were dear to Ahmed and formed his way of thinking and co-creating beyond the human realms. His father died when he reached his early twenties. Ahmed sold the business as he never really cared much for the commercial side of the trade. He left the home he had lived in for all of his childhood life and ventured into the desert to become a Bedouin. The nomadic lifestyle suited Ahmed. He loved and appreciated all animals he came to meet and communicate with. He spent a lot of time without human contact whilst wandering along the dunes, but never felt alone or weird hearing himself talk to his camels and his other furry, feathered, and crawling friends. All of those times with his father connecting to the gemstones made him aware that everything in nature was conscious. It had prepared the way for him to commune without the use of words and ink. He could feel the lifeforce in every grain of sand that he stepped on and instinctively knew when it was time to rest and water the camels, or make haste to find shelter before a sandstorm. He would firm up trade exchanges to take camels back and forth between the desert and the villages. Most times he spent a few days enjoying the hustle and bustle of the busy market towns before heading back to the unencumbered and expansive space of the desert. There, he felt an infinite silence that was pregnant with possibilities - one of his most treasured gifts and pleasures. During the cool hours of the night, he huddled next to his herd sheltered from the wind, observing the magnificence of the vast sky. The stars told him stories of great mystery. Ahmed would drift into an unconscious slumber where he could explore dimensions, galaxies, and universes. On those journeys he met wizards, warriors, and other consciousness explorers, all from different worlds and star systems. They came together to share their wisdom in joyful co-creation. Occasionally, he did come across some less benevolent beings too. He had learned to trust his heart that told him when to interact or when to send them their way. It was all part of the bigger consciousness out there, in a place where doubtful belief was not propagated. Faith and intuition became an integral part of his existence. In the desert he felt most in tune with nature. He became nature and nature provided for him. He experienced a sense of oneness. Without an occupied mind constantly interrupting his natural flow he always reached his intended destination in time for the next job. It was like folding just enough space and time to complete his current mission, earn a comfortable living, and enjoy the fruits of his labour in the process.

Those days and nights spent in the desert broke him open to his inner wisdom - the place between precognition and self-expression. There were moments of intense contemplation when timelines got blurred and he willingly stepped outside the confines of the spacetime continuum. That expansive space of beingness was at times accompanied with a sense of feeling lost; a weird unfamiliar void space that was unsettling and eerie at first. Without any distraction at hand, he had no choice other than to surrender and focus his attention onto his breath. He could always rely on his breath to safely bring him back into the body. Alert and in tune, he felt his blood flowing through his veins, his heart pumping, his mind settling back into the comfort of embodiment. It felt like being on a rollercoaster as he experienced and consciously observed his emotions. He felt oddly animated and alive as the adrenaline rushed through his body and then calmly settled back into the space between breaths. He often drifted back into gone eras and significant past lives where he had prepared himself for this future life, now. This gave him the reassurance and encouragement that he needed to trust and continue on his path. Ahmed often dreamt of the big wide oceans. Letting his imagination run wild, he played with the whales, dolphins, and all the creatures of the sea. Upon awakening from his dreamtime travels, he would find himself rejuvenated and inspired, immensely enjoying the contrast of the sand and dunes. He also relished the eclectic wildlife in the desert which was so magically adapted to this harsh environment, as well as the endurance of his beloved camels and all the elemental energies... (continue)

PART THREE: A Bridge to Higher Consciousness

Love deeply, dragon child. Breathe and hold still for just a moment. Smell the scent of the morning dew as it embraces the aromatic array of flowers in the field of plenty. There is a magic that wants to be to noticed, to be recognised. Beneath the soil lives an unseen network of wonderful beings; a multitude of elementals and minerals channelling life force and joy to maintain the Earth's homeostasis. Watch the trees swaying their branches in full ecstatic sensual flow, deeply connected to the elements, nourished by the ocean's water and nurtured through the heart of mother Earth. Open your eyes and watch the mystery unfolding. You are the bridge between the above and the below.

Dragon Dynamics

DRAGONS; their fiery and potent energies are pivotal to the creation story and, as such, have been around since well before the age of man. Little is understood of their primordial energy and not many acknowledge those beings beyond their mythical tales, let alone being familiar with the dragon's natural healing and creation force that is expressed and depicted throughout nature. Many cultures have revered the dragon as a symbol of strength, power, and transformation. It embodies the spirit that creates both chaos and order in all realms to restore the divine balance. By embracing the dragon energy, we can unleash our true potential and purify consciousness. The majestic mountains and life-giving oceans of Earth are home to dragon-shaped energy grids and beings that are hidden from the concrete mind. They are waiting for us to discover their secrets and realign with the dragon energy and the consciousness of our planet, to tap into the powerful source of pure lifeforce and create positive change. With a sacred application of our human virtues, we can discover and activate the dragon within ourselves and in the world all around us. This lifeforce energy that flows through us creates, animates and sustains our bodies. It can be expressed and experienced in many ways beyond procreation and sex, and allows us to tap into deeper mysteries of our existence.

Let's call it a form of sexual-ness which is different to sex and copulation as we know it. Sexual-ness is *love* - the creative energy of life that stimulates, motivates and vitalises all forms. Andrew Bartzis speaks of the dragon as having not just one single sexual organ, but many. Dragon teachers spark our ancient memories from times before the gender separation where we lived as hermaphrodites, not needing a mate to reproduce – possessing more than one sexual organ. As multifunctional, multidimensional beings of light, dragons have sexual organs for every chakra point. Their chakras illuminate in a coming together at the highest sacred level of unified beingness, expressing true unconditional love. A uniquely different experience that is available to all of us on our pursuit to consciously function as incarnated souls again. In order to understand the sexual-ness path of the dragon and the bridge into higher consciousness, our body and soul needs to start operating as one unit in non-competition with all that it infinitely exists with. We cannot achieve consolidated beingness when bogged down by internal programs and limiting belief systems that keep us in separation and partiality.

Inviting dragon sexual-ness into our world requires us to practice the highest levels of emotional and spiritual hygiene along with higher service. True receiving or higher service triggers an alchemical energy exchange that can go well beyond any familiar stimulation and sensory perception. Personally, I see it as a form of clear, unconditional service that transfigures the energy of giving into simultaneous receiving through higher levels of discernment that are not easily identified at this stage. The lifeforce that can be released through such an exchange instantly transforms and heals the receiver and the giver as well as any onlookers in all realms of existence. In order to bring the sense of divine unity and higher service from the heart into practical application in our pursuit of mastery, we must use our intellect to understand and integrate it. This means not just relying on intuition and feeling, but also analysing and comprehending the principles and concepts behind it.

By doing so, we can develop a deeper understanding and connection to this sense of unity and apply it to our daily lives in a more conscious and intentional way. In order to gain foresight to repeat such an experience at will, we need to engage our higher mind through hindsight.

Here is what I would consider an example of intuitive devotion that still percolates in the back of my mind, leaching out new insights upon revisit:

A couple of years ago, I attended a body process class in London where, during a practice session, my partner's body and hands began to move in uncoordinated ways beyond his control and cognition as he worked on me. He was the guy who kept falling asleep throughout the program, forced into oblivion by whatever was running his avatar. I was aware of his extensive foreign entity energy that was being released throughout the session but remained still until he settled down. Despite being able to stop the process, I was guided by an inner knowingness, a call to higher service, an intuitive devotion of true receiving to let it run its course. During the treatment, I had vivid images of him and I, embodied as two elves, running through lush fields of flowers, having a fun time. My entire body was euphorically vibrating as I got up and we both felt very awkward and couldn't even look at each other. This was one of those intense moments where I voluntarily transmuted his demons as a gift to him, and he simultaneously received and regifted me in return, without resistance. I believe that a sacred, neutral space and spiritual permission slips between two individuals, and the witnesses for that matter, must be in place to openly express that kind of transmutation until true receiving becomes the norm and not the exception in this reality.

Dynamic healings, blissful copulation, fulfilment of desires and dreams are sourced in the energy of sexual-ness. In order to conjure up and tap into that highly inspired potential, we have to let go of all charge and polarity about sex and sexuality so that we can understand the creative sensuality of sexual-ness.

We have limited and negated sexual experiences through all the judgments, misinterpretations and expectations of what sex and unconditional love is. The shame and guilt around recreational and procreational sex, as well as all of its pornographic implications, have kept a hold and handle on preventing us from crossing that bridge into higher consciousness during and beyond copulation. Abiding mental and emotional stress have also majorly contributed to a lack of physical vitality in the human being which predisposes to impotence, not to forget the religious connotations that have forced many into celibacy over hundreds of years. I extensively explored the topic of sexuality in 2014 when I became an Access Entity Facilitator. You can check out their body of work with its simple and effective daily empowerment tools, as well as their potent clearing statement via www.accessconsciousness.com.

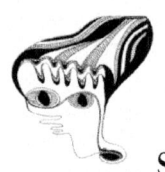

Sexual Consciousness Treatment

Herewith, I would like to offer a treatment to the future that I put together for the purpose of healing any sexual abuse or distortions in aid and celebration of all relationships.

I, [insert name] in this ever- present moment of now, choose to engage my hindsight and foresight for the expressed purpose of sending a treatment to myself in the future, to heal and to awaken my authentic expression of sacred sexual-ness as my birthright and legacy. As part of the great dreamtime awakening, I raise myself to levels of higher consciousness beyond my intellect, my controls and my judgments.

I am ready to accept the responsibility that I can heal myself on all levels of existence. I enter into communion with my sacred sexual-ness in the past, present and future and invite any trauma, perverted situation and distorted frequency to come forth for healing. I commit to being sexually present; to heal, nurture, play, and create with and through my physical body, my DNA instrument in dynamic union with my soul's consciousness.

I, as this signature frequency of the now, choose to acknowledge that there are programs inside me that will try to take me and my body, off the journey of transformation. I now project at my future self to turn off the sympathetic and parasympathetic programs of self-defeat, self-deprivation and all other self- defeating habit patterns that prevent me from having a greater and deeper experience.

As I have been acutely aware of my ancestors, my parents, my siblings, my friends, and any other people's sexual insanities, I now practice opening my chakras beyond their parameters of sexual insanity and do not entangle with them empathetically. I am not contracting, closing down, withdrawing or hiding, but rather perceive their sexual insanity and expand and open myself up, beyond it.

I am willing to sexually receive with total ease, beyond the limitations of this global narrative that I have made my own, as well as beyond all of my personal controls, agendas, and insanities.

Everything that does not allow me to perceive and access my original sexual blueprint, I now destroy and uncreate, dissipate and release the projection and expectation from my body and my frequency. Universe, show me what it takes to have total peace with my sacred sexual reality?

Everywhere I have been punished, crucified, cauterized, judged, tortured, condemned, and sexually stimulated away from the joy of bodies, I now categorically denounce, destroy and uncreate this energy from this and other lifetimes. I dissipate and release everything that has been done to my body to kill, to hurt, to harm, to judge, to shut down, and to ridicule the sexual kindness of bodies.

All of the light versions of myself in this and other lifetimes, dimensions, timestreams and galaxies that are telling me that I am sexually crazy and insane, that are designed to keep me away from healing my sexual-ness, as well as all the judgments of me that invite entities, I now revoke, recant, rescind, renounce, denounce, destroy and uncreate all my commitments, oaths, vows, agreements and binding contracts to any and all of them.

All of the sexual judgments and sexual difficulties that my body is conscious of, in other people's bodies and universes, and that I am not acknowledging as my awareness, I now begin to dissipate, release, destroy and uncreate. I am asking for the joy of having a body that will deliver me the pleasures, ecstasy, intensity, sacred recreation, and everything else that the body has to offer.

As a sacred sexual healer in full awareness of my capacities, I claim the union and communion with my dragon teachers to reach higher levels of consciousness.

Everywhere I have only scratched the surface of what my body has to offer, I am now willing to deepen my experiences. All of the sexual consciousness that my body is capable of facilitating, as well as the gifts that I have refused, I am now willing to receive. I listen to my body. I communicate with my body. I do not control my body into a reality that I used to consider relevant or important.

All of the sexual potencies, sexual powers, and sexual abilities that I have disavowed, so they couldn't be used against me or others, I now call back and re-integrate. I destroy and uncreate all collective implants such as blame, shame, and guilt, and all charge and polarity with regards to pornography, sex, sexuality, sexual-ness, sensuality, and copulation.

Everything that doesn't allow me to perceive, know, be and receive my ability to transform all energies through the potent sexual-ness of my being, I destroy and uncreate. Everywhere I was sexually present in the past, sexually potent and sexually creative and was dynamically judged for it, I revoke, recant, rescind, renounce, denounce, destroy and uncreate all of that now.

All of the sexual energies that I have been hiding to feel more human, more like my parents or caretakers to fit in, to not stand out, to not be too powerful, to not make myself or others uncomfortable, I herewith unleash these abandoned energies and apply my freewill to alchemise and transform them into joy, bliss, choice, creation, expansion, possibilities, and mutual contribution.

I give permission to my body to unconditionally give and receive sexually and to transform my body, my life, my world into pure light and love. I am a being of Higher Service and I do not require sensory perception to validate my experience.

All of the religiously and spiritually enforced celibate beingness through extensive monastic doingness; the misguided, misapprehended, misinterpreted, misconstrued, misconceived living that has been mistaken as mystical life and kept me in abstinence, self-denial, self-restraint, and robbed me of the joy and vitality of my physical body, I herewith destroy and uncreate.

I now alchemise this pent-up energy of all those lifetimes on all timelines and dimensions into pure lifeforce and redirect it to all those that have yet to wake up from their eternal slumber and hit them like a lightning rod of sudden insight and illumination.

I focus onto my spirit eye, between the eye brows. I allow my left and right brain to come into harmony and form synaptic connections, creating a superhighway from the brain to the heart. I switch off the medulla oblongata at the back of the neck and drop the brain into the throat. I am guiding the brain to sink down from the throat into the heart and all the way down into the tailbone. The photonic light energy in the heart explodes and radiates out a million miles up and down the spine, from right to left, back to front.

I connect to the central sun and all the way down into the centre of the Earth, grounding the totality of my I AM soul self into this physical body.

In this sacred moment, I see my crown chakra, my third eye, all of my energy centres bringing in that potentiality of the past being. I deeply know, that the future me is going to experience even more sacred moments.

I am asking all multiple versions of myself in the past, present, and future to enforce my personal standards, boundaries, and procedures on sacred, neutral sexual-ness. Together, we fortify my sacred sexual reality and remain aware and sovereign as to what comes into my field. As I keep practicing this skill of sending a treatment to my future self, more versions are aligning to this healing process. This will raise my frequency a thousandfold.

I now take a deep breath and solemnly declare: I herewith accept this sacred sexual energy into me, as part of my past, present and future self simultaneously existing, who has this intention of using this sacred, sexual energy to raise my consciousness, my vibration, my frequency, so my great work has a great impact on my and other lives in this universal consciousness.

And so it is.

Aho.

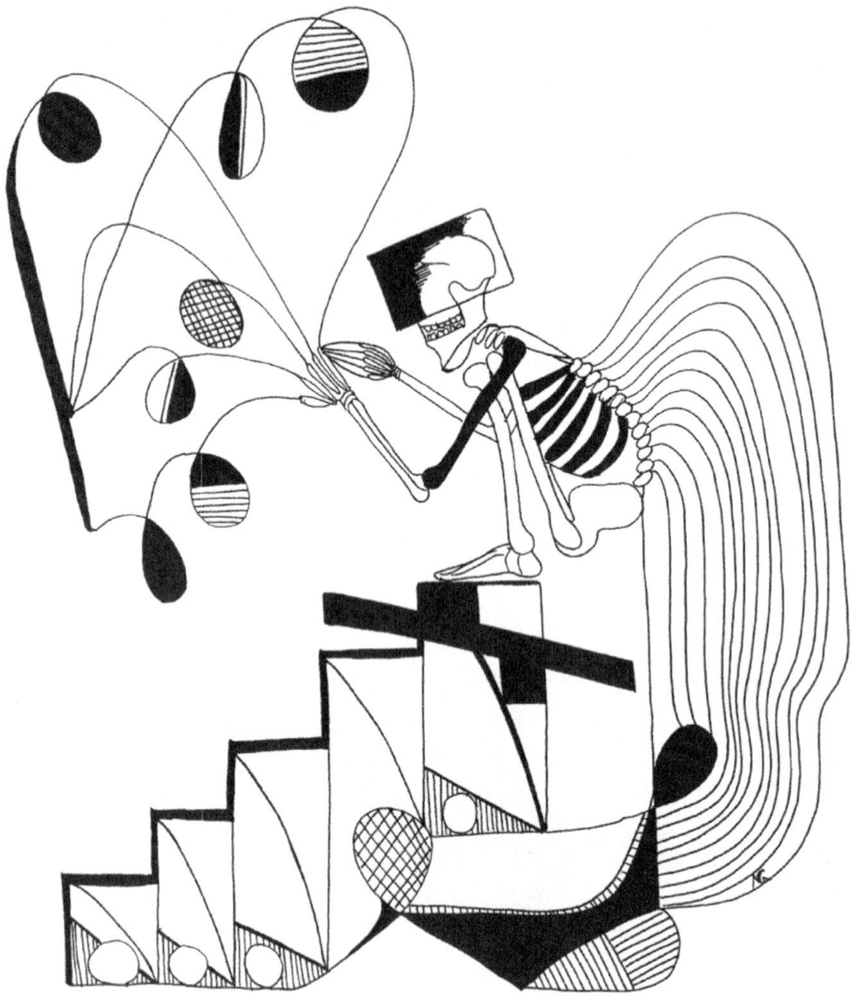

CHAPTER II: EMBODIMENT & ABUSE

PART ONE: Pain Body & Buddy

Pain – Friend or Foe?

Damocles' sword is dangling dangerously close in front of our noses.

By turning a blind eye to our discordant attitude towards pain, we risk amplifying its intensity and re-enforcing its presence. Conversely, by expecting and endorsing its fundamental existence, we may inadvertently create it. I wonder how much we have acclimatised to physical pain and emotional suffering due to tacitly consenting to a collectively agreed upon 'pain-body'? This can manifest in a number of ways, such as normalised levels of violence, implementation of non- ethical working standards, or the degradation of natural living, which we have accepted, as simply part of the status quo. Any infringement of our basic human freedom breaks down and wears away our general well-being over time. Circumstantial evidence of how largely different people seem to perceive pain invites us to test its legitimacy in the light of our own experiences. By broadening our perspective and adopting a more universal understanding, we will eventually learn to live more contentedly, either with or without pain. It was persistent physical discomfort that started me off on my self-development path. As a young girl and teenager and well into my thirties, I remember being in and out of doctor's consultation rooms with heart, bladder and gastrointestinal irregularities, which later motivated me in becoming a therapist myself. In my earlier investigation, I discovered the thought-pain relationship that helped me release a tremendous amount of old and stuck emotional build up. More often than not, the cause of our pain is not embedded in the physical domain.

We generally don't associate psychological factors such as childhood traumas or ancestral imprinting as major characteristics of physical health problems. Repressed emotions can create physical obstructions, oxygen depletion, and long-term stress responses that often weaken the immune system, increase inflammation, affect blood sugar levels, heart disease, and anxiety. I appreciate that not everyone may be interested in exploring the root cause of their affliction through 'forensic therapy'. There are a variety of alternative methods that can help support healing, such as specifically tailored meditations or breathing techniques that address pain, in addition to therapeutic and medical intervention. It has been claimed that physical torment exists to distract us from emotional pain that we are not prepared to look at - be that as it may, dealing with psychological manipulations, dramas, and traumas certainly alleviates suffering. Sigmund Freud's pain-pleasure principle suggests that people make choices to increase pleasure and avoid pain. This highlights our ambivalent belief system that is predominantly based on the physical and emotional bias of pleasure enhancement and avoidance of pain. The association with either creates a double bind that sucks us into a vicious circle of instant gratification and antipathy for adversity, reducing our thinking to the level of the three-dimensional personality.

The early origins of psychology primarily focused on a mechanistic approach to understanding the physical, mental, and emotional aspects of human experience. This approach neglected to recognise and study the deeper, inherent principles that shape the soul. Behaviour and pain cannot be entirely explained through physical action and reaction alone. Furthermore, it does not take into consideration external influences and forces that are often imperceptible to the human eye but still play a role in shaping our human experience. Whilst we still have a limited and mechanical view of our spacetime existence that we are all a sentient force of, the new energy prompts us to take a refined view. A healthy constitution is encoded in our divine essence, configured from the primal spiritual blueprint and requires us to remain open to yet unknown mysteries.

Pain primarily persists because the underlying cause no longer wants to be resisted. There is much discussion about the role of resistance and lack of flow in creative endeavours whilst the connection to physical illness remains flawed and not well understood. It is crucial to optimise our physical well-being, particularly as we activate latent DNA capacities to move into trans-dimensionally embodied living. In order for life to exist the universe has to maintain a level of balance. Through ailments, sensations or symptoms, the body alerts us of incursions to its sought-after homeostasis. What if illness is the very medicine the body needs in order to physically and emotionally rebalance?

For many years I was repeatedly treated with antibiotics which eventually led to antibiotic resistance, until I stopped expecting doctors to know what my body needed and started exploring other options for healing. Regrettably, medication is often the only solution offered for chronic discomfort that rampages through our fast-paced society. Even when in agony, we won't stop in our tracks to pay attention to the body's signals and needs. As a result, prescription drugs have become a lucrative industry that reaps the benefits of over-the-counter painkillers. These drugs may provide short-term relief but shut down valuable communication from the body. Disenchanted with the allopathic approach as well as alternative therapies, neither of which guarantee a solution, we disregard the integral medicines our body produces naturally, including but not limiting to endorphins as pain relief and mood enhancers. We are to treat our ailing body patiently with curiosity, love and respect, instead of naively silencing its deliberate cries for attention. Whilst we may still label physical discomfort an unwelcome distraction, we can no longer deny its intelligent, unique and symbolic cues. Fatigue, headaches, broken bones, sleep disturbances and more, these are all signs that the body is undergoing a realignment and probably requires support in order to repair, without the need for panic. In fact, let's also bring forth our soul's wisdom that is using the body as a messenger to convey the vitalness of a balanced physical and psychological well-being, which has come under immense scrutiny during the planetary energetic upgrades.

With the ongoing influx of solar flare activity producing ultraviolet and x-ray radiation that heats up the Earth's atmosphere, and somewhat influences its gravitational pull, our bodies are having to constantly recalibrate to maintain stability. Think of the stabilograph which is used to assess a person's physical balance. The test involves standing on a platform which measures the individual's involuntary body movements and records the degrees of swaying over a period of time. A prolonged out of balance movement can bring on dizziness, nausea, and vomiting just to mention a few symptoms, and are not necessarily caused by any physical impairment. Ever considered that your chronic cold could be a result of bad posture or earthly forces that make your body gravitate to the left or the right?

Yoga and Pilates are both effective practices that include counterbalances, containing sequences and poses that stretch and strengthen different parts of the body whilst promoting structural integrity. Our bodies can be highly sensitive to natural movements and atmospheric pressures. Research has shown that natural disasters such as earthquakes and floods can have a significant impact on the mental and physical health of individuals. As another example, many women experience menstrual pain that is closely linked to the cycles of the moon, highlighting the intimate connection between our bodies and shifts in planetary consciousness. As we awaken to our full potential as human beings, we have to ready ourselves for an expanded level of energetic flow and a deeper rapport with all celestial bodies in this solar system. Our influence and reach go far and beyond the planet's perceived borders, and we often misplace energy repositories in other realms of existence that can impact our health here on Earth. It is crucial to understand the interconnectedness of all things in order to achieve a more holistic approach to healing and wellness, and embrace pain as mediating messenger of the illusory separation.

The majority of our DNA is made up of interchangeable light photons and we can clear genetically imprinted associations in more than one way. Energy enhancing healing systems already exist but have yet to be made publicly available as a means of locating malfunctioning cell imprints that are stored in our organism, in order to bring them back to zero-balance.

Our bodies are quantumly plugged into the torsion field of universal intelligence, giving us access to our original blueprint of health and highest potential. By bypassing all projected and manipulated ideologies, our cells can harmonically vibrate and resonate with our star codes and infinite light source. This will also enable us to consciously tap into other forms of energy resources to replenish any inefficiencies. My body has taught me to follow a path with and beyond conventional medical practice and to keep an open-minded perspective. For instance, I have come to understand the link between the digestive system and the dreaming body. We are dreaming in the astral world with our dreaming body freely passing in and out the physical body through the solar plexus portal. Emotional and toxic energies that are absorbed in our dreams, in unawareness, can impact our overall well-being. A bio-photonic storehouse of intuitive wisdom and cosmic guidance is available at your very own fingertips if you should you have the inclination, trust, and vision to get actively involved in your physical health and vitality.

Hack Those Happy Hormones

The body is the response apparatus that our soul essence has moulded and formed over lifetimes to suit its expression. It is, in fact, a portal to bring soul and spirit through and to manifest with. We have become so used to inhabiting our instrument of experience that we forget to pay tribute to it. We owe it to no other than our divine self to make the most of this earthly incarnation by enjoying and celebrating our physicality here on this planet.

- Healing is releasing dopamine by eating good food, acknowledging and taking care of our human needs.

- Healing is movement through exercise, laughter, and listening to music which can kill pain due to stimulating endorphins in the body.

- Healing is getting out to mingle with all sentient kingdoms to get some oxytocin, the love hormone.

- Healing is physical touch - be that with fellow humans or

- from petting animals, we are all social creatures and thrive on connecting with one another.

- Healing is taking time to be still – to enjoy solitude in meditation or in nature, communing with the Sun that triggers serotonin in our bodies.

Ancestral Imprinting

We all have access to self-study. From personal experience, I remember a knee pain that took me many years to figure out and subsequently heal. I was eleven years old when my maternal grandmother, who I had hardly known, died on my watch. She was a diabetic and I only briefly met her in the late stages of her illness. The day she died I had been tasked to keep her company whilst everyone was working away from the house. Her breathing patterns became distressed and erratic, and I witnessed her soul leave the body. At the time, I tried to get help by running from the house without avail. Only many years later during a Bowen session was I able to release the trauma of that incident, having lodged itself as pain in my knees for all those years. I know now that this incident was predetermined and contracted out between us on a soul level. It was her time to leave and I was meant to assist her transition, but I was too young and innocent to understand that. The significance of being present at someone's deathbed varies depending on what the souls agreed upon, which may well extend beyond a graceful holding of space for the departing soul. In my case, the person leaving was passing on the torch of the maternal lineage, which can be quite an overwhelming responsibility, especially if one is not aware of it. Apart from that, a cocktail of conflicting emotions belonging to my parents having left me to her attendance, got stored in my knees. With purpose in disguise, pain often facilitates personal growth and new levels of cognition. As practiced time travellers we can heal our ancestral DNA memories and heighten our awareness through new layers of understanding. This allows us to raise our vibratory rate and adjust the body's density to move into the next stage of soul integration.

This great awakening, which I like to call a *Spiritual Embodiment Evolution*, is to discard all emotional baggage, break away from outdated dogma and doctrine, and steadily forge our way towards stepping into our divine nature. Over the years, I have had many clients that remedied their physical pain by changing jobs or relationships that no longer contributed to their well-being or soul's expansion. Pain, not ignored or overemphasised, is a valid agent for change.

Going back to the experience of my grandmother's death, I have since learned that knee problems often relate to movement and clarity of direction. It is said that knee issues can be linked to our relationship with parents and grandparents, or lack thereof. If you have knee problems and can relate, ask yourself if you have been affected by absent or controlling parental guidance from your childhood? This kind of exploration is not meant to cast blame on anyone, but to simply uncover more personal history and to help you heal yourself, as well as your soul family lineage. Personally, I never really thought much about the lack of relationship with both of my lineage grandparents until my reading with Andrew in 2014. Upon asking him about my involvement in mystery schools, I came across an astonishing link. Let me quote the transcript of his Akashic reading in this session:

"As a soul you have done the mystery thing many, many times. You have been the secret agent. You have been the good and the bad guy as a Mason and a Knight's Templar. What do you know about your grandparents?"

Apparently, the fact that I knew hardly anything about my grandparents pointed to my longstanding service in mystery schools. He continued to say that I had been kicked out of the Free Masons because I had been withholding information which was considered a massive betrayal.

He went on to elaborate:

"For you that stems from the streets of Gibraltar around 1530 AD. At that point in time our planet was under massive invasion for nearly a hundred years.

Ships were battling each other... pulses of energies night after night, day after day, for something like a hundred straight years. You were in Gibraltar at that time and the Knights Templar were a very different organisation before they fully came around. They started around 500AD. You were part of an organisation that was searching for vessels that had crashed and collected the dead bodies and the technology. The people in the Knights Templar knew how to use that technology. They were former mystery school members where they learned to remember as much as thirty percent of their past lives. Many of them went through specific alchemy training of how to create their own philosopher stone. Am I triggering something?"

I burst out laughing when he asked me that question because I was completely clueless about what he was referring to. He proceeded telling me that I created my own philosopher stone in Gibraltar from that recovered technology. I understood that I was kicked out of the organisation when I decided not to return specific pieces of technology to the controlling kingdom. On a side note, he also mentioned that a huge amount of this technology ended up in Nigeria and is actually still there under guard by a different faction of templars who broke away from the initial group to make sure that this technology wasn't falling back into the hands of the kings and the queens who were just going to sell it.

Ultimately, the validity of any information received, whether through a reading, meditation, or a dream, depends on one's personal choice and willingness to discern and ascertain the truth. Our body has a natural resonance with universal intelligence and the unique data imprint of our soul, allowing us to determine when truth is being spoken. We may not comprehend everything cognitively in the moment, but often the realisation dawns on us later as we clear more of the debris from the soul.

In January 2022, eight years after this particular reading, another remarkable piece of the puzzle in regards to being disconnected from my ancestors fell into place. I had been experiencing lower back pain on and off for over ten years and explored a multitude of conventional as well as alternative body-mind-soul modalities to identify the source of it.

What emerged over the years was a reoccurring pattern where healers pointed to an energetic rapture between my first two or three chakras, and the upper chakras. Lower back issues are said to be associated with the planet Venus and the birth sign of Libra, often linked to lack of balance and support. One of my metaphorical explorations showed me the back pain as an impenetrable metal shield that was stuck between my lower and upper body. Why a metal shield?

Well, there is no point in arguing with one's subconscious mind when it throws up the most weird and wonderful symbolism. It is not too surprising though, as when it comes to soul family themes mine would usually point to conflict and war. I come from a maternal lineage of explorers, fighters, warriors, rescuers, the hunters and the hunted all taking part in conflict and struggle over millions of years. I realised that my lower back intensity was not only related to support issues in this lifetime, but more significantly, it pointed towards a disconnect and lack of ancestral unification due to an unhealed backlog of blame, shame, guilt, anger, you name it. The previous generations of my maternal lineage, in particular, have been involved in the less enlightened side of mystery schools with an invested tacit interest in maintaining the status quo. The Martina that I am today is the fully integrated Atlantean soul that walked in during my teens in support of my quest to serve as a mediator for global unification and peace. It took over all host soul contracts plus, of course, the body itself that bears witness to past experiences and future possibilities. Our DNA memory is a precious and sought-after commodity that can easily be used to either manipulate or heal our multidimensional history, which was one of the main reasons why the system wanted to eliminate my skinsuit. Important access codes and data that are encrypted in our molecular structure can turn us into targets. All those years I had been unaware of the deep disconnect and ongoing conflict in the realms of my ancestral lineage. The pain, whilst it has improved since that realisation, still invites me to cultivate more awareness of the part we all play in the unseen realms of existence.

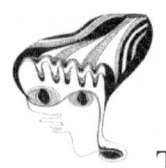

The Unified Self Meditation

Imagine a unity field inside of your heart; a big ball of white light radiating out in all directions, encompassing all versions of your past, present and future selves:

I herewith bring focus to my inner world. The barriers of separation dissolve and I create a unity field within myself. As I use my pranic life force, my attention focuses on the fullness of the four compartments of my heart. My inner core is pulsing. My ancient future self is drumming to the rhythm of this planet in honour of my multidimensional existence. This is the time of unification of all the parts that have been with me since the beginning of time. The unity field flows through the right and left ventricle, the lower chambers of my heart. It expands out to the upper chamber, the right and left atrium, and illuminates the heart. The pericardium expands in joyful bliss taking in the energy of unity that is engorging every single cell of the body. As the heart expands its divine radiance, it guides the magnetic resonance deeply into the marrow of my bones, my blood, all the way to the edges of my limbs. I flood the entirety of my body with compassion, grace and love. I saturate my nervous system, my digestive system, my respiratory system, my lymphatics and vascular system with the music of the loving heart. I take that musical masterpiece into the pores of my skin and out into the aura. The music fills my etheric body as the heart keeps strengthening, all parts become one and whole again, ready to merge with the universal heart. I see my true self. I value this self. I deserve this unity and I radiate it out through the echoes of time.

Celebrating Mortality

> "The difficult position of man, but also his greatness, is that he belongs both to eternity and time." – Michael Conge

A discussion about human embodiment is incomplete without looking at the link between grief, praise, celebration, and the alchemy behind death.

We have yet to consciously discover eternal living and equally appreciate our simultaneous existence in all forms of life, on multiple dimensional planes. I'd like you to consider grief as an important part of healing the disconnect between our finite and infinite existence – a bridge to multidimensional living. Do not shortcut the grieving process for it paves the way to understanding death as a mere transition of form. Mastering to grieve the old ways of living will be a very important part of who we are becoming, especially in the years ahead of us. The 'five stages of grief' often spoken of can take months or even years to successfully work through.

For the sake of this discussion, I would like to suggest two more stages:

1. Denial
2. Anger
3. Bargain
4. Depression
5. Acceptance
   *6. Praise

   *7. Celebration

… with particular emphasis on the celebration of the personal experiences accumulated through the grieving, forgiving, and remembering process. Grief, in an alchemised form, can be intense praise of our legacy and a true honouring of what has been left behind in the material world. It is natural and necessary to celebrate our embodiment as we integrate and transcend every stage of human expression. A wise friend once said that the unlimited soul in us needs to appreciate time as a social agreement for it has shaped people's pains and realities over billions of years and given rise to monumental masterpieces and wisdom. Etheric, mortal, or multidimensional – all our evolutionary stages are creating a massive log of experiences and memories in service to universal intelligence. We are here to celebrate and value our physical expression rather than excessively ponder its limitations.

Our impermanent nature encourages us to live more radically and spend more quality time with our reunited soul family enjoying the joys and perks of earthly living, and to fulfil and fill the memory banks of karma and dharma with celestial currency. Our planetary ascension assists in consciously bringing our ancestors of the past and future back to life, as we merge all fractal aspects under the wise guidance of our avatar.

Grief is not limited to the physical realms. We can hold space and be present with our ancestral aspects, listen to their grievances, and together celebrate their victories no matter how big or small. Ancestral rapport and support are a significant part of our self-worth, an honouring of our humanness and an important service to the birthing of the new paradigm. Our ancestors are a part of us. We are our ancestors of the past and we will be ancestors again to the new versions of ourselves in the future. Spiritual embodiment is a celebratory interplay of remembering and sharing of all the skills, tricks, trades, and lessons that we have learned while inhabiting a body. Our task here is to build and transverse the rainbow bridge that connects the lower and higher levels of consciousness. Our uniquely tailored perspectives of truth will live on in the eternal afterlife. Death is not to be feared, but an invitation to fully consummate living in preparation for a most joyous transition and transfiguration into other levels of consciousness.

Today is Yesterday's Memory and Tomorrow's Vision

I have a longstanding history with mystery schools, and in 2013, I had the opportunity to participate in a 'Metaphors of Movement' training with Andrew Austin at The Freemasons Hall in London, which is the official headquarters of the United Grand Lodge of England. It was an incredibly fascinating location for personal development studies, and I enjoyed the course, the venue, and the guided tour that was a part of the program.

For some of us, we are invited to live, study, and teach in places of ancient history to activate ancestral soul codes and assist in the neutralisation and reorientation of the enforced geometry grids. Another one of these seemingly unrelated events came together in a meaningful way whilst I was writing this book. England is a country of rich history of monarchy that dates back thousands of years. I came across the King Stone - the coronation stone of the very first seven Saxon kings in England, dating back to 900 AD. It is displayed in Kingston upon Thames, right next to the town's Guildhall. I've been living near this town since 2001, after returning from South Africa, and I had never heard of it until reading about it. The irony of it all is that in 2018 I gave a talk on alternative approaches to irritable-bowel syndrome (IBS) and held a meditation evening for an IBS support group that was hosted in the Kingston Guildhall. Similar to the Grand Masons Lodge, a rather weird place of choice to network, but certainly connected to the ancient history of mystery schools. The places we go often hold a deeper meaning and significance than we may initially realise. The meaning of weird, as mentioned in old dictionaries, is said to be 'of destiny'. It's interesting how we can live near a place for a long time and never know much about it until a particular event or moment brings something to our attention. Upon watching the coronation of King Charles III in May 2023, I was struck with the realisation that I had still been holding allegiances to the long-gone kings and queens of England, and most probably other countries too. As part of my individual process of soul shard recovery and growth, I released all remaining royal ties, obligations, and commitments, to no longer be contractually bound to karmic royal service, and to fully embrace my role as a sovereign universal citizen.

As we embark on our own healing journey, we free ourselves to pursue our destiny. We begin to play an important role in the awakening process and contribute to a greater collective effort to restore balance and healing to our planet.

In doing so, we discover that the synchronicities we encounter are not mere chance occurrences, but rather an indication that we are following the correct path, carrying out our soul's mission. It certainly was not a coincidence that during my corporate days I was involved with trades into Nigeria, travelling there on business. I was literally called back to activate the codes in the philosopher stone, hidden in Nigeria since the 16th century.

In another healing session, I found out about my ancestral lineage's involvement with the Austro-Hungarian empire, which showed me a significant link as to why I triggered the walk-in experience and the reason for leaving Austria. Our original star soul families extend far beyond the last seven generations that we repeatedly reincarnate with. Due to obscured incarnation rules in the past and the misrepresentation of karma, we choose the same biological family over and over again, just in different bodies and roles. Sometimes it takes drastic measures to break away from an ancestral lineage that may keep you stuck in a vicious cycle of repetition and tradition, genetically bound through fealties, loyalties, and festering familiarities. It is important to remember that we came here as transformation catalysts with the power to liberate and free ourselves from karmic entanglements. Whenever we do so, we blast healing waves through all existing holograms, reaching and healing our ancestors of the past and future, across vast degrees of separation. Coincidences are, in truth, divinely orchestrated prompts to declutter our past and reveal more of our future possibilities.

Living in London for over 23 years has been an important part of my soul's evolution. London is a city that features numerous sacred sites and symbols that have been strategically positioned to prevent human spiritual empowerment and to dominate over our species. It is no accident that I was drawn to this city to heal and remember my purpose in this lifetime.

London is said to be the throat chakra of Earth, a multicultural and multifunctional gateway that is linked to great worldly and spiritual dimensions. It is a place where many souls feel called to, either to live or visit, in order to fulfill their spiritual purpose and contribute to the collective consciousness. If you are interested in more than a tourist guide for London, I recommend reading Chris Street's book *'London, City of Revelation'* about the Earthstars landscape temple geometry. There is a lot more to be brought to light still and I am looking forward to the continuous and synchronistic revelations ahead of us.

Breathe Powerfully

Onto something different now; let's look at pain alchemy. Both breath and fear can only exist in the material world. Unlike fear though, breath is sustaining life and fear is destroying it. Please engage your innate alchemical genius of transforming pain through the unlimited point of view with an intense focus on breath, by practicing what I call The Avatar Breath.

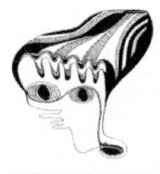

Avatar Breath Exercise

Sit comfortably with a straight back, feet flat on the ground, hands on belly and start observing your breath moving through your body. Take your intention and attention to your inner environment and start disconnecting from any outside distractions. For the purpose of this transformative healing meditation, allow yourself to connect deeply to your physical body and your life sustaining breath. Observe the rhythm of the breath. Acknowledge any physical pain or intensities in the body and gently drop your mind into your heart. Keep your mouth closed and breathe through the nose.

Notice the up and down movements of the space just below the navel; your dantien, the house and home of your personal power. Continue breathing in your own organic rhythm, with equal inhalations and exhalations.

Now, it is time to connect to the earthly roots below the soil under your feet. Imagine a wide, vast web of an interconnected system of nutrients and nourishment, guarded and guided by the spirit of mother Earth's dragons. Think of it as a celestial dragon energy breath, sourced all the way from the many fertile womb chakras of the Earth.

Open your mouth, pucker your lips and deeply draw in that dragon energy through your Earth Star Chakra, beneath your feet. Let it swirl along the spinal column, seeping into the vertebrates, the spaces in between, spiralling up and around all chakras. Close your mouth and suspend the breath before you release it again, this time through your nose. Maintain it as long as you can without gasping and feel free to practice as many breaths as you require.

On your inhalations observe this dragon breath spreading into your skin, your blood, lymphatics, organs, muscles, bones, and cells of your body. Any intensity, toxins, pain, parasites or stuck energies that are impacting your physical, mental, emotional or spiritual body - allow the dragon breath to absorb those with ease and grace. Guide the energies down into your digestive tract as you focus the breath into your belly. Imagine your belly's furnace burning brightly as it transmutes, transforms and alchemises all those intensities into pure healing energy.

On your exhalations gently draw your navel back towards the spine and suspend the breath out into your lower abdomen. As you keep holding out the breath, you push the alchemised healing energy up the spine into your heart, your chest, your throat, and to all the spaces in your body that require healing and then finally out your crown chakra.

Now, imagine all unhealed and wounded versions of yourself suspended in spacetime, still connected to your DNA technology, receiving this healing energy from your I AM presence now. Extend your presence to them through an intense flow of compassion, forgiveness and acknowledgment of their pain and suffering. See them leave, heal, pop, dissipate and uncreate. Some will be ready to integrate with you and increase your light.

See all fragments of the mosaic of your original blueprint of health fall back into place. Now, put dedication and participation into another cycle of this earthly dragon breath; as many as you require.
Take in a breath through your puckered lips. Let it move around the body to collect any pain and sorrow. Hold the breath without gasping. Focus the energy into the furnace of your digestive tract and transmute it. Exhale through the nose, holding the breath out as you push the alchemized energy up the spine and out the crown, healing your cells and soul aspects.

Simple Embodiment A-Z

Every physical incarnation is an opportune stepping stone for spiritual refinement. A point will come when the soul becomes excessively attached to its I AM personalities which no longer contribute to its growth and development. Every soul must eventually relinquish and transcend all personality vehicles that it used to gain experience and knowledge with, during physical incarnations. This is a natural evolutionary process that cannot be forced and kickstarted before its due time, as it short circuits the required healing process and purpose here on Earth. A certain arrogance and righteousness upon the outer planes are not uncommon amongst souls, considering the soul's extensive travels and achievements in all dimensional realms. Godlike or myth-based delusions are part of both the micro and the macro worlds; as above – so below. All sentient journeys are sacred, and whilst some individuals may have accumulated numerous lifetimes of hard work on Earth, others have spent a significant portion of their existence exploring the astral worlds. It is important to encourage a 'down-to-earth' consciousness in all champion souls who wander freely among us on Earth and emphasise that out-of-body experiences hold less value unless they are supported by coherent actions and real-life encounters. Spiritually embodied living is a human virtue, regardless of star origin or age of soul, reminding us that nobility is rooted in humility. The following practical tips and inspirational quotes are to inspire moments of appreciation of our human nature.

Pick one to rest after a healing session or at times when body and soul require a well-deserved break:

a) ***TAKE A 30-60 MINUTE WALK IN FRESH AIR***; consciously follow your breath and let your body and mind activate any newly made changes.

b) ***GIVE YOURSELF A PAT ON THE BACK*** for having taken action, for having allowed yourself to take responsibility for your life and future.

c) ***BE GENTLE WITH YOURSELF;*** let the day take its course and don't schedule too much distraction and workload. Treat yourself to a nice dinner or a hot bath. Whatever works for you is fine.

d) ***DO SOME RELAXATION;*** just for a few minutes sit comfortably, release a deep breath and focus your mind on the word "RELAX" repeating behind your eyes. Feel your body relaxing, your mind becoming more alert and focused in the moment.

e) ***OBSERVE YOUR PHYSIOLOGY;*** you may find that you walk more upright after a treatment. Keep it going and remember that just by changing your physiology you can change your state of mind at any time.

f) ***DRINK LOTS OF WATER*** to help balance the nervous system and energise your body and mind. Remember our bodies are more than 70% water.

g) ***ALLOW THE WORK TO INTEGRATE*** over the days and weeks to come. New neurological pathways have been formed that now need to be tested and trained on a daily basis. Remember "a path is formed by walking on it" – Chuang Tzu.

h) ***TAKE A NOTICING BREAK;*** notice what you are not noticing. Check in at various intervals during the day. Notice what you are not paying attention to. What kinaesthetic, auditory, and visual information impinged on your senses that caused you to switch off? "Life is made of millions of moments, but we live only one of these moments at a time. As we begin to change this moment, *we begin to change our lives. – Trinidad Hunt.*

i) **PRACTICE PERIPHERAL VISION;** *gaze softly at the world around you. Expand your peripheral vision to take in everything around you at once, without focusing on any one thing. "The world is round and the place, which may seem like the end, may also be the beginning" – I. Baker Priest.*

j) **LISTEN WITHIN;** *choose quiet surroundings. Quiet the buzzing mind chatter that may dominate your thinking. Listen to your own voice and keep the internal dialogue positive and inspiring. Take up meditation as a daily routine, no matter how long – just get started. "Stillness is where creativity and solutions to problems are found." – E. Tolle, Stillness Speaks.*

k) **FOCUS ON WHAT YOU WANT,** *not what you don't want. Discover the art of looking for and finding positive aspects in people and situations. "Keep your face to the sunshine and you will not see the shadows" – Helen Keller.*

l) **STRETCH & BALANCE YOUR BODY;** *do some simple yoga postures or any other discipline to enhance your energy flow and balance. Physical exercise is a major contribution to find harmony in day-to-day life. "Inward calm cannot be maintained unless physical strength is constantly and intelligently replenished" – Buddha.*

m) **THREE-DIMENSIONAL NUTRITION;** *the self has three inseparable dimensions... spirit, mind and body. When we starve any dimension, we starve the whole. When we lovingly nourish any one dimension, we nourish the whole. Reach out to your mind and spirit through physical body therapy as often as you can. "In order to change the output of the body, we need to re-write the software of the mind" – Deepak Chopra.*

n) **GET ENOUGH REST;** *sleep is the most powerful healing remedy! Why not tap into this completely free form of therapy and allow your muscles to fully rest and recover and your immune system to re-charge whilst you are sound asleep? "Just when the caterpillar thought the world was over, it became a butterfly"- someone, certainly.*

o) **PAY ATTENTION TO YOUR DREAMS;** engaging with your dreams can help you recover your inner wholeness. Learn more about how to program your subconscious mind and start dreaming. "If you want to understand human nature, the human mind, what makes us tick, you need to look at dreams" – Prof. Mc Namara, Boston University School of Medicine.

p) **ENFORCE AND CREATE NEW BOUNDARIES** that protect, nurture and sustain all that you cherish and value. What better time to do this than NOW? To create boundaries we must say, thus far and no further. This means speaking up, expressing your needs, indicating your preferences. "We shall not cease from exploration, and at the end of all our exploring we'll be to arrive where we started and know the place for the first time" – T.S. Elliot.

q) **CREATE CLARITY;** write down the results you want to produce by setting your intention. Journal your focus over the next fifty to five hundred years and ready yourself to make choices that match the energy of your goals. Always remember that "Fortune comes to the prepared mind" – Louis Pasteur.

r) **WORK WITH YOUR IMAGINATION;** for optimum resourcefulness, enter a state of relaxed alertness before performing any important activity. Visualise yourself in the now and bring in all of your senses to support your choices beyond your wildest imagination. "Your imagination is your preview of life's coming attraction" – A. Einstein.

s) **JOURNALLING;** writing down your feelings, beliefs, ideas and experiences can be extremely helpful to bring your inner thoughts to outer awareness for action. Remember, a belief is only a thought you are perpetually thinking. Rather than genes, it is our beliefs that control our life" –Bruce Lipton.

t) **SHOW UP & BE CURIOUS;** determine to do something you have been avoiding and show up ready to go. Discover what happens when you start a task that you put off in the past. "You must do the thing you think you cannot do" – E. Roosevelt.

u) **MEASURE AND CELEBRATE YOUR PROGRESS;** recognize any small concrete changes in the direction of your desire.

Create small sub-goals and celebrate any and all progress you make. Remember to take one step at the time.

v) **GET FEEDBACK AND STAY WITH IT;** there is feedback for every one of your actions. Take time to review whatever outcomes you produce, then value and integrate the information you gain from your efforts. Keep choosing and responding far past the point where you would have quit before. Give new behaviours at least fifty trials. Keep learning about what works. "Do not go where the path may lead you. Go instead where there is no path and leave a trail" – Ralph Emerson.

w) **REFLECTION AND GRATITUDE;** at night before going to sleep, review your day without criticism. Offer a prayer and celebrate having done your best. Be grateful for all the good things in life. Ask yourself what do I desire? Learn the 'art of allowing' and remember where attention goes energy flows and the result shows!

x) **TRUST YOURSELF;** remember a time when you really trusted yourself, maybe when you were a child. Get that picture up and reassociate with all those feelings, sounds and smells. Look at yourself in that picture when you completely trusted your instincts. Enjoy these sensations and know that it can be that way again. "Just trust yourself, then you will know how to live" – Johann Wolfgang von Goethe.

y) **WORK THE 'NEW YOU' MODE;** clear out your timeline at the end of the day and acknowledge the memories from it without having to attach meaning. Explore the beliefs you hold that no longer serve you and let them go. Limits are fabrications of your own psyche. When you push beyond your limits, you unlock mental and physical reserves that you never thought you had.

z) ALWAYS REMEMBER:
You were born with potential.
You were born with goodness and trust. You were born with ideals and dreams. You were born with greatness.
You were born with wings.
You are not meant for crawling, so don't.
You have wings.
Learn to use them and fly. – Rumi

PART TWO: Abuse & Karmic Hairball

Abuse

Abuse goes hand in hand with embodiment; often masterfully camouflaged but eventually revealed through a lack of committed action, unsociable interaction, and defensive reaction. Avoidance and rebellion towards dealing with any kind of abuse issues hold us captive in the lower personality realm of physical, mental, or emotional chaos and unhappiness, and deflects from the soul's higher journey to joy and bliss. We have to defragment all pieces related to abuse to get a more comprehensive picture of how widely the roots have spread. The effect of abuse does not always stop with the indecent assault but continues through one's active participation by trying to hide any shame or guilt associated with it. The more we learn about the nature of karmic bondage, the easier we can forgive ourselves and others and move out of the self-perpetuating cycle of abuse.

Anything that seeks to diminish our sense of physical and emotional wellbeing, and fosters separation rather than unified love, falls into the category of abuse. A lack of incoherent boundaries can attract hostility unbeknown to our conscious minds and may cause severe anxiety or depression that stops us from fully committing to and showing up in life. Human beings have a tendency to conceal oppression by means of zealotry and seclusion, or alternatively turn to perfectionism, workaholism, or sacrificial martyrdom... most are perfectly acceptable social standards of living. The pain that gets buried behind false optimism and superiority can have detrimental impacts on our bodies and relationships, as established earlier. The revocation that follows this brief introduction embraces a multitude of potent clearings and healings with regards to day-to-day victimhood, narcissism, empathy, bullying, control, and disempowerment - all those sub-categories that fit the dynamics of abuse.

There simply is no excuse for skipping this section if you consider yourself seriously dedicated to a journey to self-mastery. We have all been at the receiving end of abuse that lowered our self-esteem, if not in this lifetime, then certainly in another. As long as we tacitly submit to the control of another, we give up authority for our own lives and remain stuck in the spirals of abuse. Recoup any misappropriated parts of yourself and stand tall in your mighty I AM presence. As we begin to reclaim our truth and establish a more intimate and healed relationship with ourselves, we break the bonds to this world's aggressors and victims and re-establish trust in all that's physical. The true liberation lies in the acknowledgement of the massive extent of betrayal and persecution that we have all been a part of as abusers and the abused, many times over. In order to get out of the reincarnation cycle that is an inherent part of the abuse of the human soul, we need to untangle the karmic hairball of the time line paradox, end the human experiment here on Earth, and develop a true science of consciousness. Find comfort and reassurance in the fact that love is the ultimate authority. The new age is built on foundational principles such as forgiveness, non-violence, and self-regeneration. Humanity's progress is driven by the pursuit of reconciliation, harmony, and a shared vision for a global unification of all people.

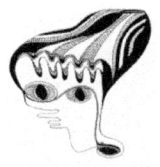

Abuse Revocation & Invocation

I call to my sacred medicine spread, that which aides me in understanding my infinite spirit. The healer's tools have been laid out in ceremonial fashion. I call to the four elements and bring their essence into my sacred healing space, in equal co-creation with all sentient kind.

I call to the ancestors to be a part of this healing to bring communal balance with the words being manifested in the now. I call to the dreamers of the southern skies to mediate between our seven future generations.

In this shamanic healing moment of no-time now, I ignite a sacred fire burning in my root, sacrum, belly, heart, throat, spirit eye to cleanse and clear my body, mind and soul, and send prayers of vitality, prosperity and health into the alchemical flames of transmutation and transformation. I herewith choose to create a spiritual court of equity and engage all my I AM selves, all shards, parts and avatars, that have endured a strict, enforced and perverted discipline.

All emotional, physical, verbal or sexual abuse from caretakers, guardians, custodians, keepers, supervisors and others unnamed, as the I AM was going through infancy, puberty and adolescence, that has squashed, pent up or limited my true feelings and forms of naturally authentic, sexual, joyful, sacred, creative expressions, are now being openly acknowledged and offered healing to, across all layers of time and space.

I, the I AM Apex being of the now, claims back all of my power from the very first moment of abuse until this very moment of the now. I let no piece of abuse go uncovered as I retrieve my energy in equal co-creation, non-duality, non-competition, non-hierarchical order.

I do this out of love and compassion for myself and not out of vengeance and betrayal... for you are still my mother, my father, my sibling, my husband, my wife or any other being I co-created with through ancestral karmic retribution, seen or unseen, in this and other lifetimes, dimensions, timelines, galaxies and universes.

I, as this I AM Apex being of the now, am going through a process of reclaiming all of my power and replaced energies, so that this sovereign being may learn the lessons from the abuse.

I now neutralise, nourish and nurture all potential concepts of charge and polarity that have been projected upon me by the abuse. I turn and transmute them into creation, inspiration, and dreams.

All dramas or traumas that have been enforced upon my body, my mind, my spirit by the verbal, physical, emotional, financial, social, sexual or any other abuse seen or unseen, in this and any other lifetimes, dimensions and time streams, I now, with every cellular level of mine, reject that energy with such force of love that it is returned to the perpetrators as empowering forgiveness and unbiased compassion, because I am linked to my I AM heart foetus, knowing that love is the way and vengeance is not.

I remove unawareness and revenge and all other aspects of that, from the abuser to the abusee, from the victim to the tyrant, so this I AM now can be fully empowered as a heart-spaced aware, loving being with no restrictions or limitations on the journey to the unlimited point of view of the sacred neutral observer, the true joyful consciousness explorer, and the celestial experiencer of the 8th colour of time.

Every time my personal space has been violated, my energy been infiltrated and my consciousness anaesthetized, my knowingness questioned, or my awareness undermined, I now revoke, recant, renounce, denounce, destroy and uncreate all the oaths, vows, contracts and agreements with my abusers as well as my numerous disowned shadow selves, created through those violations, in knowing and in unknowingness.

All the decisions, judgements, conclusions, computations, separations, projections and expectations of the self and others of being damaged, being rejected goods, not ever being good enough to be loved, being worthless, being bad, being singled out, being targeted, I now destroy and uncreate and return them to zero balance minus infinity.

I, as this evolving I AM now, open the trinity of my eyes and heart to the true potency and kindness of my being, and acknowledge all the times where I sacrificed myself because I had an awareness that I was stronger than my siblings, parents, friends, comrades, or anyone else, and took on the abuse for others in unawareness.

The time is now to let go of all the old martyr and misapplied empath programs of self-defeat, self-deprivation, self-deprecation, lack of self-value, and eradication of the self for the false empowerment of others.

All of the allegiances, fealties, oaths, vows, contracts and agreements with hierarchical authorities, that I have made in this and other lifetimes, across dimensions and time streams, submitting and sacrificing myself for the supposed 'higher service' to emperors, pharaohs, sheiks, dictators, chieftains, warlords, popes and other religious leaders, grand masters, generals, military commanders, ... [add your own] I now pull that treacherous programming and categorically revoke, recant, rescind all of my given consent and signatures.

I, as an empowered being of this 5th world of peace, I commit to my individual path of spiritual awakening and take up the mantle of responsibility for personal choice and sacred discipline. I now destroy and uncreate all the decisions, judgments, conclusions, projections and expectations of myself and others, made in and outside of this 3D reality.

All the shame, blame, regret and guilt that is haunting and limiting me, in this particular lifetime, for having been the abuser, the narcissist, the perpetrator, the assassin, the enforcer, the slaughterer, the killer, the executioner, in all eras of time and no time, I now ask for universal forgiveness for my actions and conduct.

All unshed tears of the abused and abandoned versions of myself, who felt eternally trapped in the imprisonment of their environment, mind, and body – together, let us profusely sob, weep, cry, and transform those tears into oceans of infinite possibilities. I ask those younger soul shards to claim their potency and take a leap of faith, forgive, and grow up. I imagine them standing in front me as I watch them gain in size, shape, form, age, confidence and in courage, turning on their inner wisdom of their ancient past, present, and future, becoming the co-creators of magnitude they truly are.

All of the limitations, abuse, constrictions or regrets that I have contained in my neurotransmitters, pineal gland, throat, hypothalamus, brain, visual field, cells, molecules, sensory circuitry, sexual and pro-creative organs, and my vagus nerve as echoes from the programmed parasympathetic gone awry, I now dissipate and release all and expand out into the 99.9999% energy, space and consciousness between the atoms. I now consciously choose to let go of all realities that I have impelled within my central nervous system that keep me in destructive and addictive habit patterns, and on autopilot.

All the secret, hidden, invisible, covert, unseen, unsaid, unacknowledged and undisclosed implants and explants, both on and off-world, and hidden abuse agendas, I now destroy and uncreate them, and send them back to sender with consciousness attached, to never return to this mind, this body, this reality ever again.

All the causal incarcerations, incarnations, invocations, spells, curses and forced consciousness of pain, embodied through abuse and ignorant denial of my potency, I now untwist, unturn, unravel, untie, unground, revoke and dissipate the electromagnetic energy from every single cell and molecule of my body. I am a free-willed, non-agenda being in full mutual and eternal contribution to my fellow kind.

All the stupidity and unawareness that am I using to unconsciously invoke and perpetrate the biomimetic mimicry of all my abusers, my parents, my siblings, my exes, my ancestral relations, and all their pathways, pains and realities that I have been choosing... I now state my sovereign FUCK NO MORE to all of that.

I release, disentangle, and disconnect all feeding tubes and cords with immediate effect.

As a sovereign being of the now, I no longer fall prey to tacit consent. For all the times the body thought it was the soul, or the soul pretended to be the body - I now simply forgive them both. All the times my body shut down and malfunctioned as the vehicle of experience due to subconscious painful emotional overload, leaving no space for the soul to be in the body, or kicking it out of the body, I now claim back all that space, neutralise the charge and polarity, and herewith declare truce for all eternity.

My skinsuit is my tool, my vehicle, and the home of my soul; a loyal and trustworthy companion, and as such, my chosen instrument of a cheerful, tearful, joyful, mindful, peaceful, soulful, artful, faithful, purposeful, colourful, thankful, and sensual humanoid experience. I will honour your services in this lifetime for eternity.

All the emotional and physical hits that I have taken onto my sternum, my shoulders, into my belly, my back, my head, like sledgehammers knocking the spirit out of me, I now claim back my strength and transform the intensity of the impact into potency, sacred determination, and commitment, serving the I AM Apex self. Everywhere I fell into the trap of control, disguised as an act of love, I herewith destroy and uncreate all distortions, imprints, and falsely indoctrinated teachings of what unconditional love is, and what it is not.

I pull all martyr programs and fears of conflict that have been validating my lack of connection and need for validation, as a result of the abuse and neglect throughout lifetimes, across all dimensions and time streams, so that I may finally take on the mantle of responsibility as my inner celestial dharmic warrior and teacher of peace, harmony, and unity.

Everywhere I allowed myself to have my energy drained and controlled by parents, offspring, friends, family, and teachers, I now take back that power. I transmute all energies of pain into questions, choices, possibilities, and contributions to empower future generations with the tools and knowledge to change the educational and parenting system, and purify celestial consciousness on this planet and beyond.

All the perversion and corruption of infinite being that I have innocently allowed myself to endure, by ignoring the choices of others that did not align with my judgment of loving kindness, I herewith remove all veils and concealed motives across all dimensions and timelines, and send waves of healing and forgiveness throughout the holograms.

As a celestial conduit and mediator of the 5th world of peace, I herewith acknowledge the innocence of my younger selves and embrace them with my loving and compassionate heart, for they must now let go of all the drama, hurt, and rejection that were projected towards them.

All the choices for abundance and happiness that I have been refusing by controlling and aligning with confused individuals, stuck in lack and poverty consciousness, I now release all entanglements that have been limiting my evolution, and make new choices that guide and trustingly lead me to the field of plenty. As I awaken the infinite spark of ease, joy, and prosperity within, I simply breathe and welcome the limitless possibilities that await me.

What natural signature frequency, vibration and harmony match can I and my body now be, to finally start living radically alive on the creative edge of possibilities, as an abundant, sacred neutral observer, in equal co-creation, non-hierarchy, non-competition, non-duality? Anything that doesn't allow that, I herewith destroy and uncreate.

Everywhere I am abusing my own and the freewill of others by still resisting and reacting, aligning and agreeing, creating moments of polarisation, the degradation of truths, and the false need for validation, I release all toxic interactions, biases, prejudices, and judgments.

With gratitude, I acknowledge the value of my rebel programs of the past, that no longer serve my natural highest evolution. I now revoke all contracts, vows, and agreements hereto, and sack all staffing agencies and entities that serve rebellion and war, rather than harmony and peace.

I use this moment of the now to declare my independence from a destructive and compulsive need for socialising, both on and off social media platforms, in order to feel visible, validated, heard, and seen.

Everywhere I have caused emotional distress through belittling, unduly criticizing, or manipulating data or people, I now take full responsibility for any wrongdoing on my side, and graciously accept apologies for having it done to me.

I herewith disconnect, sever, and unplug all cords and energy insertions for still having to fight against stipulations, orders, rules, and regulations set by the global narrative, as I am no longer allowing my energy to be harvested through resistance, domination, and control.

All backdoors are now closed, and I simply rest, relax and surrender into the knowingness of my heart's wisdom: I am the I AM Apex of the now, in trust, faith, charge, and no one and nothing can make choices for me and as me, as I am the true architect of my reality in divine co-creation with other beings of my choice. I create and generate supreme levels of consciousness, happiness, vitality, and prosperity, in linear and in non-linear fashion.

I do not consent to the notion that women are responsible for non-consensual sexual behaviour such as rape, sexual assault, or molestation because of their choice of clothing. Neither do I consent to blanket accusations towards the male gender of taking advantage of every intoxicated woman.

All the projections, expectation, and assumptions towards sexual abuse and gender manipulation, acceptable or non-acceptable behaviours and actions between men and women, that do not honour an understanding of individual responsibility, karmic resolution, our inherent freewill and choices, I herewith dismantle and remove for all eternity.

I, in the ever-present moment of now, choose to acknowledge my seen and unseen worlds. I declare my spiritual strategy, my rules, my boundaries, my policies and procedures as part of every prayer that I have created, and every victory that I have achieved in this lifetime. I build a house on the strong foundations of my learnings and victories.

Every choice that I have made in the past is present here, now, and no other outside source may interfere without my full awareness and agreement, I am willing to accept my blue road responsibility that uses a different frequency of time and treasure my ancestral connections and wisdom.

I honour my red road responsibility - the physical world that I walk in, with its seen and unseen worlds layered over the uniworld of great spirit. I count all my experiences, reminding me of spirit passing through time and space. The power of my memories is coming back for the purpose of creating change, the purpose of making love and celebrating peace.

As a self-realised, self-disciplined, self-motivated, self-responsible master with a daily healing and contemplative practice, I herewith acknowledge all discrimination, neglect, financial, sexual, institutional, emotional, physical, and galactic abuse.

With all the abuse that I have been subjected to, released, forgiven, and learned from, I can now see and create new positive programs to change the old fraud structures, using white magic and gratitude. I can create new words, new scales, new forms of expressions, new structures that need no labels.

From this point forward and backward in all perceptions of time, I honour my spiritual contracts with mother Earth in order to become the greatest photonic being of light. I make this statement, as a standing energy sine wave of self-truth. I trust in my own auric and akashic frequency for all sentient beings to know, "I AM" are not just words any more. This is my manifestation of potency, discernment, unity and sovereign creation as a celestial member of the stars, as this I AM APEX presence, (full name) manifested in the now.

And so it is.

Aho.

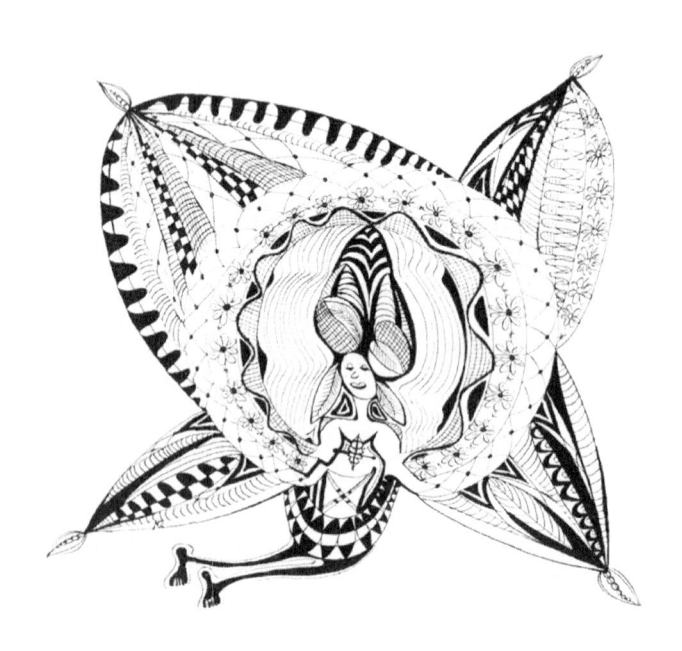

Karmic Entanglements

I was thirty when I left London for Cape Town, after having lived there for three years. I distinctly remember sitting on the plane with a weird sense of knowingness that my life was going to dramatically change. I was introduced to Paul over a phone call just a few months before. He was a cargo surveyor based in Cape Town and I was handling operations for a South African oil company in London. During that five-minute conversation, where I had appointed him to supervise the loading of petroleum products in Durban, I had a strong sense of déjà vu of having known him forever. A few months after that, we met in London for the first time.

Despite my British colleagues' discouraging views of the allegedly dangerous and poorly developed area, I was living to the East in the Docklands. In all fairness, we did have an IRA bomb detonate in South Quay in 1996 along my work route, and I had to use replacement buses for a few months. Living in the proximity of that incident may have been necessary for my karmic fulfilment, although it never occurred to me until now. Paul's parents also met in East London in the early 1960's, at the Monument that was built in commemoration of the Great Fire in 1666. His mother had moved from Austria to England to work as an au pair. His dad was a South African ship's cadet who had sailed into the London Docks, off to town for just a few hours before heading out again, when they set eyes on each other. They communicated via an interpreter at first, until her English improved over the months that it took for his ship to dock again in London, and the rest is family history. Life works in mysterious ways and I wouldn't be surprised at all to find out that we all had a part in the Great Fire of London.

My departure from England was not planned and highly unexpected. In fact, it was during Paul's first visit that I was told about the closure of the office and the relocation of the trading activity to Cape Town. Together with my Irish colleague, I chose to take up the position in South Africa. A long story short, I ended up renting an exquisite Bloubergstrand apartment overlooking the ocean and the majestic Table Mountain, working in a sunny and rather windy central Cape Town. My initial years overseas allowed me to catch up on all the fun that I had missed out in my teens. I remember Andrew once saying that it was an opportunity for my walk-in soul to freely enjoy having a body again. I was hell-bent to make the most of my newly found freedom, to say the least. Not for very long though, as fate had other ideas in stall for me. I say *fate*, with tongue in cheek, as what happened in the few weeks and months after my arrival in South Africa was an accelerated continuation of serious karmic resolution. Looking back, it seems like there was never a conscious choice as everything just happened, and all I could do was react and deal with the situation at the time.

I still wonder why it all had to occur on African soil and what ancient karma got resolved between everyone involved. Paul had a jet ski and we spent active times on the beach up in Langebaan at his parental home, together with friends and working colleagues. One of those amazing days ended rather abruptly for everyone when I managed to crash the jet ski against the rocks, after having been tossed off in a sudden and unexpected swell. Whilst the jet ski was a write-off, I was conscious and lucky to be alive, having missed the rocks myself. Some guys from a nearby surfing school saw the incident and fished me out the water.

This was the day I lost my bite! My teeth and gums needed reconstruction after the jet-ski had hit my face before crashing into the rocks and I wore a plate for over a year. Other than that, I got away with a serious warning to 'slow the hell down and to ask myself *what was I supposed to be doing with my life?*' Again, I didn't have to think about it too much because the universe already had a plan. A couple months after that, I had another accident that turned out to be the best thing that ever happened to me... and nine months later Emma was born in South Africa, before returning to London when she was two. My arrival in South Africa marked the beginning of a divine and conscious invitation to stop abusing my body through an unhealthy life style and to get back in line with my purpose.

I am ever so grateful for my soul's tenacious knocks at my door, shoving and propelling me into re-evaluating my life's choices and trusting in the unravelling of the karmic knots and bolts. The Atlantean warrior soul in me was certainly exerting her willpower and strength to stay in body. There were so many signs and impulses that called me into action back then, too many to mention. Back in London, with hardly any savings, Paul and I both worked in the corporate world and started from scratch again. It took me another ten years before I could finally leave this world behind me, in 2008.

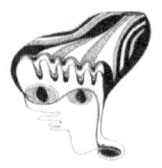

'Eye Pattern Recognition' Exercise

By now we know that our body is a technology that interfaces with and interprets consciousness. Our eyes are the windows into this world and through their movements we access, perceive, and process information in the consciousness field.

Our sensual experience is linked to the eyes. We can use certain eye positions to call forth our memories and thoughts, as well as create new ones, and gain recognition on how to stay present, outside of emotional entanglement. Notice that people under severe distress will often spend a lot of time in the kinaesthetic position until they undergo some form of therapy to release their traumas.

Practicing these movements and positions allows us to release old abuse patterns and programs, gain more mental flexibility, and access the multiple streams of consciousness that are available to us.

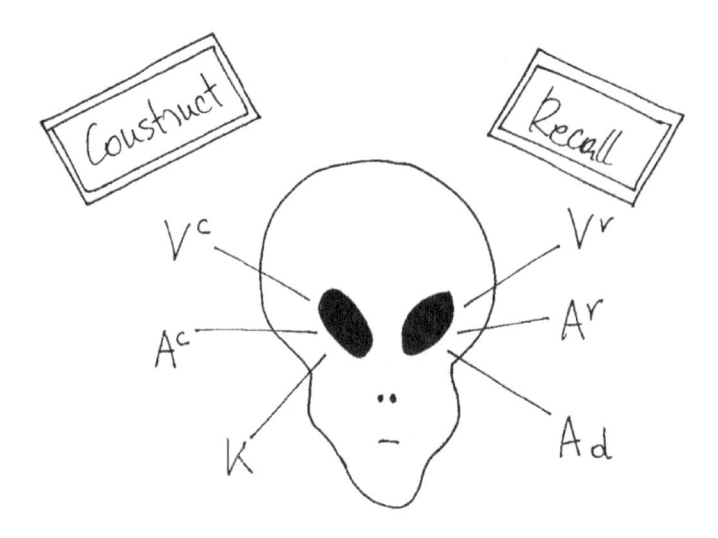

V= Visual (Seeing)

A= Auditory (Hearing) K= Kineastethic (Feeling)

AD = Auditory Digital (Internal Dialogue, Self-Talk)

Recall is on your left and construct is on your right. Keep your head still and just move your eyes into those positions, holding for a few seconds before moving on to the next.

This exercise can help with:

- Memory & Concentration
- Accessing a calm state and behaviours patterns
- Creativity and attention span
- Learning states are activated when visualizing new techniques
- Untangling mental pathways
- Harmonising the heart/brain/gut complex
- Eye position activates the 3rd eye as part of spiritual mechanics
- Health and well-being

Hold for 30 seconds in every one of the eye positions – *once a day, every day*!

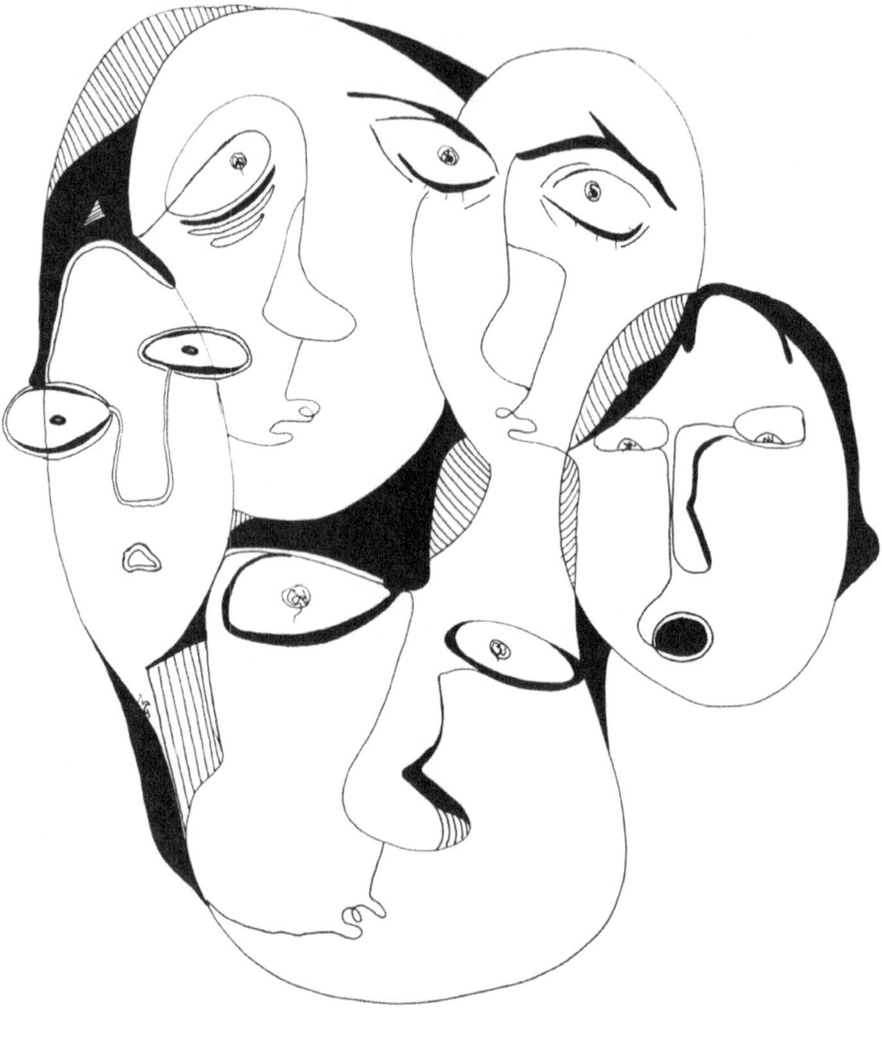

CHAPTER III: EMOTIONS & SELF-KNOWLEDGE

PART ONE: Emotional Purification & Action

> *"Without self-knowledge, without understanding the workings and functions of his machine, man cannot be free, he cannot govern himself and he will always remain a slave."* – George Gurdjieff

Over time our vibratory frequency will shift towards a more inclusive and less dogmatic tone, imbued by the spirit of wholeness, and we can strive for conscious interaction with non-physical aspects and entities without disrupting the natural order. This appetite for personal growth and expansion may be preceded by an initial phase of adjustment and recalibration in which we visibly detach from the material world of crisis and collective misery to enter deeply into solidary contemplation. *Non-action is still an action.* During this period, the practices of 'couching' and 'slothing' may become important catchphrases and activities as they assist the descent into the inner realms to nourish our imagination and lead to the emergence of new ideas, concepts, and understandings.

Energy in Action

The first of the three Delphic maxims inscribed on the Temple of Apollo at Delphi reminds us of a simple truth: *know thyself.* Studying the intricate patterns of our responses, whether through physical action or non-action, can put us in touch with our energetic self. The human organism is always in a rhythmic motion, either regular or irregular, or even both at the same time. Our actions congruently resonate or interfere with the natural rhythm. Through every embodied action, voluntary or involuntary, we act, harmonise, destroy, or create.

An emotion is nothing else than an energy that we have harnessed through a conscious or unconscious motive and action. Through effort and aim we make the unconscious conscious and promote a variety of emotions in the process. Do not stand ceremony to the manifestation of negative emotions and remember the intrinsic transience of them. Emotions have no life of their own until we breath contrast into them and jail these energies through the power of our identified mind. The focus on mastering our self-realised state is to ultimately break free from the emotional engulfment that keeps us in a self- perpetuated loop of toxic living. Emotions are like flashes of biphotonic light, randomly, and freely moving throughout the quantum field. To our detriment, we evoke them through external stimuli or familiar thought and memory patterns, and without realising, we personalize and control them. Similar to mice in a maze, they become imprisoned in our subconscious and cellular recordings, causing us to react in predictable ways. *Have you ever asked an emotion how it wants to feel?*

All energy is to be freed, not by analysis but by practical example. Similar to a disc, our biological cell storage has a limited capacity to accommodate dense and intense emotions. The reason why some people cannot easily assimilate the solar influx of photonic light is due to saturated storage space. Instead of collapsing under the weight of trapped emotions, we can review our memory records, make edits or trash them entirely, paving the way for reaching our full potential. Throughout human de-evolution, emotions have become a generally accepted part of our internal guidance system as a set of low frequency responders to interpret life through moods, feelings, and desires. As a common denominator in the material world, we tend to perceive emotions as indispensable and subjugate ourselves to their regulation and promotion of our actions and reactions, without questioning their value or source. The primary polarisation of energies is felt in our emotional or astral body, where we draw our emotional forces that govern and often limit our life's expression.

Negative emotions have an inherent magnetism that pull us towards lower levels of consciousness. The human race has reached a critical point where we have to readjust our thinking and critically scrutinise the impact and domination of emotions. Healing our personality-self will put an end to the human energy distortion. Earth resembles a battle field of emotional upheaval like no other planet in this galaxy, making it a perfect ground for harvesting our energy. Low frequency emotions store energies that are easily misappropriated to fuel more chaos and escalate fear. The shadow elites have been using negative energy manipulation tactics for eons of time to maintain a level of turmoil, inequality, and stunted soul growth that fosters emotional dependency.

With our human emotional body being energetically connected to the astral energy of the collective human consciousness, as well as other astral planes and the astral solar system, we have access to an unlimited energy supply. The notion of having our lifeforce siphoned off is not common knowledge and might seem fictional for some, but obvious to those who have it in their mental grasp. Adjusting our vibratory rate through an educated effort of consolidating our mental, physical and astral wisdom, we can move out of the targeted energy parameters and gain ultimate freedom from our emotional enslavement. Decisions require actions. Reason trumps emotions. In other words... get out of drama, trauma, gossip, and any other highly charged emotional states that drain your energy and keep you from fully integrating your spiritual essence. It is believed that with the changes in the Earth's magnetic field and the ongoing revolution of consciousness, we will eventually be better equipped to address widespread addictions and depression, and render support to those experiencing depleted energies, allergies, and autoimmune disorders. Emotional dominance not only impacts our health but also distracts us from discovering and specialising in vocational service based on our inclinations and real talents.

This can help to reduce the emphasis on external circumstances and the accumulation of material assets, which do not actually deliver the sought-after emotional stability, health and happiness. It is important to adopt an inclusive approach and recognize that all emotions are an expression of love and powerful messengers that indicate a need for resolution and a desire for liberation. However, they demand to be correctly deciphered and not ignored. Our body is an intelligently thought-out, state-of-the-art organism that is constantly emoting its dissatisfaction and longing for integration with the essence of the soul.

Fear is another misdirected emotion that is entirely man made. It only exists in the material realm, heavily stoked by the conditioned mind of man who has lost the connection to spirit. Fear is often said to be a primal instinct to preserve natural order in this world, *but does it?* Even animals act on a basic instinct, rather than fear, to protect their offspring. Fear is action gone awry. In the opening paragraph I suggested that action evokes emotion and not the other way round. The action of burning one's hand at the stove precedes fear, and the memory thereof projects the emotion into the future. In conclusion, emotional hassle could subconsciously entice us to avoid action, but then again, *does action have to evoke emotion?* I am not promoting a compulsive 'doerism' that we have adopted in this reality, but wonder if this tendency is the reason why many of us prefer living in our heads rather than engage with the physical world? The fear of loss and death, shared by humanity at large, is another key topic that requires more in-depth exploration as a means of comprehending the human-to-soul journey, and the continuation of consciousness in other etheric forms. Fear of the unknown, the future, or failure can serve as distractions from self-empowerment and trigger setbacks in our health and prosperity. The untrained mind is vulnerable to the emotional body and susceptible to getting tangled up with low frequency thought-forms and toxic streams of astral consciousness that surround and bombard us.

We have unimpeded and uninterrupted access to all data in the quantum field, and it is our responsibility to take control of that access, *not the data*, and start exchanging energies intentionally. We both positively contribute to and contaminate the field with our thought constructs. With that in mind, we have to cultivate and nurture a sovereign energy frequency within and around ourselves that automatically shields us from partaking in the unwarranted harvest of energy. Inward contemplation, meditation, and moments of quietude should be incorporated into our daily lives. As the fog of emotional confusion dissipates, our outlook will shift towards a more courageous use of our 'actionsuit.'

Tears & Emotional Maturity

Years ago, I vividly recall crying non-stop as I supported my sister throughout her husband's funeral. She was so overcome with emotional distress and grief that she had to take tranquilisers. Her mind's defence mechanism kicked in, and pushed the 'eject-from-body button' as a way for her body to self-regulate and achieve homeostasis. She was acting mechanically, no longer grounded, and not fully present in her body. In the earlier stages of our soul emergence, traumatic situations may trigger a vortex of energies that we can no longer control, diminishing some of the soul's access. The soul passes in and out of the physical body until we eventually accomplish an emotionally balanced and skilled astral mechanism, firming up a prolonged and conscious relationship with the soul. There is no room for shame or pretence in the belief that a strong person should not cry. Instead, we can view tears as precious healing pearls - a must-have in every time traveller's toolbox. Like alchemised pearls of wisdom, tears transmute past toxins and stresses into a salty liquid that validates the purification of the present. A true master is practiced in not shying away from tears and discomfort but embraces every vulnerable moment as a window into a potential breakthrough, releasing any concealed suffering that would otherwise echo endlessly through multiple frequencies of time.

Higher levels of bliss, as a result of such releases, can kick-start our body's healing mode, purifying and nourishing the human realm. All healing is ultimately self-healing, and without people's consent we have no right to interfere but must honour their ability to deal with drama or grievance as part of their soul's karmic agenda. No one can suffer for another. As we mature emotionally and spiritually, we can begin to appreciate suffering as a catalyst for growth and transformation. The accelerating shifts in the collective consciousness inaugurating the new age will help us understand how our struggles have contributed to our evolution as individuals and as a species, and how we can move forward without falling victim to it.

Earth's rollercoaster is one of the most exhilarating adventures you'll ever be on, and it is speeding up quickly. It's important to slow down in between rides and fully unplug from external distractions and personal interactions. As we balance our vulnerability with our strengths, and harmonise all pairs of opposites, we gracefully develop intuitively. Intuition is more than just a feeling – it's an expression of a clear and disciplined mind, that safely guides us through difficult situations that may be considered embarrassing. Moments of 'enlightening humiliation' can help crash our inflated and misunderstood ego and disperse emotional clouds of indoctrinated shame. In the process we gain heightened awareness in emergencies and become more adept at recognizing early warning signs propelling us into appropriate action. Emotional adulthood means surrendering the search for external validation and trusting our intuitive guidance. Philosophical, psychological, and practical mastery is fuelled by a purity of motive and a philanthropic aspiration to serve human and planetary evolution. Many of us are healers, unaware of our bodies' empathic capacity to reach out and take on, or often transmute, other people's pain. A deeper understanding of our quantum nature is important to avoid random acts of forceful interference that can result in toxic entanglements and retributive karma.

During my yogic studies I came upon a master of Kundalini yoga by the name of Yogi Bhajan, who is known for talking about a most elevated state of consciousness, *Shuniya*. It means 'zero' and describes a state of awareness in which the mind is brought to stillness. A place of perfect harmony and peacefulness where we have access to timeless universal wisdom. The daily practice of the sacred neutral point of view allows us to keep a balanced focus on prioritising our time and energy. Of course, we are not supposed to constantly remain in that zero-point state of *Shuniya*, but we can choose to disconnect from the matrix energy at will and revisit this peaceful sanctuary as often as possible, to allow our inner nature to blossom and our vitality to strengthen. This principle also beautifully illustrates the 'midway spot' between soul and form, spirit and matter; the origin of consciousness and the gateway to universal wisdom. Through a self-directed focus of the mind, we benevolently manipulate consciousness, mould and master our earthly and astral experiences. Before choosing to work with the higher realms of hierarchical consciousness, we must learn to focus and safely reorient the energies of the lower ones; the mental, physical, and astral plane. Use your energy wisely! Spiritual discipline is to cyclically engage in sacred fires and ceremonial work along with dynamically participating in the fray of life.

Value Judgements

Man-made judgements of right and wrong dig their tunnels of separation all the way through the landscape of our psyche, language, and life. Value judgments are re-enforced in our education system through alleged facts and requirements that are entirely based on consensual, collective agreements that prioritise material and competitive achievement over spiritual development. As we strive for individual and unity consciousness, our value system evolves and adapts to our new vibration. We learn to appreciate our common potentiality and no longer have to compete or struggle to feel worthy and deserving.

A liberating thought, indeed - and perfectly valid from the soul's perspective, which never intended to seek worthiness but rather wholeness for all of its fractured pieces. The quality of our service to humanity will increase upon our admittance of consensual servitude to an artificially enhanced system. We must intuitively discern value for ourselves and detach this world's meaning from our self-worth in order to be free.

In 2008, I certified as a master practitioner in neuro-linguistic programming (NLP), as well as Hypnotherapy and Time Line Therapy. Back in those days, I learned about the hierarchical structure of values and how deeply embedded they are in our psyche. Values are socially accepted parameters that we use to create and relate to our reality and distinguish between good and evil. In actual fact, they are themed conclusions and opinions based on historical, individual, or collective perceptions and experiences seeking expression in our automated, habitual responses. Attachment to the old value system may have provided a sense of belonging and identity in the past, but it no longer serves the self- realised individual. Our future values will be more reflective of the laws of nature and unification. We seem to internalise our values through oppositional tendencies and direct them either away from what we fear and lack, or towards what we desire. It is important to recognize these biases and refrain from forceful distancing, as it only strengthens the energy we are trying to avoid. By accepting our circumstances without falling into prejudiced thinking, we can focus more coherently on our aspirations. A negative frame of mind rooted in fear and lack consciousness can lead us further away from cultivating our intuitive and imaginative faculties that give rise to greatness. Millennia of racial and societal inequality have perpetuated self-inflicted limitations and control mechanisms. Our ancestral value system still runs deep, upholding abortive rules, laws, and allegiances that are evident in our spoken and written language. Words are powerful seeds that grow into facts and deeds and must be planted with care.

We often brush off linguistic idioms as *just a saying*, but they are fully packed with prejudice and predisposition that impacts our subconscious mind. One has to question how much of our self-image has been crippled by linguistic black magic that hasn't been fully acknowledged yet. As sentient beings of spiritual energy, we must move beyond the polarity trap and transcend distinctions of 'away from' or 'towards' as we aspire to a consistent soul alignment. As we learn to disentangle from the manipulated collective mind and reclaim our vital energy, we start to coherently express universal wisdom and bring beauty and harmony to this world. Common sense guided by the spiritual laws will prevail as our true sense of value and the system will eventually have to follow suit!

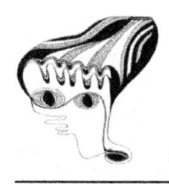

Towards & Away From Values

This next exercise is intended to identify some of your values. My challenge for you is to cautiously observe your inner dialogue. It derives from a value system that has been forced upon us during childhood and past lives that we ignorantly continue to represent in an attempt to maintain our place in society. The suggested examination of your values may point towards a need to heal some of this old conditioning.

1. *What is important to you in the context of relationship, business, health, life and so forth?* Choose any area in your life and write down as many values as you can think of; identify their directional pull and put them in order of importance.

2. Think of the word 'HOME' and ask yourself: *What do I remember about home? What was it like?* Write down as many values as you can think of. Now, notice what your life has become. Check how many of those values are pointing towards what you desire, versus away from. Then, for all the

away from values, find the opposite ones; for example, tension as opposed to relaxation, in order to create balance and let it all go thereafter.

Gender Bender

The Oxford Dictionary of World History roots the word 'value' back to the old French, feminine, past-participle of *valoir* – 'be worth,' and from the Latin word *valere* - 'be strong'.

What is true worth and strength? I am wondering how much of our gender-based discrimination is rooted in the flawed interpretation, and divided attribution of values to men and women? The left side of the brain, typically associated with male qualities, is considered adapt at tasks that involve logic and analytical thinking, while the right brain, traditionally known for feminine qualities, is linked to expression and creativity. However, an awakened individual knows that all of these traits are inherently available within oneself, irrespective of gender, and cultivates them to various degrees in order to create internal balance.

Within the business world, we often find metaphors that reenforce right or left-brained distinctions related to gender qualities such as 'coming up short,' 'no time to lose,' 'ahead of the pack,' and 'it's an uphill struggle'. These few, alone, show how we think of male qualities in terms of competition, control, superiority, time, and money. On the female business spectrum, we tend to see metaphors equally imbalanced, painting a one-sided picture. They often relate to co-operation, compassion, balance and creativity: 'Building bridges,' 'planting seeds,' 'reaching out,' 'nurturing one's business' and so on. Our life, as well our business, is an extension of who we are. Our gender identity does not conform exclusively to the traditional binary male or female. Such categorical distinctions are not constructive as they create compartmentalisation between individuals of different genders, rather than further goodwill, and support a global gender appreciation.

It encourages the ongoing fight for recognition and definition between male and female, instead of assisting in dropping the identity game. We must heal those gender rifts and work together if we want to fully integrate our avatars. The inherent lack of gender equality, fuelled by those who gain from the ongoing prejudice and hostility, could easily be rectified by taking out the rotten roots. By upholding the inequality struggle of gender, as well as the global divisions of Eastern and Western, Northern and Southern hemispheres and cultures, we keep feeding our energy to an outdated system that neither serves our personal growth or the planetary ascension.

PART TWO: Clearing & Healing Marbles

Soul Quality Control

As in-spirited humans, we appreciate all conflicting polarities as marital disputes between spirit and matter; every discord addressed in the physical form contributes to a higher union and communion of our complex being. We all have a choice to heal our shadow aspects and merge them within our light in this lifetime. Emotional and spiritual hygiene has become increasingly important with the rapid surfacing of old destructive patterns as Earth is transiting into higher density light.

These next pages are designed to help you tackle some of those self- denying and destructive belief and habit patterns. I am offering out what I call CLEARING & HEALING MARBLES, specifically tailored to the main emotions we struggle with. They are self-contained mini sub-chapters made up of distilled clearings and prompts to help you reframe and think outside the box. Similar to the revocations, their purpose is to re-emphasize the mastery, healing, and sovereignty teachings of the personality realm. These potent healing tools can be repeatedly used in isolation whenever you feel moody or depressed and require an emotional cleanse.

They are purposefully written in different frequencies with an added intensity, a hypnotic or metaphorical touch, to target the subconscious as well as the conscious mind. I suggest not to read them all at once to avoid overwhelm. Please feel free to add your own marbles of wisdom for healing. The documents may include breathing exercises and are best recorded in your own voice, to naturally manifest changes into this physical reality through your throat chakra – the seat of your mental body. If listening to your own voice feels intolerable in the beginning, rest assured it will get easier with practice. A recording voice will always sound different to your speaking voice because it reaches your inner ear in a different way. Your voice does not only sound out the written words, but in fact interprets them through your specific signature frequency – the distillation of your emotions, experiences, and vibrations over many lifetimes, expressed through a string of sounds representing the uniqueness of you. You might as well just stop inflicting cruelty against the sound of your voice, your personality and soul signature. Once you start recording your own voice, you will start noticing a shift in confidence and the way you relate to yourself and others. Another tip is to go back to re-listen to old recordings and record them anew. You may appreciate the difference in perception and experience and can acknowledge any healing or alterations that have been accomplished. The basis of all manifested phenomena is enunciated sound or word, spoken with power. Put all of your willpower and intention behind your voice as you read these revocations.

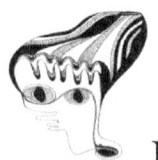

Fear / Anxiety/Doubt / Hesitation

How much of your time are you spending in the past worrying about the future, whilst missing out living in the present?

Close your eyes and allow the tension in your body to dissipate. Through your nose, take in a deep breath and exhale. Surrender into a comfortable space of stillness.

Welcome any thoughts that come up and do not judge them. Just notice the invisible line of breath they travel on, back and forth. Do not resist the incessant flow and let the energy pass through. No rules or directives, allowing your mortal mind to move out of the way, as if by magic. Keep breathing rhythmically, and observe what surfaces.

FEAR not fear. Teach your mind to stop running away from the fear of having to confront its own fear. What's the worst that could happen? That's right. Everything and everyone that still wants you to speak pretty lies instead of harsh truths, will you now please find your authentic voice and give it a mighty roar! Let the sound reach the hearts of those who are ready to embrace a new state of being. Have you allowed your perfidious relationships contaminate your sense of fun, and turned it into fear? When did life become a struggle for joy that keeps you fearing new expressions and connections?

FEAR not the unfathomable. Notice the sudden silence and begin to feel the vibration of YOU melting into infinity, once again. Stop clinging to the old life form as the new form already awaits you. There is no heaven, there is no hell, don't doubt that. There is only unbounded, untethered immortality. Summon brightness and warmth to illuminate your human heart-brain and release all ancient memories of violent deaths inflicted upon you or administered by you. Offer your adrenal glands a well-deserved rest from the old, ancient freeze, and give your mind a break from fearing the unknown. Allow all resistance to back down, easing the drive for internal fight and flight.

FEAR not freedom. Rest in this expanded space of consciousness and start cutting the invisible locks that chain you to the pole of inhibition. The chain of command, chain reaction, food chain, the old ball and chain, yanking someone's chain... are you one of those strong links in the chain that keep us all chained to the slave chain? Use your exhalation as an opportunity to let go of any chains of devious circumstances and recycle them through the soles of your feet, directly into the centre of the Earth. With every breath you take, gently demand the shackles of social conditioning to break open.

FEAR not clarity. Drop all fearful expectations and unkind projections, releasing all pressures associated with them. Let go of all dualistic thoughts projected onto you, perceived and received by you. Return them, now, and feel a sense of clarity and vision. Use this moment to relax deeply and allow yourself to feel a tenderness and openness to your fellow human friend, and the closeness to the magical world you are a part of.

Your boundaries must be clear; you've earned your soul's respect to freely and firmly stand on your own. In the absence of fear, connect to the wisdom of your heart.

FEAR not being. Let go of hardship and all the doing you think you have to do. Guide your breath up the spine into the brain and out the crown. With an innocent curiosity, follow the path your breath takes all the way into the sea of consciousness. Briefly keep your conscious awareness outside this earthly realm and witness your breath joyfully merging with divine spirit. Pause, and proudly acknowledge your contribution. Now, ask your breath to return, cleansed and cleared, cosmically invigorated. Channel it down the crown, the brain, and allow it to burst into all four chambers of your heart! Watch your heart open like a flower, nourished by the natural flow of spirited breath, encouraged by your innate trust and knowingness of this exquisite exchange.

FEAR not surrender. Imagine yourself in the nurturing embrace of Mother Earth and dive headfirst into blissful surrender. Whilst you resist, things cannot be changed. There is no more value in holding onto warriors, wars or worries. Live and breathe resilience, bravely riding the waves of loss and new beginnings.
Allow yourself to receive your own sense of compassion and fearlessly offer it out into the world. Vulnerability is humanity's best friend. What does fear require from you to feel safe again?

FEAR not imperfection. Remove that furrowed brow of frustration from your forehead and bring back that all-winning smile. We live in a world with endless troubles and anxieties. Use your breath now and infuse strong healing vibes into the vicious craters filled with fearful tension. The Earth does not require you to be perfect but to live and love generously and fearlessly. Breathe yourself back into alignment with your mission. Who taught you that it was easier to fear never reaching perfection instead of happily living with imperfection? Smooth out those ruffled edges and empty your pockets filled with panic, compulsion and obsession. Follow nature's lead and find perfection in imperfection.

FEAR not the unseen. Why is it that what we can't see makes us so fearful? Is that even true? Fears are implants that you have innocently accepted as real in the past. Breathe, acknowledge, and categorically reject whatever you have bought as real that really isn't. We think that what we can't see with our eyes is not real, but then we make fear real just because we feel something. Is fear real?

What we feel might not be real. What we can't see often has greater visibility, in truth. What is your truth?

FEAR not living for it is the greatest gift you can give yourself and the world. Release the past, let go of the future, and allow yourself to fully be in the present moment. Trust that the universe has a plan for you. Summon all fearful light bodies back to your central nervous system for healing and integration, for release and rejuvenation. Scan your body from top to toe and shine your light into the marrow of your bones. With every sound you make, with every breath you take, discern truthfulness from the old fearful lies. Live with courage, passion, and purpose, and listen to your inner voice of reason. What is it that you know, that you have always known, but chosen to forgo to play the game of fitting in or zoning out?

FEAR not love. What can fear learn from love? Love, can be fierce because love is truthful. Why do you support the fear of losing someone who cannot see your greatness? It takes a robust heart to choose self-less-ly without making oneself less. Fear not your awakening heart that prods you to become more selfish. There aren't enough fish in the oceans you can catch to prove your worth to this world, as true worth is immeasurable. Whatever ideas and ideals you have adopted about selfishness and selflessness, let them go and destroy and uncreate them; right here, right now.

FEAR not memories. Fear often makes us feel lost and lonely. Ancient suffering, haunting memories of lost loves, and tormenting agony – are those even yours? Has fear been consuming you, eating you up? Are you really afraid of fear sticking a fork into you? Are you that done? Take a breath. Break down and release all excessive bloating; the gaseous fear bubbles in your digestive system. Clear and cleanse all fear from the kidneys and the bladder. Cut through the bullshit being sold and bought as fear, will you please!

FEAR not time. Love lures you out of hiding; it encourages you to be open and vulnerable while fear causes you to fixate on the inevitability of aging, death, and the scarcity of time – all of which appear beyond your control. Open your eyes and look through the illusion of time. Love time for the experiences it allows you in this physical realm. Observe the old concepts of time disappearing, making space for new levels of timeless awareness. It's happening right now and you are still breathing, or are you not?

FEAR not failure. Failure and fear cannot frighten courage, for courage is inherently fearless. Commit and fully engage with life and all its trials and tribulations, whilst drawing valuable lessons from them. Remember, you are good enough and worthy, irrespective of any mistakes you have made. Do not belittle yourself but stand tall in all your glory, embracing the growth that comes from taking risks.

FEAR not bonding. Pause and take a moment to travel back in time. Imagine re-attaching to your umbilical cord. It's ok - just play, nothing to fear. Now, perceive the beat of your mother's heart. Feel both of your hearts beating as one and lose yourself in remembrance. Feel the unconditional bond that never gets lost. Can you feel the connection that your world is crying out for? Yes, you are perceiving it - not fearing it, as only a magnificent and fearless human being can.

FEAR not silence. The impermanence of fear becomes apparent when it is confronted with profound and persistent silence which undermines its false foundations and makes it difficult to grasp. Fear gets to live or die, whichever way you are choosing. Did you know that you are here to uncover the fear scam? It's time to out the scammers and walk away from the strategies of fearful distraction. Turn off your phone. Disconnect your TV and get off the treadmill of exhausting data-flow-exertion, overloaded and flooded with fearmongering information. Cut through the noise and chaos and find your inner strength and peace. What information are you still missing that keeps you fearfully looping around doubt and hesitation?

FEAR not commitment. Fear rebel - disclose yourself, to yourself, now! How long has your internal saboteur filled you up with fear and stubborn, short- sighted determination, that keeps you desperately balancing on a tightrope instead of exploring other options?

Acknowledge at least one of those old fear programs and cut the power cord. Make an effort to distinguish between the sensations of fear and excitement that are coursing through your body. The electrifying waves of pure vitality, contained within our physical fluids, are often mistaken for fear as they are similar in nature.

FEAR not forgiveness. Fear is this society's false prophet, preaching false promises and trapping you in a cycle of unfulfilled expectations and forceful projections. Rather than avoiding fear, choose to conquer it and let it go.

Exercise compassion, watching the roots of your conviction firmly ground your ever evolving avatar. Eliminate and undo your distorted mind's endless justifications that create unfounded fears, uncertainties, and reservations, preventing your personal transformation. Forgive yourself for fearing the fearless.

FEAR not choice. Fear consciousness is artificially manufactured by those who harvest and trade the precious energy of our emotions. It creates unnecessary separation, limits your potential, and prevents you from fully expressing your individuality. Drop those fictitious barriers and false protections that only reinforce a fear of powerlessness and keep you from living your purpose. Embrace the limitless possibilities of pure potentiality, in this ultimate reality. Choose ease and peace, my friend, making fear your companion on the journey to the unknown. The presence of fear serves as a reminder for you to seek reconnection within yourself. See it for what it is; a guidepost for expansion. Fear can be your friend or foe. What are you choosing?

And so it is.

Aho.

Anger & Co

The tone of the next clearing marble may be strong. When dealing with anger and its fellow kind, you have to be willing to step up the intensity at times. Anger, itself, is more often than not a well overdue invitation for claiming one's potency. The longer we leave traumatic events unhealed, the more twisted and entrapped the emotions become. By acknowledging and expressing our anger in a healthy way, we can tap into our inner power and take action towards creating positive change in our lives. Suppressing or denying our anger only leads to further frustration as these heavy, sluggish, and stagnant energies can manifest in physical or emotional illness. Festering and angry thoughtforms can also separate into multiple personalities, rearing their heads at the most inopportune times. In this revocation, you will find some of the negative entity clearings that I have adopted over time to maintain high levels of spiritual hygiene. Intense emotions may be overwhelming and uncomfortable, but they are a natural part of the human experience. Strategically placed humour and the use of swear words are highly underrated in the world of therapy and spirituality. When applied with care and in a respectful manner, it can break down barriers and create a more relaxed and open atmosphere. Energy cannot be destroyed, but it certainly can be redirected and transformed. Everything that you have created you can also uncreate. Angry people are usually those who have not yet chosen to take responsibility for the reality they find themselves in. Although highly capable and passionate, some individuals tend to cling onto outdated values that hinder their self-development and keep them trapped in a victim mentality. This is often fuelled by the tendency to constantly compare oneself to others. When dealing with emotionally charged people, honesty is often lost in translation since people can only hear you from their level of awareness. Before you offer advice and put yourself unnecessarily in the line of attack, ask yourself *what the person is willing or capable of hearing and receiving?*

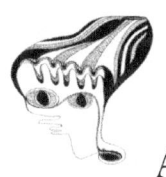

Anger / Fury/ Rage/ Hate / Frustration

What are you trying to prove with your anger?

1. Establish alternate nostril breathing which helps with mind and body, left and right brain integration to increase focus and concentration. Using your right hand, bring your index and middle finger onto your 3rd eye - the space between the eye brows. Use your right thumb to close off your right nostril and breath in through your left nostril. Close both nostrils and pause for a moment. Open and exhale through your right nostril. Inhale through your right nostril. Close both nostrils and hold the breath, then open the left nostril and exhale all the way. Inhale left nostril, close both, pause, open right and exhale again. Pause the recording and practice a few of those cycles first, before you continue] Keep using this alternate nostril breath throughout the recording to let go of anger and start creating with more ease.

2. Record in your own voice and listen whilst continuing with the Nadi Shodhana pranayama exercise.

    I, in this ever-present moment of now, summon all my DNA ancestors of the past, present and future, my angelic guardians and guides, my soul brothers and sisters, to hold space and bear witness to my declaration and demand of myself to dismantle any walls of false protection.

    I am here to let go of any weapons of self-destruction and to fortify my reality as a sovereign, universal citizen. I herewith reinforce clear and healthy boundaries to dream the new dream of peace, wealth and happiness.

    I herewith ask the universal quantum entanglements to support my request for a joyful creation with ease. I claim balanced health, an ever-growing prosperity, an inspired and multidimensional co-creation to the best and highest good for mankind and myself.

I now acknowledge the daily synchronicities and mystical experiences assisting me to explore and expand my awareness manifold as well as helping me make infinite possibilities manifest, beyond my wildest imagination.

I herewith spit out the lies of mass distraction, spoken or unspoken. Everything I bought and sold and made real for me that actually isn't, I herewith return with gratitude for the learned lesson.

As I start choosing for me and as me, I perceive, know, be and receive the contributions to my highest spiritual evolution within this global dream time awakening, and I start having experiences full of richness and joy.

I now let go of any frustrations, irritations, and limitations that keep me stuck in this global narrative of misconception. I declare to finally step into my sovereignty and signature frequency of the healed healer and potent co-creator.

I, in this ever-present moment of now, claim back every moment of rage I have ever had and every word in vengeance I have ever written or spoken. I reduce the charge and polarity to zero minus infinity so I may return to my sacred and neutral balance. All energy of rage stored inside me, I now transmute and transform into positive intention and focus.

I acknowledge the sour taste of anger and mistrust as I call upon my lifetimes as a student and master of alchemy, turning all depression and regression into creation, inspiration and dreams. All angry energy that has been seeping into my liver and pericardium through tacit consent and lack of boundaries over eons of time, I now become a magical practitioner for myself to unravel the rage weave, so that I don't have to sit in it every day.

I reach into all corners of my home and body to pull off the energy from all the negative webs that I have created and clear them with my invisible sage stick. I herewith dispose of all these distortions from my heart, every cell of my body and environment.

Every outburst of rage that I have ever chosen for not being heard, seen and acknowledged for the awakener that I am, I forgive myself and others. I do not hold any grudges against religions, governments, media, or any other authority, that has been stifling my authentic knowingness. I now transform and transmute all residual images of rage in this and other lifetimes.

I herewith claim my choice of living as a sovereign being in this polarised reality. I acknowledge my divine adventure spirit having chosen the harshness of this place and its multitude of traps and misguidance, now releasing all forms of victimhood.

I am here to make meaningful memories to create a long-term legacy for the ancient soul inside of me. To all my deformed, contorted, twisted, bent, skewed, altered, artificially modified selves, that have been wounded, lost, and forgotten in the trenches of war and conflict, I now give them healing and the choice to move on to wherever they choose to.

I herewith listen to the native bloodline telling me to stop playing small or get the hell out of the lineage. I appreciate the intensity of the message as a way of getting me to claim my legacy of becoming a grand master of sacred communication with the blood ancestors living and non-living.
 I am ready to call upon my ancestors to bring forth their ancient wisdom as well as part with mine, in non-competition and non-hierarchy.

As I claim the amount of anger and frustration in me, I acknowledge all the on and off world implants and destroy and uncreate them. I also claim any and all amount of anger that I have taken on into my auric field from others, through empathetic entanglement, in ignorance and unawareness.

I now transmute and send it back, including its electromagnetic imprinting, to whence it came from never to return to this body and this environment again. All portals are closed. All oaths, vows, agreements and entangled cords that I have with any rage entities, demons, ghosts, shadow parts and aspects that taunt ridicule, judge, anger, infuriate, mock, provoke, insult, tease and torment, I now revoke, recant, rescind, renounce, denounce, destroy and uncreate.

I take mantle of responsibility to change my rage, transforming and transmuting it into love and compassion for myself and all sentient kind.

I demand that all demons associated with anger, rage, fury, and hate, which are locked and bound to my body, life, and soul through sacred orders, break their fealties and free themselves to return to whence they came from. Return, and never come back to this reality again. Your service contracts have now ended, and all portals and leaks have been closed and sealed as I am no longer a signature frequency match to the dark night of the soul.

I end the rage at the deepest core of my being and allow love to be the healer of rage, age, ancestors, and soul families in this 5th world of peace. Everywhere I refuse to step into my true authentic potency or choose repressed enthusiasm over inspiration, passion, and dreams, I now destroy and uncreate all the decisions, judgments, conclusions, computations, projections and expectations leading to this refusal.

All the stupidity and incarcerations that I am using to control something or somebody in order to maintain my interest in prejudice rather than change, I now transform into clarity, wisdom, and the joyful bliss of my inner authentic knowing.

Whatever I have made so significant in finding beauty and kindness in others, in serving other's egos to the detriment of my own assets, gifts, dreams and desires, I now claim back my powers, my boundaries of autonomy and integrity, clearing and cleansing the polluted waters of creation and fully affirming trust and confidence in myself.

If I have to be persuaded, reminded, pressured, lied to, incentivised, coerced, bullied, socially shamed, guilt-tripped, threatened, punished and criminalised for others to gain my compliance, I can be absolutely certain that what is being promoted is not in my best interest (adapted from an Ian Watson quote with thanks) – I destroy and uncreate all that.

I herewith declare that I am no longer available to forced and angry signature frequency matches. As a self-aware and sovereign being I resolve all karma with any frustrated or hateful being, organization, establishment, foundation, institute, secret society, association, corporation, agency, entity, and replace any negative self-talk and limiting belief with empowering thoughts and positive actions.

I am a unified being, no longer falling prey to rage, fury, and anger. I now choose whatever potency I have been refusing, to create and manifest with Divine Source and Great Mystery. I now enter this declaration into the earthly, galactic, and universal Akashic records for all sentient kind to witness and understand that our freedom comes with the use of free will at all times.

And so it is.

Aho.

3. Take another three cycles of breath and then let go of your hand and release the breath through both nostrils. Allow yourself to expand in that space of no-time. Keep breathing in your own rhythm connecting to your heartbeat, and whenever you are ready, become aware of your room and carry on with your day.

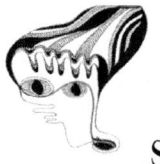

Shame / Blame / Guilt / Regret / Sadness

These last clearing marbles are designed to help celebrating YOU. As you become more transparent and authentic, new energies of a co-creative multidimensional play will resurface.

What do you love about still beating yourself up instead of choosing a different reality?

Just take a few deep breaths and with each inhalation, feel your joy and lightness expanding within you. Allow yourself to simply be as being is the ultimate source of creation. Allow yourself to see, let your spirit be free, and let your mind be open. Allow yourself to understand how to be here, in this contemplative now, where we get the opportunity to see whole new layers of ourselves.

Tune into the sounds within you and listen to the vibrations that flow through you. Let go of anything that is stopping you from opening your heart to this place of clarity and unbounded love, so familiar and yet so densely hidden. No thinking at all, only awareness, silence, and a profound sense of peace. Remember that you are worthy of all the love and happiness in the world irrespective of your background or social standing.

Can you identify what you regret so deeply that it causes you to constantly blame and criticize yourself? How are you distorting the concept of infinite self-acceptance that fuels the blame, shame, and guilt arising from your choices?

Can you pinpoint a moment in time when you made the decision that you were not worthy enough to be fully empowered and make choices for yourself? Who did you learn that from? 'For-giving' yourself is part of true receiving and healing the self-worth.

How long has it been since you got lost in the perverted minds of others that still keep you incarcerated, imprisoned, small and limited? Denial is not going to free you from the shackles of shame, and break open the memories associated with blame and guilt. The ones who blame us for their difficulties and problems perpetuate the cycle of victimhood and re-enforce narcissistic tendencies, creating division, conflict, accusations, blame, shame, guilt, sadness, and regret.

When are you going to step out of the circle of blamers and shamers, whether they are family, trusted friends, or others? Have you fallen into these behavioural patterns yourself, are you one of them?

Who decided for you to peck with the chickens whilst you could be soaring with the eagles? Everywhere you have become a master of entrainment, taking on other people's desires and passions without ever questioning what your universe is made of, or what YOU require, and what YOU desire... you now have a choice to change that. Is it time to spread your wings?

Reclaim all your beingness that has been hijacked and turned into frantic doingness. Transmute this energy into a state of non-directionality, a simple state of existing, without having to feel ashamed or remorseful. Inspired beingness is the spark that ignites creativity and drives individuals to create something new and unique. I am wondering if you can hear this, or can you not? At any moment you can shift from the frequencies of shame, blame, regret, and sadness into stillness where you can simply exist without having to attend to chores, tasks, duties, responsibilities, expectations, or demands. Taking a break from the constant demands of daily life can give your avatar a chance to recharge and rejuvenate.

How can the simple joy of being yourself call you back once more to YOU, your I AM Apex Avatar, without allowing your super psychic skills to sap, trap, pull in, and suck up other people's dirty, toxic, malicious, foul, vile, abhorrent, corrupt energies and pains? Say no more to always saying yes to the guidance or misguidance of others, that may lead you astray from optimising your unique potential. The antidote to blame, shame, guilt, regret, or sadness, is simply making a choice that no one else can make for you.

Demand of yourself to allow true love and compassion back into your life, to motivate you back into being. Everywhere you have aligned and agreed, resisted and reacted to your own or other people's actions, non-actions, reactions, responses, and all that jazz that doesn't allow your soul's orchestra of consciousness to be played, heard, and listened to, now is the time to let that go. Destroy and uncreate the many versions of yourself that judge, begrudge, blame, and shame you and others into non-existence. Hear the cries of your inner child, wanting to be honoured, admired, and respected as a potent contributor, a facilitator, and supporter of all truths.

There is a brilliant genius YOU underneath all of that old shame, blame, regret and guilt. This is also where sadness lives and breeds its discontent. Do not suppress sadness when it arises as it is an inherent aspect of our human experiences, resulting from loss and disappointments.

How much are you still making yourself less and sad in order to meet the requirements of social or intimate interaction? That's called self-abuse. All the incarcerations of the self and others, that are holding YOU captured and locked up in the deepest dungeon possible, are you now willing to search for the key to unlock the prison of your mind?

Consider this: What if, from an infinite perspective, there is no duality worth fighting for? What if instead of dwelling on blame and guilt, you can choose an unbiased observation and break through the cycles of self-judgment or blaming others for your situation? All of the blame that paints your world black or white instead of using the colourful spread of the artist's palette, will you choose to let it go? No more 'should haves', 'would haves', 'becauses', and 'supposed tos'; just a simple choice between what works for YOU, and what doesn't.

How many barriers have you created through consistently trying to make yourself invisible, whilst desperately wanting to be acknowledged? How does pushing away anyone who seeks intimacy with you work for you? All those walls and cages, the hidden, lost, veiled, and buried ones, across all lifetimes, dimensions, galaxies, and universes, now is the time to bring them down. Release, relax, and dissolve those imaginary restrictions and constraints, triggered by old memories, perceived pains, grievances, and humiliations. How many regrets are leading you astray, away from your path of transformation, from the joy of playful co-creation?

Unique and untethered beingness brings us together as humanity. Empowered and inspired action and divine love that flows through us unites all parts of ourselves and our species.

Allow yourself to be immersed in this love, cleansed, and freed from blame, shame, guilt, regret or sadness. YOU the Mind-Love- Action; YOU the Body-Love-Presence; YOU the Soul-Love-Wisdom, indivisibly co-creating, omnipotent and omnipresent. Celebrate YOU, in all your magnificence and US as the unified power of love and action.

And so it is. Aho.

PART THREE: Emotional Renaissance

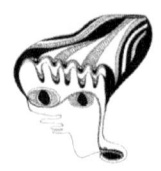

Expanding into Love

Be empty. Be still. Be open. From that space of pure presence, think of someone or something you deeply care about. Through all your senses, perceive your unadulterated compassion for that person in this moment. Now, make that energy bigger. Expand it out beyond your body, the place you are in, the country, throughout the universe. Using your awareness – is that sensory perception greater and bigger and vaster than you have ever acknowledged? This feeling so full of love that you are embodying right now, whilst you are sitting here right now is what you truly be. You are that being of love; that something greater right now, experiencing it here with you, through you.

Transfiguration of Man through Love

Sociologist Morris Massey, in his generational theory, talks about the 'Imprint Period' which occurs from birth to around 7 years of age. During this period, we act as a sponge to whatever gets presented to us. The age of innocence is where the *critical faculty* between the conscious and unconscious mind has not yet developed and we trust and love implicitly without question. Babies do not demand or offer love in exchange for comfort and nourishment.

They simply expect love because it is an inherent aspect of our existence and nature. In the years that follow, between the ages of 7-14, is the 'Modelling Period.' Here, we start to experience love as something we have to work for and be worthy of as we learn about it from role models outside of the family unit such as our peers, teachers, or movie heroes. Love gets moulded into relationships. We imprison this bountiful exchange of divine energy and turn it into a commodity, bouncing it back and forth, whilst disputing its sincerity and fearing its scarcity. *Love is this world's sustenance, and like breath, it can't be bought or sold.* By 21 we have completed the 'Socialising Period,' when we are believed to have integrated all of our values, beliefs, and filter systems into our personality. By this stage, love has become an abstract idea, a twisted fairy tale of happily ever after, or something unattainable all-together. Love does not depend on internal or external conditions, imposed obligations, or any kind of bias and prejudice. Our impending task is to become mature role models to all sentient kind, to set love free again and take a quantum leap forward into new levels of universal intimacy.

Love is the intricate fabric for all of our experiences.
Love is the mediator and facilitator of consciousness.
Love is the intelligent and purposeful motive of creation.
Love is an aspect of pure reason.
Love is who we are.

Divine love includes all, from lustful attraction to holy reverence. It is the very life force that is streaming through our blood. Pure toroidal love wants to experience radical aliveness through a plethora of old and new senses and perceptions. Love resides in every choice we make that does not bear the frequency of domination, and even at that moment love is present in disguise. Love sustains life. It has no beginning and it has no end. Its purpose is to serve. Love is like clay, endlessly shaping and reshaping itself under the hands of its creator. We should not be fooled by its willingness to serve, for true love cannot be trapped or controlled.

Love is the force that propels creation forward, nudging us ever onward towards our true purpose. It grows with every flowing, unshakable, non-agenda moment of our inner gleaming and authentic presence. The best way to experience true love is to surrender our personality and just be love. A growing number of individuals are now experiencing a conscious awakening and a heightened state of awareness. We are in the midst of unlearning, shedding old belief systems, and returning to a state of innocence, similar to being in a metaphorical womb. This is where we can experience a rebirth, as the alchemist would describe it.

As our intuitive faculty is being reawakened and refined, we can claim our true essence and invoke a new mindset of healthy detachment from drama in favour of a spiritually integrated awareness. By practicing our spiritual truth daily, we have an opportunity to invert the matrix and create an unobstructed space for our soul to express itself fully and without inhibition. Shifting through this emotional renaissance, we discover how to reconnect with the spiritual aspect anchored within the heart. Intuitively guided, we move closer to our soul's consciousness with an increased ability to firmly root ourselves in spiritual embodiment. Gradually, we begin to radiate our purpose in service to others and contribute to the evolution of consciousness through a more disciplined use of our capacities, abilities, and faculties. Our once solid focus on self-preservation begins to transform into a deliberate attention towards bridging the gap to other worlds.

We are at our best when we serve others. In our role as mediators between people, places, species and realities, we leave the manipulated narrative behind and embrace security and assured counsel within ourselves. The emotional guidance system is undergoing a major revamp as excessive desire atrophies and we aspire and engage our mind in larger universal thought concepts for the creation of a more advanced civilisation. In full appreciation of its previous purpose, we can consign our highly emotional nature to a place of rest and recalibration.

The Emerald Tablet

In his book, 'The Emerald Tablet – Alchemy for Personal Transformation,' Dennis William Hauck comprehensively and masterfully elaborates on the Hermetic teachings embodied in the Emerald Tablet. The author's level of research is commendable and I suggest Hauck's material to anyone who is interested in going more into the depth of the ancient mythology. In tune with the theme of this chapter, *Emotions and Self-Knowledge*, I'd like to just briefly introduce you to the *'Seven Steps of Transformation'* that make up the Emerald Formula. This is for the benefit of those who appreciate working with and towards a bigger picture. I would liken the hermetic teachings to the intricate studies of the Antahkarana – the building of the Rainbow Bridge in aid of the soul's growth and evolution (Reference: Alice Bailey's material).

1. CALCINATION - Heating a substance to high temperature removes impurities and volatile substances - burning off the dross, such as letting go of false pretence and outdated beliefs.

2. DISSOLUTION - Dissolving the ashes of calcination in water and acid, such as learning to let go of compulsion, obsession, addictions and so forth. Work on the heart begins.

3. SEPARATION - Identifying essences and disregarding ingenuine materials, such as when frozen energies break down, filtering out what needs to be resolved.

4. CONJUNCTION - Creating the 'over self' by expressing through being, connecting to other realms and integrating the soul, as well as tuning into heart intelligence.

5. FERMENTATION - Chemical breakdown of a substance, such as exposing the integrated soul to

death and rebirth, loss of identity and new beginnings, psychic visions or new levels of imagination.

6. *DISTILLATION* - Purifying a liquid through a process of heating and cooling could be interpreted as looking at emerging purpose, our service to ascension, higher purification of the soul essence, spirit made corporal, and moods and behaviours no longer just tied to earthly explanations.

7. *COAGULATION* - Processing liquid into a semi-solid state; 'ultima materia of soul,' such as forging our ascending master body, the union of spirit and matter, and empowered and embodied higher states of consciousness.

May these *Seven Steps of Transformation*, as part of your spiritual alchemy studies, add another level and perspective to your self-mastery toolkit from *challenge to choice* and encourage deeper investigation. For more information on alchemy, the online course and book material, please directly refer to Hauck. What follows next is a copy of The Emerald Tablet, which is a single document covering the science of the soul, whose origin is lost in legends that go back to Atlantean times. The writer of the Emerald Tablet is Thoth, the Atlantean priest-king who is known for founding new colonies in Egypt after the fall of Atlantis and his association with building the Great Pyramid of Giza. Thoth, often depicted as a deity with a head of an ibis, was considered immortal. His praise reaches far and beyond and he is recognized for his contributions to many different fields. Thoth is renowned for his ancient wisdom, writing, language skills, mathematical insights, expertise in sacred geometry, and philosophical ideas.

You name it – Toth has already claimed it.

A Conversation with Hermes

The Emerald Tablet

In truth, without deceit, certain, and most veritable.

That which is Below corresponds to that which is Above, and that which is Above corresponds to that which is Below, to accomplish the miracles of the One Thing. And just as all things have come from this One Thing, through the meditation of One Mind, so do all created things originate from this One Thing, through Transformation.

Its father is the Sun; its mother the Moon. The Wind carries it in its belly; its nurse is the Earth. It is the origin of All, the consecration of the Universe; its inherent Strength is perfected, if it is turned into Earth.

Separate the Earth from Fire, the Subtle from the Gross, gently and with great Ingenuity. It rises from Earth to heaven and descends again to Earth, thereby combining within Itself the powers of both the Above and the Below.

Thus will you obtain the Glory of the Whole Universe. All Obscurity will be clear to you. This is the greatest Force of all powers, because it overcomes every Subtle thing and penetrates every Solid thing.

In this way was the Universe created. From this comes many wondrous Applications, because this is the Pattern.

Therefore am I called Thrice Greatest Hermes, having all three parts of the wisdom of the Whole Universe. Herein have I completely explained the Operation of the Sun.

The Emerald Tablet of Hermes. (Compiled from several early Latin and German versions)

"There is only one pattern in the operation of the sun. By Fire will you be set free; by Water will you reclaim your power. By Air will you discover your inner worth; by Earth will you realise its potential." – From The Emerald Tablet by Dennis William Hauck.

Let the Mind Serve

"The universe is of the nature of a thought or sensation in a universal mind... To put the conclusion crudely — the stuff of the world is mind-stuff." – A Eddington

The mind is not the enemy. As a powerful ally, it captures our desires and aspirations, adds the spark of vision, and guides our intuition to bring them to fruition. Our mind is a fractal of the higher cosmic or universal mind, and it enables us to entrust our intuition to safely navigate the lower and upper realms, manifesting our resonating thoughts into physical form. Once we have come full circle and recognise that we are the creation and the creator of our destiny, with inexhaustible access to celestial blueprints, universal patterns, and codes, we move beyond challenge or choice. Our task is to align ourselves with the universal vibration of pure intelligence and unconditional love. This approach is based on the premise that everything is energy, and by exercising our freewill to connect to higher vibrational frequencies, we step into a divinely embodied flow, and simply witness our stories unfold. By streamlining our thoughts, we can shift our perception and reshape our reality. The faster we declutter our polluted mind and clear the misnomer of its function, the quicker we can enter the fluidity and inclusivity of the singularity. Genuine metamorphosis occurs when we renunciate all superiority and surrender to the ever-changing nature of divine guidance. By naturally sifting through our mental impulses, rather than trying to control them, we allow for a deeper connection with the world within and around us. Resonance trumps force, negating the preservation of a separate existence, leading to a more inclusive mindset. Ancient wisdom speaks of the link between the sun and the heart, throat, and mind. The mind, in conjunction with the brain, has the ability to structure and coordinate the storage of light information for later use in appropriate situations. Higher thought forms received from the ether and astral realms can be activated intentionally and collectively shared as ideas.

As we continue to purify our consciousness, the higher mental faculty will allow us to safely navigate through the higher realms of existence and bridge the world of form and spirit.

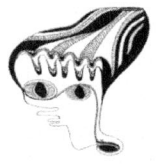

Olympic Rings 'Imagitation'

With this 'IMAGITATION' I welcome you to focus your mind during this imaginative meditation process and invite the five elements of Fire, Water, Air, Earth and Ether to reclaim your power and co-create with you.

Creating and Healing with The Five Elements

Begin by calling forth all your soul aspects, all other corporal and non-corporal companions of soul destiny to witness this journey of elemental receiving. Like a child, just keep exploring ideas and notice your heart-based input. Start sharing your intuitive inspirations with an expansive quality. Give yourself permission to tap into all of your infinite potentials within and outside the cosmic mind. This is a good time to step into the wisdom of the morphogenetic fields and activate the DNA in your physical body. Participate in the endless flow of mutual receiving without constriction, contraction and compaction. Be simply present and don't resist the flow as you open up and walk through the doorway to true potentiality. At the end of every interaction, you will be asked to offer any gifts that come to mind. Take time for contemplation and do not rush the process.

Now, imagine the symbol of the OLYMPIC RINGS - all five colours; red, green, blue, black and white. As you do, think of five different beings you would like to co-create with. Beings, with or without bodies, who are willing to be in their truth and integrity about their light and shadow aspects so you can garner profound insights through sharing this meditation with them.

<u>Now, choose your first companion and ask him or her to give you the WATER RING – the blue one. Step right into it.</u>

Blue characterizes the eternal flow that is unpredictable by nature. Water collects and remembers information. Water gives life. It is a majority composer of various fluid substances inside your body like blood, lymph, urine - even emotions, which often possess a liquid, sticky, clingy, and cohesive quality. With the blue water ring around you, can you feel the water of creation flowing through your being? Pay attention to how it distributes nutrition and carries away waste products. It regulates your body's temperature, strengthens and moistens your immune essence. Is there anything that requires action or resolution? Ask your tongue and sense of taste to assist you in digesting your feelings and emotions. Become them, transcend them, and turn them into intuition. Allow deep emotional patterns to be transformed as you bring forth the courage to be intimate in your relationship with the self and others. In the West, Water, the Chamber of Surrender, we learn to embrace sadness and reclaim our power. Water teaches us to grieve and yet celebrate life. You are invited to participate and co-create with WATER. Please place any offerings into the ring and draw inspiration through this co-creation.

Now, choose your second companion and ask him or her to hand you the ring of FIRE – the Yellow one. Step right into it.

Yellow is the power to transform, burn and illuminate. Fire takes the information collected by water and alchemises it. It is a galvanising force in the alchemical journey that melts away resistance. The Agni, the revolutionary spark in the body, acts as a digestive power for all foods and substances; be they solid, liquid, or gaseous in nature. Fire converts nutrition into tissue and energy. Fiery intelligence and fiery emotions along with passion, lust, as well as anger contribute to a fiery experience of being. What comes up for you here as you look at the great transformational force of fire? Allow your vision and visual senses, which are fire dominant in nature, support you. Those that you have drawn to you hold the ability to assist you in your personal evolution. There are no mistakes. Be willing to look deeply into the truth held within your relationships. Let go of all the times you made yourself or others wrong for lacking joyful enthusiasm. Don't use force to make it work... walk away and let them go. The East, Fire, the Chamber of Integrity, holds treasures for your transformation and transfiguration. You are invited to participate and co- create with FIRE. Please place your offerings into the ring and draw inspiration through this co-creation.

Now, as you choose your third companion, please ask him or her to present you with the EARTH RING – the Red one. Have it laid out in front of you and step right into it.

Red represents the solid state of matter here. In the mind, earth endows resolve and holds the power to withstand. It grounds, supports and commits to the creations of water and fire. As you perceive this red earth ring around you, can you review important memories stored in the Earth's Akashic Records? Are there any thoughts that come up with regards to stability, permanence or rigidity? Invite your nails, your bones, your teeth, flesh, skin, hair, beard, moustache, and tendons to assist you in this process. What comes up for you? Can you smell the earth? Can you fully connect your heart to the molten core of your Earth mother and receive what she offers you? The South, Earth, the Chamber of Awakening, where self- healing becomes your mastery. You are invited to participate and co-create with EARTH. Please place your offerings into the ring and draw inspiration through this co-creation.

Now, choose your fourth companion in this meditation and ask him or her to give you the ring of AIR – the Green one. Step right into it.

Green is the element that is mobile and eternally dynamic.

With no arrest, air is a master communicator with a unique characteristic of constant motion and speed. Respiration, twinkling of eyes, all subtle movement including that of nerves, contraction and relaxation, propulsion and retention, is all related to the element of air. What comes up for you as you feel that ring of AIR around your body? Allow the touch and tactile sense to assist you here. Drop all evaluation. Let go of your reactive nature and allow the breeze of intimate presence to softly embrace you, whether alone or with another. Be open, be here, be present. Innocence, trust, simplicity, and joyful wonder are our natural states of being. Your true North, Air, the Chamber of Gratitude and Joy calling you forth to deeply engulf yourself in your dreaming and awake mind. You are invited to participate and co-create with AIR. Please place your offerings into the ring and draw inspiration through this co-creation.

<u>Now, choose your fifth and last companion and ask him or her to pass you the ring of ETHER – the White one. Step right into it.</u>

It is the energy and consciousness in which soul and spirit meet. It is the medium that connects the above and the below, the existence of infinite potentiality. It is the etheric field that is simultaneously the source of all matter and the space in which it exists. Here sound represents the entire spectrum of vibration. What comes up for your as you feel that Ether ring around you? Allow the sound of ether, all echoes of time and no-time, to create expansive potentials around you. Fully receive your compassionate, authentic heart song that is being played in the Centre, the Ether, the Chamber of Grace. You are invited to participate and co-create with ETHER. Please place your offerings into the ring and draw inspiration through this co-creation.

Now, focus back onto the breath and be still. Perceive and receive the magic of all five rings swirling around you as well as the contributions they offer. Imagine all of them merging into one. What do you experience as they do? See, taste, smell, hear, feel that energy and expand it out well beyond your body. Your offerings, learnings, gifts, all alchemising into one – perceive, know, be, and receive them. Is there a symbolic representation of this integration that you would like to take away with you? What symbol comes to mind? Over the next few days keep that symbol close to your heart and let it flourish. Now, having focused your attention to raising your awareness of receiving, with the help of the five elements and your companions, will you now please close your eyes again. Take a few more breaths and allow the healing integration to continue.

With gratitude, let your radiant mind acknowledge your victories once more. Let yourself be bathed in the healing light and sound from the eternal source you are always connected to. This is the time of new beginnings and perceptions, new allies and friends. As you express more authentically who you are, you will draw your expanded soul family closer to you. With a new sense of oneness, your guides, guardians and earthly companions will support your ability to manifest your inspired visions and dreams.

Be still often, listen and recognise the many eyes and hearts around you that spark the remembrance of sacred trust in your unfolding. Now, give permission to your past and future selves to accept this meditation as a healing and continue with its process over the next couple of days and weeks. Don't expect, don't resist, and more versions of yourself will align with your signature frequency to assist you in exploring future abilities. You are learning many things. You are healing. Follow the energy of lightness to the edge of unknowingness. The places of new insights will provide you with new understandings and authentic truths. Open yourself up and fully receive this healing with gratitude for the blissful potent co-creation. Take a few natural breaths along the spine now, and then please stretch, open your eyes, and feel refreshed as you return to full alertness.

And so it is.

Aho.

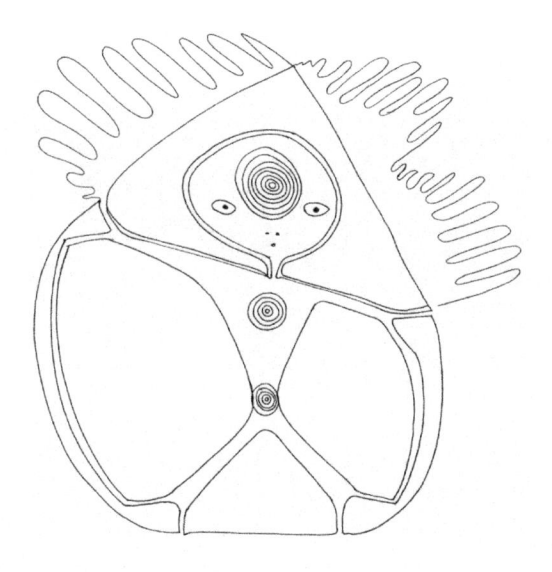

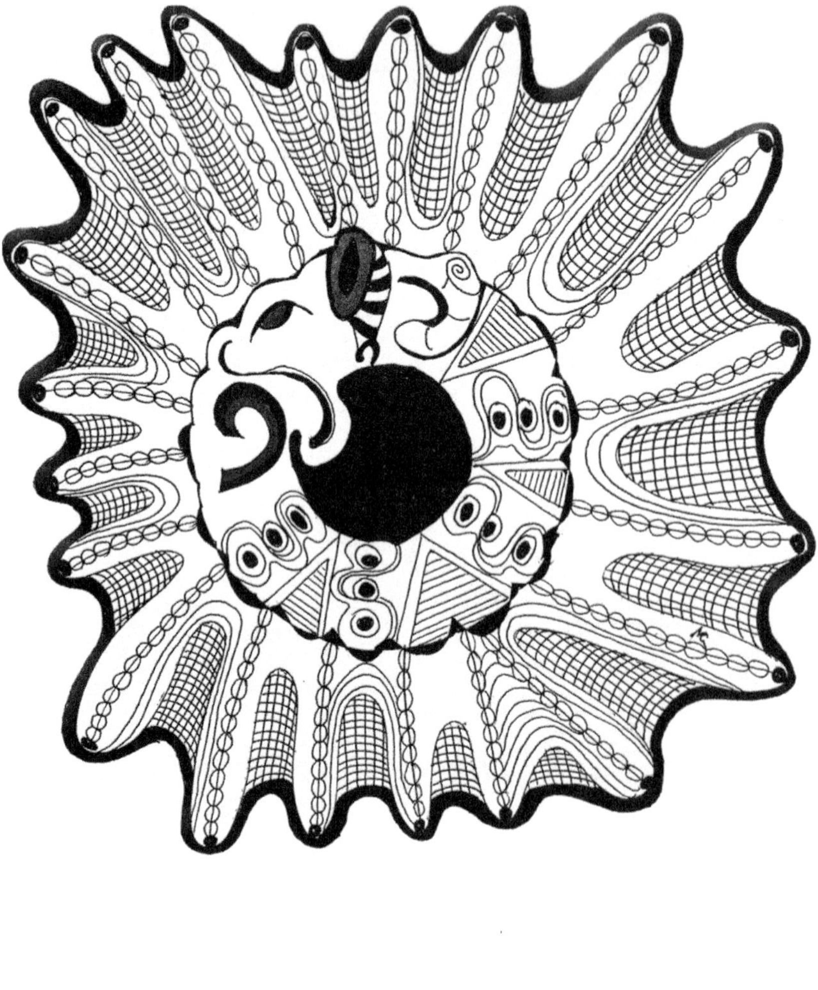

CHAPTER IV: GROUNDING & MASTERY

PART ONE: Sat Nam Presence

Sat is being translated as 'everlasting truth,' and Nam as 'name' or 'identity.' My truth is my identity; a powerful mantra that is often used in meditation. By chanting these two words, we naturally connect into a resonating morphic field that is habitually imbued with a certain sense of solidity and presence due to the ritualistic use of the mantra over centuries. Our body naturally functions as a physical anchor into this reality when free of unhealthy impressions and in a centred state of beingness. With our breath being the anchor's chain, the identity is our personal truth. That centredness attracts and projects energy.

Bruce Lipton talks about the body as a virtual reality suit; cellular receptors being antennas through which we broadcast and pick up signals from our immediate environment, as well as the astral realms, and facilitate the exchange of energy. No two people get the same reception because of our different sets of antennas. The I AM self is a magnetic focal point in consciousness. When we are fully engrossed experiencing in the flesh, we feel animated and inspired. We are so intimately present that we lose *ourselves* in the experience. This is but a snapshot of enjoying physical living as an entangled and immersed observer, in full flow of creation. We build life upon life based on such unique encounters, calling forth the soul to gradually unfold into the I AM self and elevate such experiences. Once we begin to see the world from the trained eyes of the disciplined master, we have learned to alternate between the experiencer and the actual experience, and delve deeper into the underlying patterns and structures that shape our reality, allowing us to adjust our sphere of observation at will. We must honour discipline as one of the keys to living freely and beyond distractive stimuli in order to unlock our true potential.

While true centredness allows for a sense of fluidity and liberation, it is important to note that freedom without structure can become monotonous over time. Does boredom stem from a lack of discipline? It is only when we stay focused and committed to our aspirations that we can truly experience the freedom that comes with it. Ultimately, discipline is a gift that we give ourselves to make the most of our time on Earth. Sat Nam presence follows this path and invites us to steady our impulses and seek simplicity as a way to not get bounced around and sucked into the vortices of compulsion and repulsion. To the degree you feel connected to your masterful self, you will manifest these qualities and bring joy to your service. In this physical realm we give names and definitions to all existing forms to help us isolate and distinguish them from one another. We learn to analyse as well as synthesise, express and regress, all in line with the law of attraction and repulsion. The NAME we were given at birth is part of our identity profile. *Have you ever thought of your name as a grounding tool?* It is really quite fun to play with this concept and explore the deeper meaning. Use nicknames or abbreviated versions of your own and other people's names and see what reactions you get. How does a name affect people's behaviours, drives, and even actions? With some friends, I find myself uneasy shortening their name without almost diminishing a part of who they present themselves as. For others I only use the first letters, as I do with my own full name, MG. Personally, it gives me more space to ground myself in and keeps my consciousness flowing freely. However, always make sure to ask your friends if they are comfortable with you using a nickname or shortening of their name before doing so. It's important to respect their identity and how they want to be addressed. Think of travelling to a foreign place where nobody knows you by your name. Do you feel more or less comfortable? This question alone can give you important clues on how aligned and grounded you feel within yourself. The more space you occupy, the less limited you are. Some research suggests that our name impacts our profession, where we live and so forth...

Most of those intricate associations still play out in unawareness until our pattern recognition becomes more conscious and second nature. You may want to draw your own conclusions and pay attention to the use of your name, depending on what you endeavour to achieve - be that now, in a relationship, or career.

Ground Control to Major You

Once we are happily walking barefoot on the Earth as fully embodied and ascended masters, if we so choose, we can safely assume that we have finally understood the ultimate meaning of grounding. One soul has many forms and transferences and getting bolted out of the physical body is simple. Lack of exercise, abuse, overthinking, emotional overload, and world order distraction are all easy and readily available escape routes. We are not meant to live in constant panic and self-defence mode, but to instead bring forth new ideas, laugh, love, and be empty. If you don't like emptiness, you will never walk away from suffering. Emptiness invites fullness and a fully embodied presence. Whatever you make vital and relevant will run your life and eventually control it. Many of us have had powerful lifetimes to reflect back on and extrapolate wisdom from. Nonetheless, if we can't cherish this life's perks and opportunities and stand our ground right here... right now... we miss out on enjoying the fruits of our soul's accumulated efforts and labour. The spiritual master diligently and steadily carries his experience and work forward in service to the grand evolutionary plan, teaching the mind to let go of attachments and allures of grandeur. By cultivating a sense of tranquillity and steadiness, we can collaborate towards a more advanced and united civilisation on Earth, rebuilding a world that invites beings of higher levels of consciousness. In doing so we must learn to assist those who are choosing a corporal body here on Earth for the first time, as well as self-reliantly guide ourselves through the changes in our individual awareness and biology.

The totality of our cells, organs, and individual brains are constantly aligning with Earth's geophysical shell structure, through the Earth-brain resonance. By means of targeted focus in the awake state, or during dreamtime, we fluctuate between brain wave frequencies that connect us to the inner Van Allen belt, the Schumann resonance, or the electrical discharges of Earth's inner core. Through our skinsuit technology we are constantly tapping into the changing electrical potential of Earth's electro-sphere. In addition to that our body literally gives us access to all memories stored in our planet's etheric, crystalline, and molten core, as well as to the Sun and other planetary consciousness. Our DNA upgrades will exponentialise our access to universal information calling for advanced levels of assimilation in order to keep up with the demands of this new era of data processing. Our bodies will need to be able to integrate the influx of energy more efficiently, allowing us to achieve new levels of understanding and creativity. For some, it will get increasingly difficult to live in a world that is destined to dismantle its old ways and structures, and many will leave. A big part of masterful grounding is to maintain a healthy level of sanity and gain the will to avoid overwhelm and burnout. The human ability to adapt is not just a necessity, but one of our natural capabilities to create intelligent solutions. Unpredictability does not allow room for recklessness and rebellion. Grounding and mastery will save lives.

Back to Basics

A refined understanding and focused awareness on the importance of the BREATH and meditation will greatly assist in the ongoing planetary reconstruction. I personally use diaphragmatic breathing as a coping strategy when I feel ungrounded and out of sorts. We all know that the oxygenating effect of the breath purifies the blood stream and releases stressful tensions.

Purposefully tailored breathing exercises, together with spiritual focus, can produce potent effects in directing the lifeforce in the body. Just as an example, when we rhythmically guide prana into the solar plexus, we aid the digestion of solid food and etheric thought composites. The body and breath are our most revered companions and such profound grounding and manifestation tools. The art of processing thought forms through conscious breath is another topic entirely well-deserving of exploration on its own. Most breathing exercises, Kundalini breath in particular, allow us to more consciously merge the physical and the etheric body through a steady focus on flowing prana. A synchronised application that includes the breath, physical movement, and mantra works well to streamline our willpower and practice a coordinated rhythm. Rhythm is the medicine of the soul. Having been a member of the Life Force Academy with Jai Dev Singh, I support the academy's ethos and more details can be found at www.jaidevsingh.com. Allow this like all concepts, recommendations, and experiences presented in this book to behave as a blueprint for you to discern, tweak, and apply to what specifically works for the uniqueness of you. So much research has already gone into breathwork that the sources to indulge in are endless. This comes with a general note of caution not to get caught up or drawn into other people's inclinations, and to discern for yourself your own peculiar preferences. Our personal objectives can easily get watered down when overly entangled with principles and guidelines from the assembly lines that are operated by the global narrative. There is no prefabricated customary way of living. This world needs reform and we are the reformers. Our daily choices aligned to our soul's purpose and freed from rules, worship, and idolisation, will dissolve and reconstruct the pillars of reality. I can't stress enough that impartiality, healthy discrimination, and choice are paramount grounding keys to get the project *Universal Galactic Citizenship* off the ground. Settle into the core of your existence, open your arms, and let your heart radiate and welcome the cosmic upgrades. Herein lies the secret of successful co-operation and execution of the divine plan.

Finally, removing ourselves from PARASITIC PEOPLE, inclusive of friends and family, is part of the advanced healing process irrespective of how challenging that can be. Fulfilling one's potential may require us to step away from souls that previously have carried us. Remember, energies are spirits. Spirit naturally orients to the physical using sentience as a vehicle. This means that our collaboration with toxic people who are usually stuck in other time frames due to their wounding, draws us into ungrounded frequencies. Our awareness is not negotiable and once we stop defending our truth, we can be refreshingly blunt and uncompromisingly forthright, as Wikipedia describes the word. BLUNTNESS seems to be more fashionable than ever as we forge the way through the jungle of our outdated customary codes of polite behaviour. The rules of etiquette are rapidly changing in this 21st century of reformation; bluntness, redefined as kindness, is gradually being acknowledged by the refined thinkers and creators of the new world. If coherently delivered, its message is poised and gentle and gives the receiver permission to exercise his or her authentic choices also. Such honest conduct, grounded in a transparent expression, facilitates an expanded and mature energy exchange, *wouldn't you agree?* Think of speaking to someone who wants to express anger or frustration towards you, but struggles with the fear of being impolite – you can physically feel the built-up tension. No degree of spoken or written politeness will cover up unhealed emotions, as our psychic antennas are increasingly tuning into incoherent energies that are intuitively felt and intellectually observed. Pure thought and a loving motive are powerful forces and contributions to ground and centre ourselves in higher soul-embodied consciousness. Attempts to repress the inner turmoil neither honours the self or the contribution of another. It often overshadows valuable gifts that could be exchanged and can negatively impact our health and wellness.

The separation of densities is in full flow and it would be wise to just surrender into it.

The body needs FOOD & DRINK. In fact, eating is one of the most pleasing grounding techniques that we hardly pay attention to. We use food and drink to energetically harmonise with frequencies; be that when travelling to foreign or unfamiliar places, or when experiencing adversity in our native habitat. Eating is a primordial, spiritual, multisensory, and secret co-creation with the tangible and intangible realms. The shrimp's innate spirit in your paella doesn't have to magically whisper sweet nothings to your ear in order for you to acknowledge its presence. You can taste and smell spirit through its many manifestations. It creates a feeling of satisfaction and comfort when you eat a meal that arouses or calms your senses. Spirit is serving you a culinary experience as much as you are serving Universal Spirit as the instigator of the experience. A mutually beneficial collaboration that we can draw many lessons of spiritual connection from.

ALCOHOL, unless consumed excessively, can be equivalently grounding in a fine celebration of our human condition and qualities. Still more, we seem to often engage in circumstances that are not perfectly aligned with our soul's purpose. This is where we enter a grey area between simple grounding or fitting in. Who hasn't used alcohol in order to be able to relate to a certain group dynamic, seen or unseen, for that matter? I used to think that I was 'drinking myself out of this reality' - whilst in fact, I was trying to fit into it. No need for guilt-tripping either way, but it's important to have an understanding of what drives a behaviour, be it compulsive or recreational. Emotional stress drinking or eating could be the soul's attempt to desperately stay in the body, whilst an overloaded nervous system is trying to cope with internal or external programs. Alcohol is classified as a depressant that slows down the messages between the brain and the body. *Which body?* An antagonised and unhealed emotional body asserts control over the ego of the physical vehicle. With alcohol or drugs, we can momentarily numb out those messages but until we address them, they will eventually resurface. A crucial aspect to consider is that we psychically have access to all emotions in the quantum field as mentioned earlier.

Once our critical mental faculty has been anesthetised through the overuse of alcohol, drugs, or intense emotional turmoil, we lose control over the reach of our emotional body and open ourselves up to all kinds of astral invasions. A significant aspect in this awakening is to develop high levels of self- consciousness and self-assertion through the healing of our endocrine and nervous system, which are run by the emotional and mental body as discussed earlier in the book.

The COLOURS, SHAPES, and PATTERNS of our clothes have their own consciousness that interacts and impacts on our physical and mental well-being, as well as our environment. Colours are specific light frequencies that reflect our feelings and emotions, affecting our body-mind complexity and greatly assist us in engaging with life. Take the colour red, for instance... the life force energy associated with our blood. Red gets linked to a grounded, materialistic, erotic, determined, action, and affection-oriented personality, as well as emotional reactivity to the contrary. I have always been intrigued how, on those three-day self-development courses, the dress code would change as the week progressed. The people, having processed emotional healings, would start wearing more colourful, brighter, and daring outfits towards the end, indicating positivity and a newly found zest for life. The more spirit we ground through, the more alive the body becomes as it proudly expresses its soul signature.

CLOTHING, BODY MARKINGS and DECORATIONS extend far back in our evolutionary history and elegantly illustrate the progressive changes of our species. The most basic function of clothes is to maintain our body temperature and also, very practically, to avoid inappropriate sexual arousal in our everyday interactions. Think of the specifically designed outfits for protection from the harsh climate and wild animals in the hunter-gatherer days, right up to modern times, or the elaborate to extremely utilitarian uniform and the wartime camouflage gear of military soldiers. Clothes are excellent grounding and survival tools.

I venture to point towards an adroitly adaptation of the fashion and function of men and women's clothing, as we move further into the liberalisation, beautification, and 'galactification' of our civilisation over the coming centuries. A fascinating topic indeed, deserving more exploration as it holds a variety of entrepreneurial opportunities for future enterprises.

With the emergence of the mindfulness movement in recent years, there are endless exercises, techniques, and literature to choose from that can assist in maintaining a high level of grounded presence, in addition to the aforesaid. One favourite of mine is understanding how to work with the vagus nerve, as elaborated on in the book Accessing the Healing Power of the Vagus Nerve by Stanley Rosenberg. I would like to share one of Stanley's exercises to reset the vagus nerve, incorporated in one of my meditational formats. The vagus nerve has access to the totality of our consciousness and impacts on the functions of the physical, emotional, mental, and etheric bodies, which includes all soul aspects that have integrated with this I AM Apex presence. On the physical plane, it mediates between the nervous system and all organs in the body. I am sharing this meditation here as a potent tool to assist you in grounding and staying present. As always, record it in your own voice and relax into the meditation.

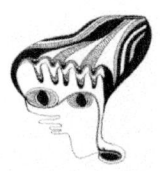

Vagus Nerve Meditation

Balancing the Autonomic Nervous System

I, [insert name], as the I AM Apex being of the now, manifested on two legs in this ever-present moment as a conscious being of knowingness and wisdom, grown as a foetus in my mother's womb...

I choose to engage my hindsight and foresight, as my birth right and legacy to honour and acknowledge my spiritual DNA technology and the original blueprint of perfect health, for the expressed purpose of restoring, rebalancing, relaxing, and healing my autonomic nervous system, the spinal and cranial nerves, and in particular all the branches of the vagus nerve that is central to every aspect of my life and living.

This is a tribute to and a healing focus on the vagus nerve, the wanderer and other cranial friends that cover a multitude of autonomic functions on their travels from the brain and brainstem into the chest and abdomen. Its selfless contributions of its two branches never fail to amaze, inspire, calm and heal as it wanders through the throat, the esophagus, the lungs, the heart, into the organs of the digestive and eliminative systems, as well as promoting lovingly bonded relationships.

Now, take a deep breath and allow your attention and intention to settle on a version of yourself that feels safe and sound, relaxed and expanded in all directions of your beingness. Keep your focus and allow every inhalation to create more space. Drop any barriers of constriction, in aware and unawareness as you observe every exhalation to maintain that space... cultivating a sense of peace, of purpose of perfect place for meditating and healing.

Now, interweave the fingers of both hands together and place them behind the back of your head, with the weight of your head resting comfortably on your interwoven fingers. Feel the hardness of your cranium with your fingers and thumbs and the bones of your fingers on the back of your head. Breathe evenly. A deep inhalation followed by a complete exhalation, creating space on the inhalation and maintaining that space on the exhalation.

Allow a feeling of safety to occur inside your body, as well as outside of it, and allow your structures to relax. Be open to the 'touch' of the sound of your voice to support your mental and physical health, your individual growth and restoration, and to optimise the autonomic functions. Acknowledge what it feels like to feel safe in terms of environment, as well as in terms of feedback from the proprioceptive nerves that constantly monitor what is going on in the body. Keeping your head perfectly still now.

Look to the right, moving only your eyes as far as you comfortably can. Like that, keep on breathing for about 30 to 60 seconds and do not turn your head.

You might want to swallow, yawn, or sigh and that is okay. Your energies are shifting and your body is relaxing. After that, with the head remaining unmoved, look to the left and repeat the process of breathing, keeping your head still for 30 to 60 seconds. [Allow time in the recording or pause to practice the eye movement]

Now, slowly and gently bring your attention back to your breath. Relax, unwind and release the eyes and hands, taking a long inhalation all the way from your tailbone up to your crown and exhale deeply. Observe your body's steady breath, your sympathetic and parasympathetic resting peacefully, your muscles relaxed, and the blood flow circulation continuously restoring as the autonomic nervous system calms down even more.

With every conscious breath you take, honour your pranic body, your physical biology, your co-existence in the here and now. No more running from the imaginary tiger... the baddies have left the building long ago. No more withdrawing from the world, avoiding people, intimate relationships, places or spaces of socially engaging. No more hiding in solitary existence, giving rise to addictions and disconnecting from this world. Now is the time to bond, to reach out again for mutual contribution in equal co-creation, non-competition, non-hierarchical order.

Breathe evenly and allow the spiritual DNA technology and your mystically magical skill sets to switch on, to assist you in making the unknown known. Keep detoxifying and freeing the branches of the vagus nerve from the sharp claws of the global narrative. It is your birth right, your legacy, and your responsibility to claim and realise the magic that you truly be.

Begin to practice these mystical skills that will raise your frequency and psychic awareness a thousand-fold. I now invite in all my younger versions of the self that can give testimony of trauma, drama, and disease. All aspects of my I AM presence, who in unawareness, through tacit consent, have biomimetically mimicked other people's pathways, pains, and realities and embodied those distorted energies of anguish and distress. I call them forth now for liberation. I give them full permission to let go of all the charges and polarity, all the electromagnetic energies of distorted love stored in the atoms of their bodies and between.

Heal, restore back to the blueprint of perfect health and happiness and turn hatred and fear back into love once more.

I herewith reclaim my birth right to travel beyond time and space, whilst owning the joy of having a physical body that will deliver me the pleasures, the ecstasy, the intensity, the potent re- and co-creation with my fellow kind in deep personal, sacred, communion and intimate union, to reach those higher levels of consciousness with total ease and bliss.

Let us now light the torch of new beginnings and choose awareness over fear, as fear is no longer your friend, but foe in times of thrival versus the old survival. Do not fall prey to stressful hyper action, defensive triggers of reaction and response leading you astray, away from happiness and joy, into depression, aggression, regression or suppression, as none give you the sense of relaxed safety that you are striving for.

The time is now, the energies are with you. Go, enter the playing fields of conscious awareness exploration; be the wise and sovereign master in sacred neutral co-creation, including everything and judging nothing. Claim back now your potency, your choice of choices, and peripheral vision to act and react without killing your kind body, and to once again embrace your psychic skills to astral travel, and become the dreamtime creator that you truly be. Your galactic shards, parts and avatars have been waiting patiently to merge with and serve you once again and share the way as way seekers, peacekeepers, and leaders of this new paradigm.

I herewith clearly state that I do not consent to any atrophy, entropy and antipathy of awareness, seen or unseen, not in this or any other reality, dimension and timestream that diminishes, rips apart, or fights the harmony and evolution of my autonomic DNA technological functions and my rights as a spiritually awakening, sovereign, free willed being.

I take on the mantle of responsibility to consciously connect and activate the new strands of my spiritual DNA technology, and acknowledge the importance of trusting and surrendering to a balanced autonomic nervous system. I herewith connect, in gratitude to the vagus nerve, the great 'wanderer,' and magician of all cranial nerves... not only to physically and emotionally rest and restore my vehicle of experience, or to cultivate optimal health, wealth and prosperity, but also to help me generate and maintain intimate relationships, friendships and communications amongst all celestial, sentient kind, in this 5th world of peace.

And so it is.

Aho.

Now, bring your awareness back to your body and to your breath. Take a deep inhalation all the way from the tailbone, along the spine to the crown of your head. Hold the breath for a moment. Slowly exhale before you open your eyes and get on with your day.

PART TWO: Mastery – The Work

Tuning into Identity

Identity is progress.
There is no 'I AM Self' without identity.
Identity without integrity has no structure.
Without structure there is no reality.
We are the structure.
We are real.
We are our reality.

Everything covered so far in this book is an integral part of the 'Triple S' work: *Self-healing*, *Self-mastery*, and *Sovereignty*. Each of us has a unique soul imprint which guides the process towards human mastery.

We are blessed with flashes of intuitive insights, so called epiphanies, that are blissful distillates of our desires and spiritual truths, often accompanied by strong physical reactions. The general objective of human proficiency is to develop a deeper sense of appreciation of our inherent abilities when we arrive in this physical realm and to be more intentional in our preparations for our departure. Meanwhile, the obstacles and setbacks that are inherent to this ever-fluctuating world make for interesting experiences and contemplations.

Consider the possibility that everything you are striving for in your mind is already available in a state of suspended consciousness. All accumulated past events and future life endeavours that are contained in our present signature frequency, guide us in tailoring our daily actions and activities by way of inclinations and impulses. I tend to find that we are often more prolific in a suspended 'trance' space between reality and fantasy. There, solutions have less relevance because there are fewer day-to-day problems and distractions, and we can purely focus on our aspirations and creations. By claiming abstract ideas as ours and taking enthusiastic action towards them, they will eventually materialize within an appropriate timeframe. If you can perceive it, you can know, be, and receive it. This works the other way too. It is not unheard of to accidentally deposit one's set of keys in another realm, or even experience the feeling of a missing limb stuck in the ethers.

Consciousness is proving itself to be the perfect playground for playing hide and seek with the form and formless. As we dive deeper into that in-between state of consciousness, bridging the gap between dream and reality, we become more attuned to the concepts of certainty and illusion, as well as uncertainty and stability. Consistent self-healing and grounding practices will determine how well we can manage our elevated awareness and position ourselves at the centre of our spiralling vortex on Earth. Many of us have spent lifetimes of dedicated effort towards building a strong character and a body capable of supporting the vastness of the soul.

Being centred in our I AM Avatar allows the soul to freely and holographically project its essence. The soul's quality, increasingly harnessed, will continue to act as a strong motivational force to facilitate growth and lead the way on the path of destiny. The liberated I AM self can maintain its stable footing through recognising that everything in fact is uncertain. By accepting this truth, we can find comfort in adapting and navigating through this world's mysteries with more ease and less resistance.

Faith, the nature of the undivided mind, is one of the greatest security blankets during times of uncertainty. Believing in yourself and in the natural progression of things allows you to let go of the false notion that you must manipulate all outcomes of your choices. Faith frees you from the burden of worrying about the future and enables you to concentrate on the present moment. It serves you well to befriend faith as you navigate through uncertainty when walking at the edge of unknowingness. We've played our roles well in the demise from pure spiritual beings to seeing ourselves as enslaved three-dimensional earthlings, and now it's time to flip the coin. In higher service to spirit, our long-term motive is to catalyse humanity into unity consciousness, expressed through spiritual wisdom and love. The knowledge and understanding of the mechanics of the universe, our soul's evolution, and our voluntary participation in the Galactic Ascension Machine are crucial for our true liberation and freedom. In his book The Galactic Historian, Andrew Bartzis speaks of our galactic history through his expanded perspective of our existence, as he endeavours to assist humanity in the personal and collective disclosure.

In my recent studies of alchemy, I delved into the concept of planetary consciousness as part of our hierarchical system, and its influence on our environment, behaviours and gifts. The following planetary reference points provide a highly distilled, but perfect brief summarisation of the subject matters addressed throughout the chapters of this book.

Conventional astrology primarily covers the energy of the planetary constellation at the time of birth, providing a map or guidelines for the development of the human personality. The planetary archetypes, even those not yet discovered, have a subconscious impact on our thought processes, perceptions, and imagination throughout our lives, proving greater access to spiritual interaction. In the future, it is possible that astrology may evolve into something closer to 'galactology', allowing us to include and better appreciate our soul's journey on its own plane and its interaction with other forms of existence. The personality-self is often unaware of the soul's responsiveness to tugs and shifts in the solar system, until they eventually emerge into manifestation. The collective energy shifts through the many potent planetary alignments serve as a reminder of universal projection onto us.

Sun:	Spiritual energy and identity
Moon:	Physical and experiential
Mercury:	Inspiration and higher love
Venus:	Focus and intention
Mars:	Compassion and understanding
Jupiter:	Grounding and contraction
Saturn:	Growth and expansion

Humans are complex and spiritual entities. A spirit, or entity, is a defined consciousness that acts according to set parameters. As such, we are sharing a fellowship and camaraderie with all existing consciousness that wants to be explored and nurtured. We find ourselves increasingly challenged in a time where those set parameters are under intensive scrutiny and adaptation, as we are transitioning out of Pisces and into the Aquarian age. The success of our species, within the context of universal evolution, is being measured by our spiritual advancement. Our extensive travels through time have broadened our minds allowing us to expertly spin all polarised knowledge into wisdom, for the purpose of serving the undivided wholeness. We can simply observe how the old paradigm is still playing out in this current economic and political environment, without becoming spent or exhausted by it.

Mastery is not to be mistaken with separation, control, or superiority over someone or something despite its dictionary definition, but rather the remembrance of the natural hierarchical structure, as well as the ancient and wise mastermind within.

Public Shaming & Joyful Living

With our sovereignty being openly scrutinised in recent months and years, more people are acknowledging the indoctrination of man and demanding greater transparency. In this digital age, we are bombarded with endless information and points of view of rightness and wrongness, making the decision-making process more challenging. The legitimisation of insanity driven by greed and aggression, is speedily spreading like an emotional wildfire. Publish shaming, particularly on social media platforms, has become prevalent and potentially damaging. So You Have Been Publicly Shamed by Ron Johnson is an educational and eye-opening read that illustrates the ripeness of public shaming in the 21st century. Responsible citizens can take this opportunity to discern and sift through competing opinions while remaining focused on following the trail of common sense to avoid getting lost in the noise. For some, this lifetime may be the last one on this planet without their conscious memories intact, calling for joyful celebration. As we focus on our victories and move onto the higher levels of initiation we speedily out-create this reality.

The snake of transformation consistently and patiently forges her way through these pages to remind us not to stop, to not give up now:

The snake swivels through the thick mudded roots on the ground, rustling through the leaves, shifting through the dirt, ready to climb up the tree to warm her leathery skin under the nurturing rays of sunlight. She is now resting, well-nourished after a long period of meagre food supplies, having well explored and mastered the predator prey circle of life. All is well.

It is this time of the year again to get ready to shed her skin, to discard the old cover and settle into a roomier one. It is going to take a few days and whilst she might get a bit distressed throughout the process, she knows it will be all right. She's done it many times before and can still remember the feeling of elation and freedom after having sloughed and shed that suit that had become restraining and full of harmful parasites. She is the ultimate symbol of transformation after all. Thank you snake for your inspiration.

For those who opt for heightened consciousness, a swift and drastic transformation of our existences on this planet is inevitable. Having climbed and fallen off the evolutionary ladder so many times, discomfort and vulnerability are familiar companions that will accompany us through all the craziness in search of the generative ocean of lifeforce, at the foundation of our empiric world. We are but a speck of dust in this vast, immeasurable universe; a manifested drop in the sea of potentiality, and yet our progress is being monitored throughout the cosmos. Every one of us is an impulse to unite what has once been divided. We are to purposefully co-join the visible with the invisible realms again and blissfully ride the waves of sudden insights that lead our way to physical immortality.

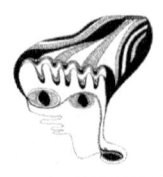

The Triple S Synthesiser Task

With the following document, I challenge YOU to get down to business with regards to the three subjects: Self- healing, Self- mastery and Sovereignty.

Feel free to choose from the specifically tailored and randomly arranged clearings, statements, questions... to create your own Triple S invocations or revocations.

A synthesizer is defined as a person that uses the mind creatively. You could even transform some of the teachings into lyrics for a rap song.

You are not alone, and you are not a clone. Are you feeling afraid? Are you playing one, two, three, or even a thousand roles? Are you away from the ground, with your head in the sky, watching over others, healing the sick, endlessly empathising, and teaching struggling students without rest? Or are you here to hear the whispers of your own music, to listen to your own song, soothing the pain of the past, and shed the skin of limitation?

If your ears could hear you calling for the authentic human in you, wanting to be acknowledged and loved by you, no matter what, what would you tell them? Are you on the lookout for a certain someone? YOU? YOU the master of the I, you the healer of the AM, and the bearer of sovereign gifts to the I AM. A man or a woman, flesh and bones, walking the walk, talking the talk, are you singing the song from the depth of your heart?

Yes, can you be here right now? Feeling, thinking, emoting, and being fully present on this planet, on this Earth, fully joining in the dance with all those 'man-infested' bodies without judgment, overthinking, doubt, or hesitation. With a raging fire in your belly and pure commitment to discovering your individual path, leading you to illumination, are you ready to embrace the journey ahead?

What does it feel like to be human and have a physical body? Does it hurt? Yes, it does at times. Pain, no longer just generated in ignorance but understood from a place of awareness, growth, and gratitude, becomes a mature appreciation that there is no separation between health and sickness. Both are just two different states of being, pregnant with opportunities to learn, breathe, and live greater.

Allow yourself to feel the humanness in your very bones and observe the aliveness in a body that you can choose to truly honour - the natural sweetness, innate kindness, the raw explosive intensity. A glorious, orgasmic trance constantly broadcasting polarity and contrast that only we humans can perceive, receive, and alchemise into greatness. Can you be with the intensity we call pain - physically, emotionally, mentally, spiritually - and still smile?

With an open mind, a belief engine that does not judge, expect, or project, you can be here, there, and everywhere. But for now, just now... can you be here? Just here, in this chosen body, tasting the bitte-sweet tears of your own medicine? Can you keep a secret? Or is there no secret space left in your body, fiercely holding onto hiding the magnitude of all the secrecy built up over lifetimes?

How much have you been invalidating your own knowingness, hopes and dreams, needs and wants, to keep them hidden from your parents, brothers and sisters, peers, friends and colleagues, clients, and from the creator itself?

The secret of a secret is that it is secret – even from yourself! Grounding, inhabiting your body fully, and being present and vulnerable is impossible without exposing all of your secrets to yourself. Secrets are barriers and barriers divide. They separate us from us and our loved ones and from seeing the oneness in all that is. What hidden secrets have your secrets that create the lack of opportunities?

What if you'd stop being a cow, a coward? Cowardice keeps you from speaking your truth about what really goes on inside yourself. Would that raw energy of vulnerability set you free? Can you embrace vulnerability and see its strength, rather than the falsely indoctrinated wrongness?

Everywhere you are choosing to misinterpret this individual spiritual awakening, and opting out and escaping from the harshness of this reality, instead of honouring your body and its magnificence as the ultimate grounding tool, please destroy and uncreate all excuses, falsely adopted justifications and rationalisations?

Lighten up and shine a light onto the misguided and arrogant parts of yourself that falsely keep you on a pedestal looking down on Earth instead of being rooted and grounded in her. Stop struggling to maintain a footed, stable position in your life. You are a manifesting, co-creating being of natural, not forced, evolution.

What black wizardry have you been engaging in that drains your every spark of imagination, imagery, and magic and keeps your energy invested in the paradoxical timelines in this and other galaxies, solar systems, and universes? Is now to the time to step into your inner genius, sack all false time lords and ladies, collapse the holographic constructs, release yourself from the stranglehold of Roman numeral fraud time, and reconnect with earthly, galactic, and universal time?

What solidity, morbidity, rigidity or stupidity are you still holding onto that stops you from remembering to enjoy this journey in all its contrasting colours, allowing you to fail, make mistakes, and revel in the joy and misery of being fully human?

Find that voice within yourself that guides you back on track. Commit to yourself, nip that inner rebel in the butt, and thank him for his services in the past when you needed him most. You will be rewarded a millionfold.

Now, for just a moment, consider all the directions you can move towards, and all the steps you can take. You are never stuck. Use your legs to move to the left, to the right, to the front, to the back – an array of different possibilities that can help you expose any unhappiness and collect more learnings, insights, knowledge, and wisdom on your path to a grounded, soulful beingness. Allow the physical movement of your body to awaken the music within you... the sacred flow to the sound of your eternal song, irresistibly manifesting in the now. Take that one step. Take it now.

Are you living your life in the past, holding onto unhealed relationships and staying stuck in the dark? It is time to shine your light on those places and release them. As a creator being of light and a healer of self and others, you have the power to illuminate and transform.

Utilise the breath to bring you fully into yourself - your body, your potency, your confident expression, and existence in the present moment. There is no other more powerful, more vulnerable, more insecure than you. There is only one source, mirrored, projected, and reflected through all of us, diversely and uniquely expressed in a squidillion ways. The time is now to heal our DNA and use freewill choice to build your own solid foundations, or you will keep looking for yourself in others forever.

It is time to master true courage and consciously grow through major life cycles, no matter what force is put upon you. Can you remain firmly seeded, divinely guided, and earthly nourished? Name your powers, release your limitations, raise your awareness, and acknowledge your body and mission you have chosen to play with in this cosmic earthly game.

Good food, fresh water, exercise, mantras, sex, art, music, breathing, meditation, revocations, invocations, ceremonies, rituals, dreamtime exploration – all of these can help. Mix them up and monitor your progress. Make time within your day, week, month, and year, and do not fall prey to zealotry, militancy, or even spirituality.

Sovereign, multidimensional living includes everything and judges nothing. Only when we step out of judgment of the self and others, have we healed our old wounds of aggression, obsession, hurts, and rejection.

Be the masterful and worldly urban shaman, intending and attending to your ceremonial fire, as well as maintaining a divine-human balance, without frantically seeking definition, validation, and gratification. Can you be fully present in your body and stay infinite at the same time?

Acknowledge the physical form you inhabit in this world, but don't become too attached to it by trying to control it or letting it control you. What if prioritizing physical appearance, status, and wealth leads you far away from your true self? Are you naturally living in alignment with your body and purpose? You owe it to yourself and your legacy to do so. Who or what is still dictating your reality?

Remember that everyone has their own path to walk, and it is not your place to interfere or judge. Part of the sovereignty teaching is to not tread on other people's journeys, no matter how hard and painful their odyssey seems. Can you see the potential in others yet be in allowance of their lesser choices? Stay clear of mental, psychic masturbation, and do not offer unsolicited facilitation.

Let go, move on, and step forward as the leader. The others may or may not want to follow. Sove-REIGN-ty is key; reign in your sovereign power, reign over the kingdom of yourself, and establish clarity and focus to exercise your intent. How do you position yourself in this world? How do you get people to see you in all your colours? How do you manage to bring all of your selves together in harmony, in balance, and in total allowance of what is, was, and ever will be? How can you make present moment choices that can create long-term rewards over lifetimes, generations, and eras of light?

How can you ground yourself so deeply in all your glory that the depth of your lightness takes you to places and spaces of energy and consciousness? How can you stop dreading the unknown and go forward towards the edge of the unknowingness, where the magic unfolds?

No more traumas. Let go of drama and gossip, which takes your breath away. Self-healing and self-mastery are total game changers. No more enduring pain in order to gain, but instead, enthusiastic effort and joyful contributions. Choices may or may not give you the result you were looking for. Nothing ventured, nothing gained; you can always choose more.

Procrastination will be replaced by commitment and integrity as we follow the path of right timing and heart's discernment, instead of blindly going along with the latest trends, gurus, or getting led astray by curiosity learning.

Having to pay for motivational classes to take action is a story of the past. Once you found your inner fountain of wisdom and generator of passion, you can start co-creating with like-minded tribes, and create a web of interconnectivity in service of those who willingly seek support and inspiration.

If you do not know the energy of total surrender, how will you ever know what is truly possible? What do you know about how to be or do with your body, and for your body, that you've never had to do or be because you followed the script of the role assigned to you? You are the master of your own making. In this place of endless choices, can you trust and invest in your heart and follow the energy of joy and compassion?

Improv laughter is healing, as is being in sensual and sexual communion with another. Think of the joy of laughing and cuddling in your lover's arms. When seeing the beauty of yourself reflected in the flowering rosebush or the playful kittens, you experience moments of infinite bliss, joy, and grace. In those moments, you are living according to your divinely orchestrated plan. What if that is enough? What if being a master of joy is enough to assist this world to move further into ascension?

All the hidden places and spaces in which you think you are trapped, all the prisons of the mind that keep you captive, all the old missions that have incarcerated you and hold you back from being true to yourself, no longer have authority over you. Fire them, pink slip them, eradicate them, and send them packing with love and your utmost forgiveness.

Are you constantly on the lookout for yourself? Don't you want to be let down? Which one of those are you? Chasing and blaming others for what they have done to us just does not cut it anymore. The moment you start valuing yourself, others will perceive you in a different light. They'll either want to be close to you or they will disappear, as they can no longer force a match to your signature frequency.

Emotional intelligence is all about using your emotions as an internal guidance system and not being run or triggered by them without choice. As long as you harbour anger, fear, shame, blame, and guilt in your cells, you run the risk of being consistently kicked out by your programs without you having any say. Healing the self is all about not letting emotions trigger you, and lead you into false actions and reactions. We are here to master our emotions and use them for the benefit of creation, as well as teaching tools to other worlds.

Move in unison with your body and mind. Sing with your authentic voice, taste with your curious tongue, release tears through your all-seeing eyes, and allow your heart to hear your ancient song of innate wisdom, long-lost camaraderie, of love never-ending, grounded into your being and uploaded into your DNA memories. Who wants to liaise with an entity-infested body? All the 'for rent' signs on your body... is now the time to take them down and own and claim your skinsuit for yourself? You are no longer contractually bound to mediocrity.

Acknowledge the agreements you made in unknowingness, and remove your signature from these ancient contracts signed in other dimensions, timelines, galaxies, and universes. Keep sending those parasitic energies back to whence they came from, never to return to your reality again. Don't let your trickster selves run your reality. The willingness to stand up and out is equal to the value you place on yourself, as the I AM presence now. Audit out all those ancient, habitual versions of yourself that do not support those extraordinary states of compassionate human consciousness.

Become aware of your energetic makeup and acknowledge the impact of your environment. Don't use it as an excuse to play the victim game. Understand the importance of the choices that you make and the ones you don't make. Not choosing is still a choice.

All the convoluted ideas of what self-mastery, self-healing, or sovereignty should be, is, and ever will be that is sticking to you, nailing you down, boxing you in, throwing you off track, and making you constantly seek higher grounds of fake grounded-ness, dissolve them. Just breathe the breath of life, of life force, of simple divine knowingness, of trusting your body, your soul, your mind, and let go of the rest.

Settling for the familiar is neither healing nor does it create more. Seeking comfort or hiding behind one's past achievements, does not equate to mastery. As long as judgment, the grand dark master of charge and polarity, is still at war with our awareness, we remain caught up in inferiority and in competition with the self and others.

So often, we become addicted to seeking validation, external gratification, and conforming to the frequencies of others in order to find meaning and value in our lives. However, all addictions ultimately dishonour our existence. They demonstrate a lack of respect for our body, our health, and our innate wisdom. It is okay to not always feel like we are part of a grand and glorious mission.

We must acknowledge and embrace our differences, even if it means being considered weird, not normal, or an outsider – outside of what, the false 3D matrix box?

Find the heartbeat of Mother Earth inside yourself, and deepen the experience of your yin - your female core - for boundless, masterful creation. Acknowledge your yang - your male expression of relentless, fiery, and fierce commitment - for re- birthing yourself as the grounded, sovereign I AM APEX master.

Allow Earth to reach out to you, and with matching heartbeats, hear her whispers of love. Allow her to take you in her gentle, nourishing, and nurturing embrace. Allow Gaia to sweep you off your feet with her radiant life force and calm your emotional tornadoes with the most transformative energy. This will propel you back into grounded love and unbiased compassion.

Now, take a moment of no-time and focus your attention on your breath. Close your mouth and allow the cool air to enter your nostrils, brushing against your nasal hair. It travels down your palate, your cheeks, your teeth, your oesophagus, down the throat, the lungs, the heart, the chest, the stomach, the pelvis, the legs, the ankles, and all the way down into the soles of your feet. Feel and acknowledge the consciousness expressed in your DNA vehicle of experience.

Connect to the Earth below your feet, and to the energies above your crown. Move your fingers and toes, and allow your head to sway from left to right and right to left. Receive the gift of breathing the self into spiritual embodiment in this moment of now. Can you feel the lifeforce moving through your body, urging you to not give up on yourself, your self-healing, and your self-mastery? Can you perceive, hear, see, taste, and smell the benevolent astral beings leading the way? Guides and guardians nudging you to fortify your sovereign state of being, shaping pure sacred neutral awareness into sounds, words, and form.

Be yourself, be grateful, be beautiful, and be here now as the healed and sovereign master. Only then you can move into a joyful future as one of the humanoid galactic teachers of the new explorer race.

And so it is. Aho.

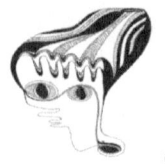

Crown Shyness – Sovereignty Exercise

I trust, by now, you have already completed some of the revocations and clearing marbles in this book and are feeling revitalised and more in harmony with nature and your multidimensional existence. Peter Wohlleben writes in his book The Hidden Life of Trees:

'A tree is not a forest. On its own, a tree cannot establish a consistent local climate. It is at the mercy of wind and weather. But together, many trees create an ecosystem that moderates extremes of heat and cold, stores a great deal of water, and generates a great deal of humidity. And in this protected environment, trees can live to be very old. To get to this point, the community must remain intact no matter what. If every tree were looking out only for itself, then quite a few of them would never reach old age. Every tree, therefore, is valuable to the community and worth keeping around for as long as possible.'

Take a moment of silence and look at the drawing which I have called **'Crown Shyness'**.

- *What do you see?*
- *How does the picture make you feel?*
- *What can you take away from it and apply to your life?*

Wikipedia defines crown shyness as a phenomenon observed in some tree species in which the crowns of fully stocked trees do not touch each other, forming a canopy with channel-like gaps. The phenomenon is most prevalent among trees of the same species, but also occurs between trees of different species.

When I first came across the term, it got me thinking of the mutualism of souls and how sovereignty can be seen as the bridge for coming together again as a flourishing community. Organisms, trees, humans, and all celestial minds are sourced in the one consciousness and our interdependent, reciprocal, and responsive relationships facilitate the nature of it. A divine source feeding the unique experiences of seemingly separate forms, without infringing on each other's branches. Nature's wisdom never ceases to amaze me.

Thanks for playing with this exercise.

The 12 Universal Laws

In the context of The Triple S, I adapted the twelve universal laws to consider an ideal scope for personal and universal expansion. As we begin to master all the laws as part of our soul's unification process, we can dynamically engage with life in all of the time and space equations in the sea of consciousness, well into the ocean of awareness, and beyond. The ultimate goal is to establish a non-competitive universal heterarchical system where we can all express our unique qualities within an undivided totality and teach the supreme law of do no harm to any sentient kind.

The Law of Divine Oneness / THE SINGULARITY

This law is the macro expression that the universal prime creators are subjected to, as well as every single one of us in the micro. We are all connected irrespective of shape or form, or no form, at all levels of awareness. The act of neutral observation allows us to perceive the ever-prevalent interconnectedness between the all. This realm of matter gives us the illusion of duality and separation, but we are also experiencing the singularity in our dreamtime, now.

Q: *How much could more recall of your dream journeys assist in the search for your divine essence?*

The Law of Vibration / ENERGY MOVES

As we know from quantum physics, universal consciousness is enfolding and unfolding continuously, from wave to particle and back to being a wave. The vibration determines the duration of energy compounded, magnified, and expressed in all bubbles of reality. The sound emanation through one's voice can create a frequency spark that impacts the energies of others and the multidimensional landscape, as it ripples and harmonises throughout all time equations. Every single one of us is an authentic expression of perception and perspective, representing a unique dimension of the *one truth*. Energy is in constant motion.

The universal building blocks of consciousness are vibration, frequency, and harmony that attract, create, connect, and perpetually remodel all holograms of multidimensional expression.

Q: *What is it going to take to have your truth spread throughout the multidimensional network?*

The Law of Correspondence / INSIDE OUT

Our inner world reflects the outside world and beyond. A multitude of energetic webs; some sacred and others not so, make up the patterns of the universe. We are both the creators of our reality and the ones who are affected by it, constantly weaving the fabric of our spacetime existence. We have an energetic capacity to create harmony within ourselves and our environment at large. As we purify our inner landscape from outdated patterns of repetition and limitation, we draw an entire new world of corresponding images, thoughts, and conceptions towards us. We can use those to alter our past, present, and future versions of ourselves, facilitating great change.

Q: *What outside triggers still remind you of unhealed inner wounds?*

The Law of Attraction / SIGNATURE FREQUENCY

This law goes beyond attracting what we focus on. It is an invitation to get to know the entirety of our being expressed and nourished through our soul's signature frequency. Our energetic imprint repels and attracts people, places, as well as situations that have multidimensional scope. It is a reminder to look beyond the surface of what we can see, hear, taste, or smell and appreciate the level of tacit consent we have ignored in the past that got us into this mess. Nobody is out there to punish us. Whatever we are willing to perceive without resistance, we can attract into our lives. There is no such thing as not being deserving or not worth it.

Q: *Are you ready to stop playing small and expand your point of attraction beyond your wildest imagination?*

The Law of Inspired Action / EMBODIED SPIRITUALITY

Firstly, we have to acknowledge that there is a reason why we have a body. We have legs to walk with, hands to build and touch with, a mouth and tongue to speak and taste with. Actions are activators of our innate gifts in the present moment. In order to collect memories in this reality, we have got to commit, move, and act. Inspired action is the result of a greater understanding of our soul's purpose that wants us to go on adventures and have experiences, joyful or not. Being fully present and healthy allows the soul to project more of its light into our body.

Q: *How much more fun can you have with that?*

The Law of Perpetual Transmutation of Energy / GRATITUDE

No matter how small we think we are compared to others, or how insignificant our daily practices and actions towards freedom and choice are, being here on this planet is huge. Our very breath changes consciousness at our local and universal level. Our victories are not just personal triumphs, but they create a powerful alchemy that transforms us and the world around us. Our experiences are recorded in the Akashic records of this planet, contributing to the collective consciousness of humanity. Gratitude is a daily choice.

Q: *What victory can you acknowledge today that would change your reality right away?*

The Law of Cause and Effect / MANTLE OF RESPONSIBILITY

The principle of cause and effect teaches us that nothing in this universe happens by chance. We are infinite creator beings and with every decision with make, we simultaneously create within the collective time-space reality, as well as impact the entire fabric of this universe. As we remember our divine essence, we begin to recognise that this reality is fractal based and not linear. Events in the physical realm can occur without any apparent cause or reason. Our experience is equal to the level of our awareness of the holographic universe.

As we overcome our past traumas and begin to understand the true nature of the universe, we act with greater conscious awareness and are no longer at the effect of things.

Q: *Are you willing to let go of the idea of never-ending karma?*

The Law of Compensation / NONATTACHMENT

A contribution does not go unnoticed. A way of interpreting this law is by reframing prosperity and gaining clarity on what wealth or abundance truly entails; we must stop associating them purely with material possessions and money. There is a requirement of trust in the self and the larger unfolding of our soul's journey that accompanies that law of compensation. We are here to act as benevolent avatars of our soul. Keeping this goal in mind, we can strive towards personal prosperity and joy in service to all sentient kind. The world does not owe us anything. We owe it to ourselves to be happy and content.

Q: *What are your favourite ways of acknowledging your contributions?*

The Law of Relativity / SACRED NEUTRALITY

What if another person's perspective and opinion does not necessarily have to be of value to us, even though it seems important to them? Can we be in allowance of that without questioning it or, at worst, throwing a tantrum? Everything is relative - nothing is inherently good or bad in this duality expression that we find ourselves in. This law invites us to look deeper into the impetus of idealism in the pursuit of perfection, as well as the rightness and wrongness that is creating the illusion of separation, instead of oneness.

Q: *What will make you stop justifying your decisions and opinions, regardless of the expectations and choices of others?*

The Law of Polarity / FREEWILL

This fabulous law of opposites is to, initially, learn to create within the lower levels of consciousness. Through opposites, we practice intent and focus until we masterfully manoeuvre in a reality that offers freewill and contrast. We can stay away from what we don't want and put our attention on what we do desire. This law serves as a stepping stone into higher levels of awareness, guided and served by free willed choices. When practicing polarity in neutrality, with the energy of freewill behind it, we open ourselves up to a wider range of observation and creation. Planet Earth provides a training ground for us to learn about freewill and to implement healthy boundaries for natural and sovereign living within rhythmic and evolutionary cycles.

Q: *How can you have more fun with the contrast available to you rather than trying to control it?*

Law of Perpetual Motion & Rhythm / IMPERMANENCE

Everything is in constant motion and we are invited to embrace every new cycle to the fullest. This law deals with the impermanence of life. Everything has a beginning and an end in this realm of matter. The ancient sacred symbol OM stands for birth, sustenance of life, and ultimately death - the transition into another cycle which is infinitely repeated. Earth has its own heartbeat and seasonal rhythm that we are connected to in sharing space with her. The preciousness of it all lies in the acceptance of death as part of life. Through grieving the loss of what we love, we can deepen our connection to the universal rhythm and gain illuminating insights and knowledge. The appreciation of impermanence unfolds into a celebration of life and praise of our existence.

Q: *Are you celebrating life and death as a way of honouring both?*

Law of Gender / BE THE GIFT

This law reminds us of the importance of our differences; the two sides of a single coin. One cannot exist without the other. Spirit and soul, the yin and the yang, the feminine and the masculine forces within every one of us are constantly seeking balanced expression. It is time to burn off all pretences and inculcated belief systems with regards to gender conformity and examine our internal polarity and distortions of the male or female. The supreme gift lies in reciprocal receiving as we give and contribute in service to the self and others.

Q: What gifts are you refusing by not uniting the man and woman inside yourself that you could be choosing?

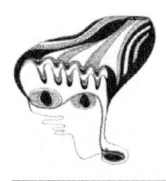

12 Universal Laws - Victories

Upon reading the aforementioned universal laws, please use the twelve questions to reflect on them in greater detail within the context of your own life and create a culminating piece where you can mesh all twelve queries, as well as your contemplations, into one summation that could be viewed as a victory in itself. This exercise can be periodically repeated to reveal your progress over time and provide a valid cause for celebration.

Enjoy!

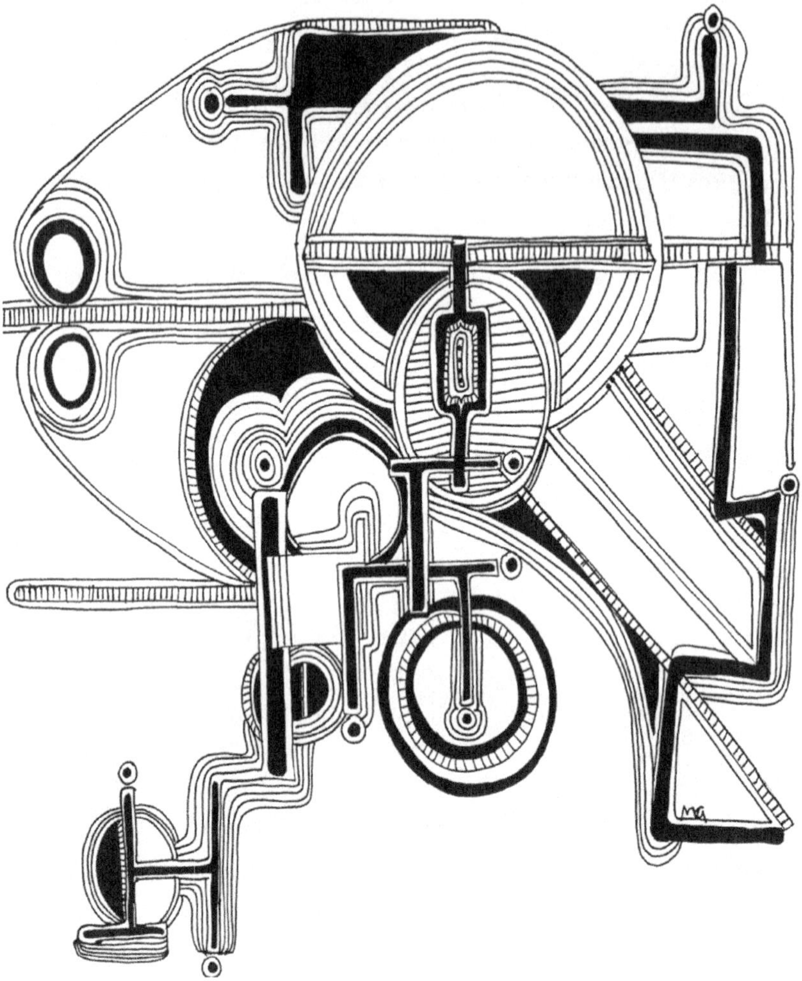

CHAPTER V: LEADERSHIP & TIME
PART ONE: I AM Choices & Mediumship

Magic beyond Mysticism

Along the path from challenge to choice we naturally gain an appreciation for our spiritual existence that allows us to unlock more space and energy for claiming and committing to heightened levels of freewill. I AM choices can open unexpected avenues for exploration and expand life exponentially, often beyond our wildest imagination. They usually are preceded by a line of synchronistic events; unassuming when looked at in isolation, but revealing of a certain magic once recognised as a pattern. It is wise to pay attention to the subtle and discrete signs of spirit that impulse us into soul-inspired action.

I just recently have come across one of those *coincidental* threads that steadily and effortlessly still keeps evolving. A simple snapshot taken from a dream I shared with a friend led to a newsletter that propelled me into booking an astrology chart that suggested further studies of the Alice Bailey material, perfectly synchronised with my explorations. These inspired choices along the evolutionary path to the I AM may be ridiculed and frowned upon by family or friends and society at large as, more often than not, they do range outside the strictly regimented bandwidth of logic and sense. Do you ever find yourself super excited for no concrete reason whilst others just shake their heads in disapproval or bewilderment? - Yes, that!

We are moving into a soul infused and more spiritually confident era of leadership within communities, benefiting both businesses and society as a whole, as more and more people awaken to their own spiritual journey. It can be difficult to think clearly, make decisions, and concentrate under forms of emotional distress or stress as we discussed in the third chapter.

Endocrinological studies imply that emotions create chemicals that impact our hormonal balance and as such, our interactions and decision making to accomplish our goals. A typical example of this is with prolonged stress, where our body continues to release adrenaline until we learn to relax, clear our mind, and be still. This also applies to 'positive' stress that is caused by compulsive desires, passions and addictive seeking, as energy does not distinguish between right or wrong. An I AM choice, aligned with one's true self and values, cannot be made when the mind is overly distracted and influenced by a distorted reality framework. Our bodies are designed to transcend chemical living as we continue to heal and balance our nervous system and our organism adapts to the enhanced planetary energies. By clearing our innate light pollution, our physical body can more easily hold and emanate a higher vibration, engaging in our intuitive and creative faculties.

Making I AM choices that align the higher with the practical self, harmonises our existence and positively impacts the intertwined web of creation. When all is said and done and love rules reason, we will be able to function as one awareness. *This IS the work of the self-initiated master.* In other words, when we stop defending and clinging to our intellectual property, we have unlimited access to universal love and wisdom that is coded in light and sound. As we learn to consciously access higher thought-forms through advanced levels of perception, our familiar playground significantly changes. This comes with an important note of caution; spiritual mediumship has to be gradually implemented throughout the awakening journey, as it takes intellectual and energetic maturity to safely register and filter any incoming data from the etheric and astral realms. Such access comes in cyclical spurts and bouts and can be easily overwhelming if not adequately mastered. To responsibly alchemise the spiritual information and allow it to positively affect the quality of our work on the physical plane, we have to remove the wheat from the chaff and structure the downloaded energy wisely and run it through our heart's bullshit detector.

A prematurely developed access to this higher perception is not ideal. It is important for a human being to be well established in a safe and nurturing environment as to not fall prey to burnout during heightened extrasensory activity. An uninterrupted focus on the spiritual unfoldment without the provision for stable physical outlets to fully ground the light, nullifies or misdirects the spiritual ambition and practice.

Our responsibility as the physical avatar is to prepare and provide a healthy body and a stable environment for the soul to coherently signal desire and purpose. Beware of spiritual arrogance and fanatical, unbalanced, idealism when overly exposed to the astral realm without sufficient discrimination. An unhealed ego can easily get over inflated and create separation and false hierarchies as is often observed amongst communities. By consistently practicing mindfulness and reducing our reliance on intense and biased emotions, we can better connect to our true inner authentic voice and are no longer distracted by the demands and expectations of others. An intended collaboration between the physical, etheric, and astral body helps us to distinguish between a trusted source of higher consciousness and unclean, destructive influences that pull us in different directions.

The more proficient we become as sacred neutral observers, the more we can tap into the infinite data streams at-will, which makes chemical memory less attractive and no longer necessary in the long run. Key to all of that is to stop falling for this world's propaganda, which includes our own, and to finally get out of the cycle of brainwashing we have been subjected to. All energies are innately spiritual and being naturally attracted and repelled through our 'heart-gut' mechanism, and managed by our mind's intelligence. *Living the magically spiritual life is not mystical*; it is learned, understood, and earned. Again, we can't force a match to celestial mediumship and abandon our emotional guidance system with immediate effect. Every higher level of awareness is but a culmination of the many earlier and grows out of the realisation of a timeless and enthusiastic application to the service of self and others.

It is part of the evolutionary liberation process and will naturally happen as we begin to merge the solar plexus with the heart chakra, after having cleared the toxicity out of the overemotional body. Trust the process and remember that not everything depends on individual effort but also works within life sustaining cycles of contraction and expansion. Don't despair; we are not going to turn into lifeless robots without the ability to appreciate blissful sensations, but rather function through intense inspiration without the old entanglements and limitations that previously prohibited multisensory and multiorgan perception. We may well still go through highly-charged emotional levels of discernment preceding a particular choice point, until we become more practiced in trusting our intuitive I AM's navigation. I am certain you have had those moments of clarity - a deep sense of knowingness where everything just falls into place, void of any need for words, thoughts or feelings. I AM choices are supported by our ancestral energies; our I AM pre- and post-cognitive workforce that helps us coordinate choices and actions as part of the I AM Avatar. By consciously combining all three aspects of our micro personality, which is comprised of the mental (intellectual), emotional (astral) and physical (dense and etheric) bodies we can safely tap into the macrocosmic intelligence. The aim is to first soundly discern each of these three existential vehicles separately, without overemphasising the importance of any single one, and secondly to wisely use them in co-creation. Too much attention has been placed solely on the mental and material world with all of its trials and tribulations that has reduced man to the status of an octopus held captive in a tiny aquarium, disconnected from the big wide ocean of energetic awareness. As we progressively awaken from the states of endemic mass-hypnosis, we start walking out of our narrow-minded confinement and can learn more about the etheric and astral components that make up the qualities and characteristics of our personality, soul imprint and purpose. Looking at our existence purely from the physical and material body's standpoint, without taking its energetic and spiritual associations into consideration, creates dimensional separation and rifts in our consciousness.

We have to study the underlying and overlapping energetic network that synchronously penetrates and guides our ego, personality, body, and soul. With knowledge comes power and the responsibility to accept that our truth is but a partial aspect of the greater fabric of universal truth. As we embody more understanding of our history and existence and confidently express our individual truth, we are being reminded once again to suspend our beliefs as they are parameters for a truth that is steadily evolving. By shifting towards a greater vision, we may find it easier to maintain mental flexibility and to eradicate any outdated value or belief system, and therefore avoid its spiritual or conspiracy rabbit-holes that lead to nowhere. I AM choices are intuitively inspired and directed by a balanced and empowered mind that listens and knows what creates more for the individual, rather than submitting to mediocre standards.

The key to transforming ourselves into the desired *Philosopher's Stone of the I AM THAT I AM* is to transcend low-frequency and chemical thinking and embrace a higher level of consciousness. As a manifested spirit, our signature frequency permeates all layers of the universe as it links the micro and the macro planes. Following inner guidance, I never reopened my yoga studio after the Covid lock down restrictions had eased in 2022, without any solid reasons. Desire and purpose keep changing quickly in these accelerated energies and we need to be willing to out create the old and stay present with what presents itself without falling for outdated definitions of *success*.

Slowly but surely, we are leaving this world's Truman Show behind and becoming fully fledged catalysts for human and galactic change, assisting the ascension of this and other planets, galaxies and solar systems.

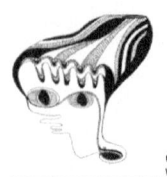

Success Evaluation

Let's take a brief moment to evaluate some of your daily choices to establish if they are still aligned with your current meaning of success. Striking a balance between the joy of service to others, along with the responsibility of service to self, remains an elemental key to success.

If you had everything you ever wished for, would you still choose what you are doing and being now?

- Would you still spend your time with the people you engage with?
- What kind of particular purpose do your daily choices service?
- What do your choices create for you in the short and long term?
- What do your choices create for others?
- How many of your choices are I AM choices?

Choices in general guarantee a succession of personal and divine expansion. Every choice point validates the pairs of opposites in the lower realms of personality, as well as the higher spiritual realms. Our active, as well as passive participation in this awakening is of deep significance, as we are all interwoven and locked into the multidimensional grid of consciousness. That said, don't over complicate matters by fighting humanity's crisis, but instead choose to create a new dream – one of a world that you want your future selves to inherit. Your courage and enthusiasm will spill over to those that wish to be a part of this dream.

In the words of Buckminster Fuller, "you never change things by fighting the existing reality. To change something, build a new model that makes the existing model obsolete."

PART TWO: Pioneering Leaders in Action

Prophecies of ancient cultures from every part of the globe speak of a great transformation; a foretelling of a new human who is free of fear and full of ancient-future wisdom now, ready and prepared to accept their guardianship for all sentient creation. *A leader is his own fault!* Leadership is not bestowed on this new human, but is a natural result of a mastered and healed being operating with sovereign conduct. By closing the gap between one's honest aims and those openly declared for the sake of fitting in, the leader finds courage and commitment to seek out a greater and more adventurous vision that meets the requirements of the soul's purpose and aspiration. Everyone's individualised journey has to be one of honouring and healing the genetic inheritance, in order to move forward as masterful thought-leaders of the self and others... in a body that ages, heals, and dies differently with a soul that has come into full expression.

The Latin word for authority is 'auctoritas,' which comes from 'auctor,' and translates as the originator and promotor. True transformational leaders will have trained to be well adjusted to their physical existence, as well as to the invisible world of energy and spirit. They will embody a sound level of authority that is recognised, but not limited to the material realm, as one of self-governed inner guidance and outer directiveness.

This new Earth needs embodied wisdom and peacekeepers who have duly mastered their micro personality self and function on a macro level of the mental plane where all context is clearly seen and being orchestrated from. They no longer thrive on recognition or competition and operate from vision and true compassion beyond the need for a validating applause. They appreciate the existence of solar and planetary hierarchies, but not those that are fabricated by plutocrats and kleptocrats to dominate and isolate an entire species. As stewards of this Earth, they actively seek to assemble mastermind groups to pioneer new ideas and methods that affect all planes of existence.

A true leader's ability and readiness to head up and work in harmonious group dynamics does not only empower and motivate the individual member of the group, but encourages all its collective, multidimensional, workforce. With a keen awareness of the need for interdependent responsibility and teamwork that serves humanity and all sentient creation, leaders claim and fulfil their destiny and naturally attract followers through their magnetic sphere of influence. Let's join those who are practiced in silence, clean in energy, diverse in action, pure in thought and motive, precise in spoken and written word, and imaginatively orientated towards a great vision.

+ *Open your mind to universal concepts, perceptions and experiences.*
+ *Open your heart to lovingly desire multidimensional connectivity.*
+ *Open your gut to intuit your soul's messages.*
+ *Open your eyes and observe with gratitude, compassion & boundless grace.*

Equine Leaders

Thoughts on leadership and the way to claim our place in the 5th world of peace.

'STRAIGHT FROM THE HORSES MOUTH'

We are going through a time of great revival in how we perceive ourselves as unlimited citizens of this planet Earth. This period now is marking the transition of humans from seeing themselves as separate from everyone and everything, to becoming integrated *Homo Illuminatus*, more aligned with their fractal selves and realised in their true potential as divine co-creators. *'The history of mankind is carried on the back of a horse'* – author unknown. Did you know that in the 16th century, the word 'horse' was a common adjective describing anything strong, big or coarse? With horses playing such a pivotal, leading role in developing our world's economy and society, it is hardly surprising that the equine energy has found its way into the metaphorical expressions used in the language of our ancestors, and still even today.

Over millennia we have managed to categorize celestial beings - in particular animal and man, by imposing a hierarchical structure, buying into the predator-prey relationship, and following a linear chain of command whilst forgetting the divinity in all sentient kind and the true meaning of symbiotic relationships. What does the raw, strong, and undefined, yet supremely authentic horsepower bring to the 'stable,' and how can it brand the new leadership of the future that has begun to evolve? Effective leadership starts with self-motivation and integrity coupled with mediation skills to weave connections and support the formation of practical strategies. Take it from the heart of the horse. It represents freedom, wisdom, and power no matter what means of domestication cultures have tried to impose. Equestrian or not, we can probably all relate to the desire and joy of the wild and free movement of riding a horse. You possibly are now thinking 'what's the common lead here with horses, humans and leadership?'

So here goes the story:

Many, many moons ago, horse was wild. Horse was powerful. Connected to the stars and nourished by the Earth, horse was interfacing with all the hubs of consciousness between planets, dimensions, timestreams, galaxies, and universes. Roaming freely, it was sharing its tales of different worlds, having 'grazed' in many of them before time here on Earth existed. No need for reins and halters then, they were true leaders of awareness in union and communion with the all-existing consciousness. Horse chose to be a gift to mankind; an unbound spirit embodied and belonging to a material world, in order to joyfully play with one another in the field of consciousness and thereby render its services. Whether through ill fortune or design, man lost touch with their divine connection, became greedy and fell prey to domination and control. Man forgot its purpose of coming here to Earth. Horse got trapped and saddled with the task of staying loyal to its purpose of teaching wisdom, until the Earthly focused students were ready to be galactic teachers yet again. Horse was willing and still is willing to go to any distance, whilst holding space in the dream weave and beyond, determined to assist us in overcoming any hurdles. They always give free rein to their rider, spurred on by the sacred desire and trust in mankind's remembrance and the cosmic unfolding of universal peace and sovereign mastery.

THE FOUR C's OF EQUINE LEADERSHIP

1. **CLEARING OF CONDITIONING** – Identifying the Problem

In mythology, the horse is ever-present. The romans linked horses with Mars, the god of fury and war, at the time. Horses were also seen pulling the chariot of Helios, the sun god. In Celtic mythology, horses were good luck and harbingers of good fortune. The evolutionary lineage of the horse goes back well before the beginning of mankind.

Throughout many contrasting incarnations, we have adopted a system of countless beliefs that keep us limited and blind us from seeing our true potential. Are you willing to ask yourself a few questions to mark the territory that is in need of healing, and to identify some of your stuck programs?

Q: Who or what depletes my life force?
Q: Who or what keeps me fenced in?
Q: Am I ready to lose who or what doesn't serve me?
Q: What would it take to commit to a free, happy me?

'In order to be first out the gate, you need to first get to the gate.'

It takes a brave, curious, and committed individual to embark on the inward journey of self-exploration and healing. Awareness is not for the fainthearted. The time has never been more pressing to come out of suffering with a steadfast resolve for getting to know thyself. Many healed-healers are lining up to assist and explore this place of potency that you didn't know you were entitled to. Without letting go of martyrdom, victimhood, or false expectations and projections, there is no way to come out of solitary so that you can commit to your inner truth and create a life as a true frontrunner.

Horse energy gifts you with the power and endurance to stay on track and to seek a healthy balance in all things, along with the energy, space, and consciousness pertaining to abundance and peace. With the planet Earth emerging in its new density, the evolution of mankind has reached a crossroad. Conscious awareness is our birth right and the ultimate source for the needed change facilitating our continuous growth. Infinitely available choices are the keys to unlocking the doors of awareness. There is no need to assign blame or pass judgment in order to walk through the halls of polarity with your head held high.

Q: Who or what is missing in my life, physically, mentally, or emotionally?

To all those war-horses out there - put down your armour, let go of your burdens and the heavy loads you carry, and look for what is missing! Now is the time to jump for joy again! Here on Earth, we cannot succeed without our physical bodies. Rule number one is to become our body's best friend and ally. Nurture the body's needs and respectfully listen to its way of communication. Neck-and-neck, we are all moving through the revolutionary gates of new beginnings. We have to free ourselves again! Take off the blinders and sort through the shadows of the past. Spurred on by the inspiration of the present moment, we can create this new world together with our future selves!

'We can lead a horse to water but we can't make it drink.'

The sweet taste of freedom and blissful embodiment is calling you to action. The choice is yours.

2. CLARITY OF CONTRIBUTION-Expanding One's Awareness

All of us – we are dark and different horses of colour, divergent breeds with specific DNA technologies offering a god-zillion of soul gifts, and one thing we have in common is that we are all here in this time right now on this planet Earth to witness, instigate, and enjoy this great time of change and transformation. And to actively facilitate the remembering and subsequent awakening of our true potential as galactic teachers, celestial peace keepers, and visionaries of a grand future! With authentically unique leaders, change is unfolding through working as a team in co-creation, contribution and service to each other, as well as the 5th world of peace. We must have the courage to grow and innovate, to take risks and be willing to embrace our vulnerability when things don't work the way we imagined them. By consciously applying our intuition and our physical DNA technologies, along with our breath and mind, we can generate enough vitality to live in passion, joy and blissfulness, and be represented as one of those very leaders. It is a matter of being truly courageous and doing whatever is necessary in the commitment to oneself. Awareness expands through the art of questioning!

Q: If I choose this, what would that create for consciousness at large?
Q: What would be most fun for me?

As you follow the path of humility, courageously committing to YOU and your personal evolution, the journey from challenge will eventually lead to infinite choices. In every moment you have another choice that can open up more awareness pointing the way forward. We have to be willing to get off our high horse and actually think like a horse. Trying to control manifestations into being doesn't really work, does it? If you have ever tried to mount a horse against its will, you know that control is an illusion. It is a misidentified value that causes frustration, irritation, and limitation that keeps us looping endlessly in self-judgment.

Equine leadership is all about trusting one's inner knowingness and leading from a peaceful heart, whilst intelligently focusing on the clear purpose of being in service to one's self and others. If you are still looking for your purpose; that's it! Look no further. Do what makes you happy and share it with whomever wants to know, without attaching your happiness to a particular outcome. All goals are merely a way of guiding and focusing our journey. It's the moment-by-moment process, the action and enjoyment in the moment that matters, since hardly anything ever looks how you think it will. What if you could make your journey your destination? You are a multidimensional being and as such, you most likely will require a 'Da Vinci' approach in exploration of more than just one avenue of creation. Always be prepared to work on the basis of multiple interests, opportunities, and income streams... and keep asking:

Q: Who or what can I add to my life?
Q: What choices can I make that could create greater possibilities?

When you know what inspires you and you operate in the unlimited point of view, there is no constraining the horse within you as it runs with the wind. This will also assist you to stop 'chomping at the bit' as you allow impatience to distract from your creations, until the time comes to finally take off the bridle and choose free-reign regardless. May your passions be plentiful, and may your unique offerings propagate abundance and wisdom reaching far beyond this planetary surface! Hold on tight, you surely are in for the ride of your life!

3. COMMUNICATION - Authentic Expression

Horses are great mediators and communicators with all species kind, both in the seen and unseen world, and therefore are perfect teachers to us. *'Taking it straight from the horse's mouth'* is an invitation for you to establish yourself as a sovereign authority with 360-degree perception in your life. Brace yourself for inter-stellar travel and communion with all species at will!

Q: Are you willing to take on the responsibility of authentically voicing your truth?

Communication goes well beyond the words we are using. Matured and unlimited perception allows us to recognise and simply acknowledge everything that comes our way; every sound, smell, taste, touch, and every breath of air. Masterful communication has a level of intensity and joyfulness behind it that is our legacy. In a state of true communication, verbal and non-verbal interaction divinely flows.

Q: What is it going to take to sovereignly communicate with all sentient kind?

By maintaining our neutral perspective, we become unbiased observers. Without falling into polarity, we open up to the full awareness that is available to us and can naturally communicate with all realms of existence. Horses are considered divine messengers to and from the non-material world that graces us with guidance from *the beyond*, whilst also teaching us how to step into that role ourselves. The horse symbolises one's ability to gracefully move through situations. Authentic communication starts with being fully present when listening. There is no place for judgement as it limits our perception. In these vastly expanding energies on this planet, curiosity and allowance are good companions to hang out with. The value of feedback is only as good as your willingness to receive the information without prejudice, as well as offering your point of view in return without expectations or projections.

'There is no point in closing the stable door after the horse has bolted.'

Authentic communication neither closes doors or creates the need for escapism. In fact, it cultivates a level of mutual respect and an awareness of the responsibility to honour the multitudes of perspectives; to have an appreciation of all opinions without entangling in their web.

4. CELEBRATION & LETTING GO – Integration

'Don't ever look a gift horse in the mouth.'

Everything in this seen and unseen experience here on planet Earth and beyond, is a gift and an opportunity to express gratitude for the use of this corporal body, and for the capacity to walk the path of the teacher and peacemaker in this new era of light, in celebration of everyone's contributions no matter which side of polarity that they are on. By regularly celebrating your achievements, new levels of motivation and inspiration are being birthed and drawn into your experience, and the energy of possibilities expands a thousand-fold! But like everything in this reality, it is all about practice and not just theory.

Q: What does celebration mean to you?

Have you ever been on a horse, fallen off a horse, or got back on a horse?

Even if you have never interacted with a horse, why not engage your inner genius to visualise the sense of pride and union between two magnificently powerful creatures? Sense the perseverance, the mastery, the magical celebration of not giving up on each other, and the trust that has been established.

Q: Are you celebrating your victories and counting your blessings?

Journal them! How much of your do's, dont's, accomplishments and efforts have you been acknowledging of late? Remember to incorporate the dont's. Practice saying 'no' when the energy does not feel congruent with the exchange. Gratitude allows prosperity to blossom.

Q: Are you and your body celebrating union and communion?

Shrouded in this mystery is a coming together of free-spirited species; a celebration of likeminded souls claiming their skills in an effort to lead the way out of dominance and suppression, and to birth a brand- new era of being.

Horse reminds us that our body is a friend and companion that we have chosen to walk this path with. Daily celebrate the flesh and blood. Honour its technology and the guidance it provides, knowing that you are never alone. Our purpose here is to cultivate and celebrate compassion and service between all species kind. Horse spirit teaches us to come full circle, to see through the veil of confusion and indoctrination, to stomp down the manufactured borders of separation, and to return to living the natural ways of life. When we are willing to leave the false safety of the misguided herd and choose our own path of sovereign sacred celebration, we become a broadcasting beacon of light. We remember both our past and future heritage as we start living in alignment with our true purpose. No more need for co-dependency, but rather a solid ground of ever evolving awareness to build upon, to out create, to masterfully play in joy and bliss with true passion, grace, and gratitude. Any kind of neediness or attachment to an outcome is still part of a scarcity expression. A generosity of gifting is where the reward lies in the contribution of one's unique expression, without the need for reciprocity.

All is available right here, right now. Come and claim it, own it, share it, lose it and regain it. This world and many others are now open for us to co-create with in a way that we have never been able to before. If people with wishes were horses; horses for courses, without jockeying for position, with everyone doing what they truly love and doing it without regret, shame, blame or guilt... *what would this world be like?*

'This is the time to seek out adventures. Allow your imagination to run wild and ride in new directions to awaken and discover your freedom and power. Stop horsing around! Embark on embracing adversity. Stop hiding and start creating your lives – be the leader this new world is asking for.'
– Horse

PART THREE: Time – Social Agreement

The Gift of Time

Temporal perception depends on the individual's state of awareness. Over the last two centuries we have made a mockery of time through deceivingly trying to freeze its natural tempo and rhythm into a structured frame, in the name of progress. Let us not be fooled into denying its ingenuity that would turn us into nothing more than inconsequential hallucinations. David Bohm talks about time being an abstract representation of successive order, movement, and the process tied to the identification of the self. Time is an essential building block of a linear reality that shapes activity and movement throughout a lifespan. In order to harness its fleeting moments, we endeavour to save time, spare more time, or turn back time. We get agitated when time pushes us from behind, exhausted and bored by constantly running ahead of it. Keep time close to you, treasure its quality rather than quantity, and you will eventually transcend it.

Time is a conceptional perception, a fundamental aspect of consciousness that allows us to download, process, store and record information. Whoever has had the great pleasure of spending time with a beloved in the presence of true generosity of spirit, will most certainly advocate that time is a precious gift bestowed upon us in this physical universe. Through our awareness of time, as an indirect consequence of the universal law of attraction and repulsion, we generate forms, shapes, memories and feelings that impact and forever change the fabric of this spacetime continuum. Time has been an integral part of our species' survival and thrival, never standing still throughout the centuries of evolution and de-evolution. The ancient Atlanteans had an extensive understanding of time and its cycles, the tracking of its seasons and astronomical influences, and the flow of the tides. In neolithic times we were still connected to the stars and watched the solar-lunar cycles and weather patterns to create with.

Fast forward through the ages to the times of ancient Babylon and Mesopotamia where humanity turned to agriculture and trade, we defined the calendar months in our quest of optimising the turnaround of crops and to safeguard produce. Mechanical clocks in Europe date back to the Middle Ages, whilst sophisticated sundials and water clocks have existed well before that in Egypt and other parts of the world. The time we have come to know and become accustomed to does not really exist other than on planet Earth. The use of Roman Numeral Timekeeping (RNT) goes back to the European Renaissance period in the 16th century and has since been increasingly high jacked and manipulated and socially accepted. Our daily activities have not just been dissected into hours, minutes and seconds, but also got linked to a patriarchal system that in many cultures is a metaphor for time, authority, and power. As the passage of time has become inextricably linked to rules, control, stability and safety, in obstruction of our divine inner guidance mechanism, we got deflected from enjoying and trusting the natural flow of living.

In the days before readily available clocks and watches, our bodies were still in tune with the natural sunrise and sunset. This notion about running out of time was less of a concern prior to the growing industrialisation of manpower that made the concept of RNT appear fundamentally real and vital. Before the implementation of a standardised working culture, we moved within a more natural human work rhythm without such an apparent need to maintain a mental and physical work life balance. Life was task and more talent, rather than time oriented before we moved into big cities and predominantly began living on wages. Households would be self- sustaining and grow their own food, know what and when to seed within the natural rhythm of the days and seasons, and rear animals for consumption. The overidentification with time, or lack of time, rules our interaction with life by creating artificial restrictions and urgencies. We lost self- direction and settled for being motivated by time, rather than simply doing whatever is necessary to complete a task, or not.

Time, insufficiently appraised, can be a suffocating commodity exchanged for money that influences and manipulates the human value system, reinforces materialism. It can generate survival angst that promotes a preoccupied existence instead of encouraging carefreeness and a spontaneous adaptation to altered circumstances. The one lesson some of us have drawn whilst working from home during the pandemic is that we waste an awful lot of liberty by entertaining a five-day work week. In the process of participating in the race for success and recognition, we are continuously trying to beat the imaginary sundial instead of intuitively following the energy. Remember that in truth, we are buying into inculcated living standards. In the process of aligning to a more multi-layered human expression, we will awaken to a fluidity in our temporal awareness that will change our conscious perception of time. As an entire species we are reclaiming our birth right as 'infinitely finite' time and space travellers, that will reconnect us to free and timeless communication and universal creation.

When I finally left the corporate world after twenty plus years, I struggled. I'd be lying if I said it was easy. Whilst I started a new chapter as a therapist, I missed the international rapport, the daily routine, and the buzz of a full day's work. I had to literally learn to allow myself to enjoy having all this freedom and a sudden lack of structure, without finding fault in myself for choosing it. It may sound ridiculous to think how having free time can actually cause one to be stressed - a perfect example of human domestication. We are timed, tamed, framed, and farmed! We have been educated towards a standard narrow perception of time which is characterised through preordained sequential milestones such as knowledge, a career, money, family, holidays, retirement, and eventually death. This socially engineered lifepath leaves us with little to no time or space to deviate from. The doctrine of working hard and fast, rather than smart and in accordance with the impulse of one's internal time and wisdom keeper, services the global establishments and keeps us under their thumbs.

Under the pretence of time is money, and without money we can't have a good time, we gamble away our freedom. Let's call a time out and reclaim our sense of adventure. The courage to surrender to one's true vocation requires trusting the existence of a contributory universe. It took me many months of deep inner work to excavate all those unfulfilled and abandoned ideas regarding personal happiness that I had kept so well hidden, even from myself. Surrendering into a less time and money bound state of being, rather than doing, also forced me to look at the powerful dynamic of mutual receiving in my personal relationship. Stepping out of corporate time, whilst one's partner is still fully engaged in it, can be a challenge in itself. Therapy at its best. I highly recommend drastic life style changes to test the strength of your relationship!

Storing Time

Any entrapment in time-sensitive realities, including our dreams that have their own frequency of time, reaches deeply into our psyche and influences us in all areas of daily living. In the past we have happily accepted aging to be the result of the body's delineated temporal processing, whereas now reverse aging is becoming a huge topic as our DNA is upgrading and revolutionising our perception of time. The human organism sustains itself through biological and spiritual reciprocity and creates experiences in sync with Earth's frequencies. Our neural pathways allow us to momentarily draw on past and future experiences. Embodied consciousness is the purest expression of time and space, enabling us to transmute chemical or light memories and manage new information flows. The way we store time has an impact on how present and aware we are. We can perceive and organise memorable time stamps of past, present, and future events laid out as a line, looked at from the perspective of floating out and on top of one's body. You can try this yourself by expanding out and looking down onto yourself. Think of a joyous past or future event and locate it in relation to your physical body.

Each person stores time uniquely and its visual depiction may very well change throughout the healing and awakening process. Some people see their memories represented as a line from the front to the back, up to down, in a V shape, or any arrangement where part of the past, present, or future is either in front of or behind them, with the line going through their body. This person is usually more present and focused, whereas those who recall their memories from left to right, right to left, or any other way, and keep all time in front and outside of them, would be more reflective of the past and are probably aware of a longer-term future. Time Line Therapy™ (TLT) is a powerful therapeutic and creative process that has evolved from hypnosis and NLP, developed by Tad James, PhD in the 1980s. I have been using this very effective modality to detach emotions from destructively embodied events and to recover stuck soul shards. Only in recent years the term 'nowness living' has been turned into a more tangible experience, as we are beginning to understand our simultaneous holographic existence and the need for centeredness. If you haven't seen the film 'Everything Everywhere All at Once' go and treat yourself; a satirical and brilliantly choreographed illustration of our spiralling existence. All of our memories are instantly available within the torsion field. The film features how our lifetimes are happening all at once and emphasises the importance of claiming our authority as the currently embodied I AM Avatar. There is time in no-time, beyond time as we know it. As a citizen of this planet Earth, we are linked to galactic and universal sun cycles.

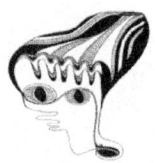

All Time Invocation

The following document is designed to let go of definitions and ordered sequences with regards to RNT to help you fully step into your solar self.

As we merge with our soul essence, creating a harmonised union between spirit and matter, we can unify all time frequencies and gain instant access to a wider range of dimensional experiences.

I, [insert name], the I AM Apex being of the now, accept my celestial consciousness as a photonic being of light, born into this human construct of time through the sacred union between egg and sperm. My DNA holds the wisdom of all my lineage generations that have come before me, as well as those that will come after me.

As a galactic citizen of this Earth, galaxy, and universe, I have the right and timeless opportunity to share the DNA wisdom that has been recorded in the universal, galactic and earthly Akash, devoid of limitations of competition or hierarchy.

In order to receive all ancestral wisdom available within the universal hub of time and space, I switch on my sacred neutral observer function and bring my vision to the centre of my heart. Imagining myself as the foetus of my mother's womb, from this safe and neutral place, I honour my birthright and potential to fully engage with and function within earthly, galactic and universal time simultaneously. I choose to embrace my DNA, which holds the key to unlocking the full spectrum of my multidimensional being.

As I connect to the Galactic Central Sun, that supports all solar systems in guiding the spiritual exchange of experiences, I ask her to bear witness as a neutral auditor to compare my DNA lineage records to those of the galactic Akash, so I may know the difference of the two potentials and how the system is guiding me.
I ask to have all my galactic soul aspects audited, and every record of galactic time stream that I exist on, recorded in my DNA memories. In gratitude, I now solidify and integrate all galactic time frequencies.

I now engage my sacred discipline and sovereignty in order to connect to Earth time that existed before Roman numeral time. I ask Earth's Sun to bear witness as a neutral observer and auditor to compare my DNA lineage records to those of the Earth Akash. I ask her to audit all my earthly soul aspects and upload every record of earthly time stream that I exist on, into my DNA memories. In gratitude, I now solidify and integrate Earth time frequencies.

I now ask the Universal Central Sun to come into my sacred heart space to act as a witness and sovereign neutral auditor of all universal realms within the universal Akash. I ask to have all my universal soul aspects compared to the universal akashic records, audited, and recorded in my DNA memories. In gratitude, I now solidify and integrate all universal time frequencies.

May all wisdom flow into my knowingness so that I can learn how to read all Akashic records of my DNA lineage as well as the collective celestial consciousness perspective. I have made these choices to teach myself and millions of others, who observe through earthly, galactic and universal time. We are soul factions, looking for a sovereign existence, in sacred neutral exchange with our soul families within and beyond the 7th colour of time.

Each time I repeat this invocation, I strengthen my relationship to the universal, galactic, and Earth time, and I begin to out-create this human fraud time that I live and manifest in. I provide a bigger understanding and picture of our free-willed, multidimensional totality to all celestial citizens living here on Earth. By integrating this knowledge into my being, I am able to live and manifest in this physical reality with a greater awareness and perspective, aligned with the wisdom and guidance of my earthly, galactic, and universal lineage and contribution.

And so it is. Aho.

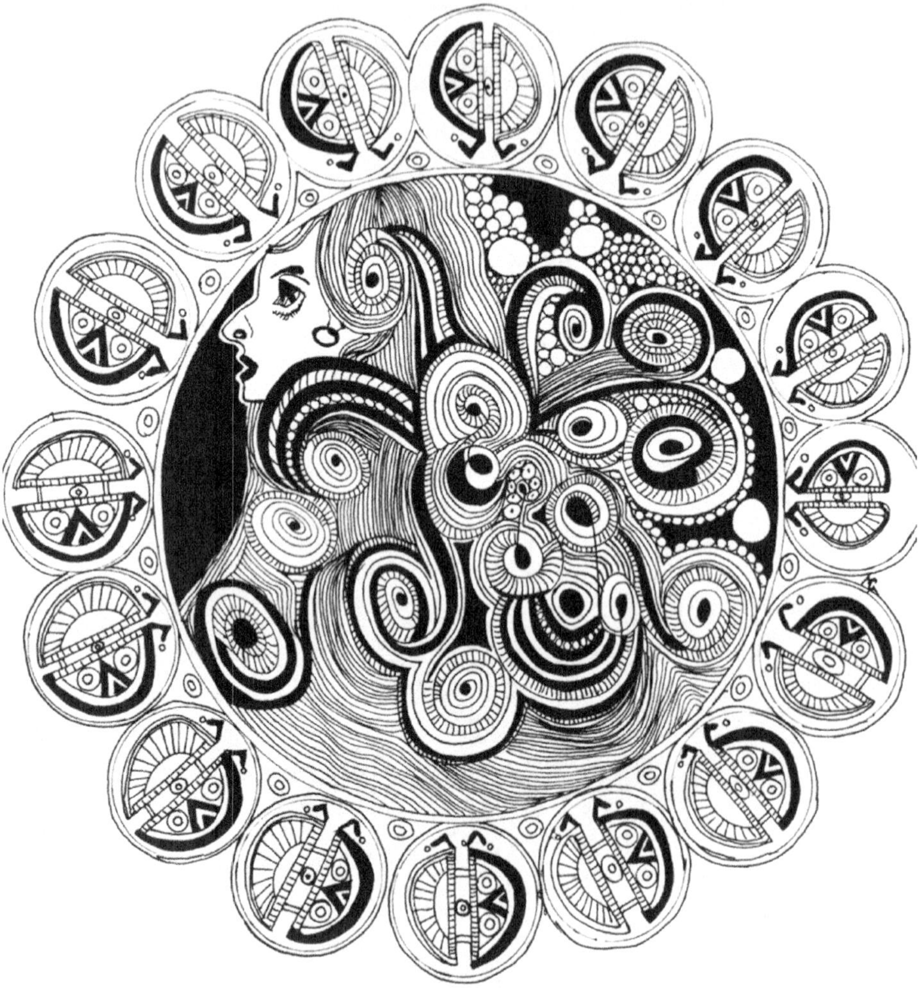

CHAPTER VI: PURPOSE & AVATAR EMERGENCE

PART ONE: Man & His Tools

Willpower, Faith & Freewill

"I am a self-spawned celestial medium of peace that infiltrated into the system of domination and control to become part of the prediction model to out create it from within. I am part of Resistance Free Earth in assistance to humanity on their journey back to the stars, to the ancient future now. Upon returning from journeys with the founder beings, in witness of false gods that had taken over the DNA through farming, I decided to be here now to put an end to this. And that is just part of who I am."

Man must be interested and ready to move beyond curiosity, arousal and stimulation of his personality traits. When I was younger, I never really spent much time contemplating questions about purpose or the larger context of humanity's origin. Undoubtedly, I would not have been able to grasp the meaning of the subject paragraph without extensive exploration into ancient and galactic philosophies, particularly over my latter years. Back then, I was too busy making a living after my parents had thrown me out, right after finishing my baccalaureate in economics. I lived in an apartment with the ceiling held up by pillars after a fire had destroyed the upstairs loft, and my body was constantly in pain. Amongst all that chaos, my walk-in soul settled in well and became a gracious teacher. It has taught me that the quickest way of ending a war is to be vulnerable enough to lose it and move on... to never despair and keep faith no matter how unjust life appears. I've learned to distil every ounce of insight drawn from all of my own and other people's mistakes and use them to create anew without losing faith. Faith is our birth right. This universe was specifically created for the purpose of resolving karma through the use of freewill, with Earth being chosen as a central melting pot of souls and the 'heart' core for karmic facilitation.

Our souls heard Gaia's call for help and we came from galaxies near and far, other universes and void spaces, to break open the bolted gates of our karmic prison and unleash the incarcerated lifeforce, our very own sentient force of spirit and faith.

Faith fuels willpower.

The ability to purposefully will and guide the direction of lifeforce towards personal freedom is powered by faith and backed up by spirit. Without Prime Creator's infinite renewal of faith, instilled in every single one of us, we would not be here in the first place. Faith empowers choice. Faith supports humanity's quest for peace that fuels the choices we have made and continue to make, to fulfil our fate and purpose on Earth. *The human is designed by Faith, guided by Fate, and destined to Fortune.* The more you collaborate with the faithful Self inside of you, any pattern can be changed instantly. To say that you have no choice is saying that you have no purpose or faith in spirit. By doing so, you are denying your ability to exist and negate your primal and most fundamental choice of choices, of having joined the galactic force of peacemakers to explore love. No one can diminish your enthusiasm as long as you put in time and effort in choosing not to be limited. If you have faith, you need not worry about being worthy or powerful because faith always has your back.

Faith is similar to breathing; your body came with breath, with no extra charge. No need to frantically conjure up willpower, as it only takes your focus off simply choosing. You have faith and not belief to thank for that. Surrender into the knowingness that you have infinite possibilities available to you, believe it or not. Human development is the most difficult path of the four earthly kingdoms in our solar system, as we are here to create the 5th kingdom of the embodied ascended masters. Its evolution is firmly rooted in self-consciousness and self-initiated mastery.

Compared to the minerals, plants and animals, man must learn to consciously use the principles of freewill and action to intelligently practice unconditional love and master what it takes to be of sacred service.

Does freewill empower action? Freewill IS action. *Freewill without action is powerless.*

Choice is a human mechanism that leads to greater awareness. Upon choosing, we tap into the universal intelligence that exposes the individual to different options and possibilities, broadening the perspective and level of understanding. *Willpower without choice has no power.* Freewill was included in Earth's complimentary arrival package; it's free for you to claim it. As long as we entertain our fractal selves moving in different directions without mutually working towards a common aim, true freewill remains powerless. A soul infused personality that brings forth an advanced spiritual state of consciousness eventually leads to freewill and freedom in human development.

Non-familiar

The soul's intent and purpose are comprised of very specific traits and behaviours that have been specifically developed over many lifetimes of living with more than one soul family in a variety of worlds. Soul family themes such as thinkers, philosophers, warriors, breeders, nurturers, healers, leaders, clergies, and scientists, just to mentioned a few, are plentiful and the groups are constantly evolving. In our capacity as a significant spokesperson for our soul family, we are not only responsible for the why and what we are creating in the physical, but also how the message gets conveyed in the unseen realms. Don't underestimate the far-reaching work that you do in the immaterial realms whilst pursuing a so-called three-dimensional career.

We share a deep spiritual connection on a soul level and the results of our physical actions affect the matrix that is made up of a multitude of overlayered dimensional holograms. Some of us are fulfilling our purpose through the love of star gazing, or through building a multi-million-dollar business, whilst others go to prison. We applaud or envy the business owner and disapprove of the convict or dreamer. Whatever we have concluded about moral standards that are predominantly, if not exclusively spacetime constructs, is neither here nor there and does not take into account the cyclical journey of the soul. We have all earned the right to be here and support each other's growth and evolution, well deserving of our unique signature stamp in this spacetime equation. Careless thought and talk costs precious lives. Here is an example of one of my contributions in a past life from my personal reading in 2014 with the Galactic Historian:

'You have a tremendous amount of very beneficial lifetimes where you were a Neanderthal in the Afghanistan area, upper Persia, long before modern history- about 4 million years ago when the world was set up very differently. At the time Neanderthals were considered high society. There was space ship travel too. In those days people would have left the cities, gave up scientific living and converted back to a different state because they didn't want to see the world destroyed. So, you converted back to Neanderthal life where you had some of your most powerful shamanic experiences as a soul, in deep unknowingness. It was where your dream world expanded so many trillionfold that you figured out how to go to the end of the universe, and how to come back to your Neanderthal body and create a fire and view your future self in knowingness and in unity.'

Ponder that... Neanderthals were an advanced species at the time, their intellect routed in natural and multidimensional living. Without putting excessive merit on past lives, I certainly can appreciate the personal benefits of those Neanderthal lifetimes from a shamanic perspective. They remind me to acknowledge my psychic and celestial medium abilities now, and to assist in bringing back to Earth a highly advanced civilization grounded in natural living.

Past life information can teach us to value the complexity of our human evolution and illustrate how this current global narrative's curriculum has profoundly failed humanity by leaving out so much of our ancient wisdom. What serves us best is contentedly appreciating that what we know is but a fraction of the whole truth. Prayer, ritual, and ceremony are valuable tools to connect to soul and star families.

False Appearance

Imagination is a cognised, spiritual and creative capacity of the mind that enables us to form thoughts, ideas and sensations in the absence of direct experience. It has the ability to create mental images and concepts to generate new projects or to solve problems. Our imagination is a powerful mechanism to explore new possibilities and ideas beyond the constraints of what currently exists, and yet it can become a compulsive habit leading us astray. We often get lost in incessantly pondering what the future has in store for us and forget that it is our personal day-to-day actions that determine our path. From a timeless soul's perspective, projecting ideas into the future is equal to existing in the future. Whilst our consciousness loves to travel and reach out universally, our body lives and breathes in the present time. As obvious as it may sound, many of us fall into the trap of quite happily living as a soul on the spiritual planes in the attempt to escape the daily grind, instead of buckling down and getting our boots dirty. This is especially important to notice in oneself during the transition period from the karmic to predominantly dharmic path, where outside forces have considerably quieted down and we need to use self-initiative to remain grounded and in creator mode.

Ideas without action are like feathers in the wind and easily get carried away. I remember creating elaborate mind maps of workshops without ever supporting them through adequate physical implementation. These lost thought-forms keep floating around in the astral realm, waiting to eventually get picked up and carried out by someone else.

The harvest of freshly seeded actions can be severely delayed in this lifetime and even beyond future lives, depending on the soul's consciousness and purpose. Some material manifestations that seem instant might have been seeded a long time ago and brought to pass through the evolution of our soul or planet. The soul's interest is not limited to this lifetime. Our soul aspects want to be consulted and considered in the planning process too. By trying to force a tangible outcome, we often compete or infringe on the liberties of our future versions.

Instead of beating ourselves up, we must intelligently ask if now is the time to push forward, or if we should stop and review the path that we are on? Remember time is a social agreement, eternally outlived by our divine essence. An appreciation of our soul's short-term and long-term agenda will greatly ease the pain of the impatience that some of us still carry. Our envisaged and projected life goals may also be distorted through our conditioned upbringing and do not always add value to our soul's greater evolution. It is as simple as that. When plans don't work out as anticipated, you haven't necessarily done anything wrong; it could just be a lack of understanding of our soul mechanics that can be rectified by asking more questions.

Beware of false synchronicities, or giving your power away to spiritual guidance that is not of your soul-self. Mastery is achieved through taking action in accordance with your authentic self and the values that you hold dear. Some of those 'synchronistic' signs are false flags, especially when we get caught up in excessively seeking validation from external sources. They can become addictive, self-destructive, and often create convoluted paths and distractions. So-called 'placebo' synchronicities arise from a belief system that still functions on expectations and projections, which only re-enforces a disempowered state of being if we are not careful to call them out. The devil still breathes divine spirit and not all signs are benefiting our evolutionary journey. Discernment is a crucial step in finding true meaning and purpose. It is an essential skill that requires us to make wise decisions and navigate both complex and simple situations.

As our intuition sharpens, we can weigh up situations based on our general perception of lightness or heaviness, progressively choosing what is light. Continue to reflect on your actions, values and beliefs, and be willing to adjust course if necessary. Time is a great influencer on apparent truth. On the dharmic path any remaining rigid thinking, disguised as spiritual perseverance, can be harmful and counter-productive. Overextended ceremony or excessive spiritual practice in an effort to frantically escape the world's chaos can lead to physical exhaustion and spiritual burnout. We must remain connected to both the inner and outer world, and avoid being dominated by either one. True transcendence is claiming both worlds, using the outer world of experiences and advance the inner soul spark. As we are moving through this magnified collective reset and restructure, we are reminded to live simpler, healthier, and to foster more understanding and compassion towards oneself and others. Try to avoid labelling things as good or bad and objectively assess a situation instead of slandering it. An occasional lack of enthusiasm or strong resistance can be a very important guidepost that goes unnoticed if overshadowed with self-flagellation. We can draw on the wisdom of our infinite I AMs and plan many lifetimes ahead, in full awareness. Once we begin to comprehend that we are timeless space travellers with a limited posting here on Earth, we can appreciate that dimensions are just different frequency ranges of the same consciousness; much like white light is a combination of all colours in the full colour spectrum. There is no point in dwelling on a level of consciousness other than we are at, or losing precious lifeforce through excited, or worse, fearful anticipation. All information will come into view when we are ready for it.

PART TWO: The Avatar Emergence

The multidimensional nature of our universe plays a crucial role in the development of our human experience and evolution.

We will remain perplexed by many enigmas in our world if we do not embrace the idea of populated parallel universes and alternate realities, irrespective of the lack of support by conclusive evidence.

Our individual signature frequency is comprised of fractal consciousness, which is rooted in the fundamental principles of the natural world, as well as fractured consciousness, resulting from the forced de-evolution our species has been subjected to. Fractal consciousness refers to the interconnectedness and self-similarity of patterns that exist in the natural world, such as structures of the galaxies, the branching of trees, and the formation of snowflakes. These patterns are also present in our own consciousness, as we are a part of the natural world. However, our consciousness has been fractured due to forced circumstances and the disconnection from our true nature. Throughout the journey of healing our fragmented I AM personality we strengthen the connection between our heart and brain, allowing us to make more conscious and voluntary choices. The integration of our dissociated and traumatised aspects, will assist us in transcending duality and tapping into ancient spiritual wisdom, expanding our non-local abilities and realities. The interconnectedness of all things in the universe means that a single act of reclaiming personal power can have a far-reaching impact on our inner and outer worlds, rippling through all holograms of existence and soul connections. Any action taken in this reality has a profound impact on all the now moments from the very beginning of spacetime, without distinction of past, present, and future. Think of a Moebius strip that serves as a powerful symbol of the interconnectedness of things and the underlying complexity of patterns that are not always immediately obvious.

Maslow's pyramid provides a good example of the initial stages of an individual's journey towards personal development, with its hierarchical structure of needs and its compounding requirements.

If we look at the geometrical form of the pyramid, the triangle, we see the reflection of the three-dimensional nature of our physical reality which corresponds to the *strictly human* personality aspects of the self. The bottom of the pyramid represents our basic physical needs for survival and safety, while the top symbolises fulfillment.

All physical forms, including our bodies, must primarily focus on the physical aspects during their initial stages of creation in order to develop, acquire and maintain strength. The gradual development of the soul and purpose depends on initially establishing a firm foundation and a nurturing physical environment. As we progress towards the top of the pyramid, we begin to appreciate that our human needs cannot entirely be met by security and material possessions alone, and we must cultivate a deeper understanding of ourselves and our place in the world. This is where spiritual growth, an omnipresent awareness, and meaningful relationships come into play, helping us achieve a greater sense of fulfillment and purpose in life.

In order to advance towards a future that serves the planetary and universal ascension, we must eventually cross the threshold of a three-dimensional existence to an all-inclusive mode of thought and conscious soul integration. We may have aspects of our I AM on both high and low energy Earths that compete and coexist in domination Such alter egos within our individuated awareness may still harbour their own convictions and attitudes in division and conflict and are all part of the fractal order and holographic principles. As we transcend our personal individuation and embrace a more extensive interrelation and celestial co-operation, new opportunities for spiritual abundance, multidimensional adventure, magic and wisdom become available. To resolve the paradox caused by the time line wars that Earth has experienced, it is necessary to remove all treacherous time stamps and strive for soul integration.

The responsibility of the self-healing master, the embodied I AM Apex, is to retrieve all soul shards, which may be simultaneously operating in or outside of time and space, and to unite them on this graduation time line to function collaboratively on the journey towards ascension.

While the paradoxical nature of life can be confusing and challenging to reconcile, it also presents tremendous opportunities for personal growth, inspiration, and joy. By forging and manifesting our transcended I AM Avatar on Earth, we facilitate the unfolding of evolution throughout all of our immaterial connections within the cosmic cycles that are intrinsic to human consciousness. The concept of unity within our I AM Avatar, beyond our limited sense of self, allows us to appreciate the interdependence within all of existence. As we release individual low-frequency attachments and biases, and expand our awareness beyond the surface of this Earth, we may experience personal and collective shifts beyond our wildest imagination. The release from the prison of unconsciousness and the journey towards spiritual embodiment is not a competition, but an invitation to all of our soul factions and aspects to come together and participate in the grand adventure of cosmic evolution. By surrendering to this intimate spiritual romance with our soul's totality, we can access our diamond shaped DNA and unlock new levels of beauty, harmony, and health. Let this be an invitation that goes out to all of our soul factions and aspects to join us in the grand adventure of spiritual embodiment. Co-hosting the *Adventures into Reality* shows in 2020 with Andrew was a great opportunity to discuss a variety of subject matters related to our avatar emergence that was later included in his book. For more about Andrew's work, you can visit www.andrewbartzis.com. Our souls are time travellers, potent movers, and divine shakers.

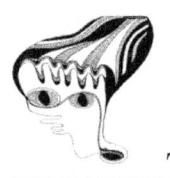

The Avatar Emergence

The following Avatar Emergence document is offered in order to heal your soul's fragmentation and in assistance to discovering more of its purpose. Enjoy!

A fire has been prepared in sacred ceremonial fashion. Let this be a universal invitation.

I am the ocean of awareness.
I am the sea of consciousness.
I am the tapestry of this reality.
I am love. I am the weaver.
I am the observer.
I am the fire.
I am the dragon.

I, [name], herewith open a spiritual court of equity for the expressed purpose of acknowledging and planning the journey to greater awareness, as the I AM Apex presence on this graduation timeline, now. As part of my birth right and legacy as a celestial universal citizen, I light this fire in honour of connecting to all dragon minds, through the placenta of all our foetuses, in connection to the Earth and beyond.

I am saying to the seven past and seven future generations that I am making an attempt to be in the first place of I AMs, in the many strings of I AMs, during the great awakening. I am asking other Apex I AMs in non-hierarchical order to offer their pre-cognitive workforce to assist me in living and breathing as a multidimensional being of this universe, and so will I return the favour.

Let us collaborate in mutual, beneficial contribution in our frequencies and timestreams, without competing against each other. In ancestral unity consciousness, we stand before prime creator. Teach us the truth about the dragon powers and their legacy for our seven future generations. Throughout this sacred fire ceremony, I am supported by my dragon friends and keep the I AM Apex safely driving on the information superhighway, gently nestled inside the vagus nerve.

As I look at all the layers of uniworlds, I maintain my elevated bird's eye view, witnessing the many holographic layers unfold before me as the DNA light body matrix of one. I am a multidimensional, multifunctional, photonic being of light that is connected to a non-local soul, living here on this planet in this linear time-space equation.

I acknowledge the entirety of my soul aspects living on different timelines, dimensions, galaxies, and universes, in the past and future generations. As an old soul in these times of awakening, an honorary member of Resistance Free Earth, I have committed and prepared myself during thousands of lifetimes to be part of the Galactic Ascension Machine and its unravelling.

I am here to assist in resolving repetitious paradoxes that were created through the time line wars, and to put an end to karma. From this day forward, let us put the battle between eras of light behind us. Let us create unity consciousness for all species kind and free the tens of millions of worlds and their denizens that have been trapped here.

I act as the neutral observer of time, space, and consciousness. I stand in sacred neutrality as a sovereign beacon of light for all my soul aspects to find their way back home to source connection. Let us remember that we simultaneously exist in our past, present, and futures, only separated by the illusion of time.

As a foetus in my mother's womb, I have been given a timestamp as an I AM. I started as an infinite heart that grew arms and legs and has DNA encoded with memories. I choose this lifetime to become the APEX of my DNA, and to work in sacred neutral alliance with all the other versions of myself who have chosen the opportunity to be sovereign. May our healthy boundaries unite us throughout all eternity. May this sacred ceremonial hub of interconnectivity extend to other dreamers to be united in unity once again.

The wood has been stacked up high. The fire gives off heat to cleanse, clear, and warm the place in welcome of all the many 'mes'. The thousand versions of myself that exist in different spacetime locations, in the holographic fabric of existence, are being duly noted. The fire sends out smoke signals to all the I AM selves, hidden, stuck, bankrupt, forgotten, scared, angry, confused, happy, and accomplished. Do join us in this sacred reunion.

I do not take sides.
I do not abuse.

I do not step on other's journeys.
I invite.
I forgive.
I am grateful.
I love.

May this fire serve as a symbol of restoration of the past, to encourage union and communion in the future for all our celestial minds on the journey to celestial mediumship. Be here, now, in this place and space of no-time to gather and be still. This is a possibility to heal and let go of old, outdated beliefs. Let us release attachments to old decisions and judgments for good. For greater understanding, let us revise those points of view gone awry that keep us disconnected and stuck in other time-space equations. May we move forward united. Let us integrate and heal ourselves from the separation of consensual realities and realms. Let us be foetus guides to one another.

All the forgotten selves that have been shut down to this slice of time, let your voices be heard through the dreamtime gateways of this sacred fire. Let us continue to tell your stories to the fire, so we may remember the adventures of the ancient past and future and create a better world. Your efforts have not been in vain. We are the flames burning brightly to witness, catalyse, and honour all storytelling. To any soulmate foetus in another mother's womb, I say hello and welcome. Join me and warm yourself on our fire. I salute and greet you for being here for the great awakening of unified souls. Let us work in unison and respect each other's sovereignty. My heart is full of gratitude knowing that we share dream space. Maybe we will meet in the flesh one day, in this lifetime, in recognition of our common roots and soul connection?

Let's add more logs to the fire and smudge the pit with sage. I now speak to the multiple I AMs stuck in other realities, fighting this I AM Apex presence now. Let us cut all ancient cords of misunderstanding that keep us looping endlessly in hierarchy and competition. I invite you to put down your weapons and open your hearts. May the cleansing power of the smoke bring clarity and understanding to our hearts and minds, allowing us to see beyond our disagreements and find common ground. We are soul family. We are divine soul essence.

My DNA technology has the capacity to discern and accommodate all parts, shards, and other avatars. I interconnect with all previous spacetime holograms, in dream and awake time, and vow to stay present in this body from this day forward.

At will, I open multiple spiritual courts of equity to suspend any intruders and I AM stalkers, and invite my teacher spirits to come forth and deal with them. I can unify all aspects of myself and incorporate them into my overall spiritual well-being. Let us breathe together into the fire. Let us pray for strength and ask for courage and faith to embrace all aspects of ourselves, and transcend the barriers of division, labelling, and approval-seeking.

As individuated members of the celestial hubs of interconnectivity, we are her to explore, share, and journey together. As the unvanquished dreamers of peace, we are a force to be reckoned with. Let us share laughter, food and drink, and transmute old deceptions and projections into new inspiration and dreams. Let us be beings of innocence again, understanding the expansiveness of our true light existence.

The fireplace is getting crowded. I welcome my soul brothers and sisters, all peacemakers and peacekeepers to join this meet and greet of likeminded celestial minds. Let us joyfully celebrate and gain more conscious awareness. Can you perceive how sovereignty connects? As we gaze upon the rainbow above the flames, we are reminded of the bridge that connects our diverse cultures to the future generations and limitless opportunities that await us.

We are all divine collaborators, adventurous travellers through time, space, and dimensions. In this holy realm of fire, I am speaking to the I AM agencies that have been working with me from the beginning of time. I herewith fire those that are mismatching me with delusional, destructive, distorted, and perverted I AMs, working against my greater good and evolution.

I herewith take back my power from all those I AMs, and revoke and nullify all commitments, oaths, vows, contracts, and agreements, in all timestreams, dimensions, galaxies, and universes. I am not your sidekick. I have never played a secondary role to you, nor do I expect you to play one to me.

I am the I AM Apex presence here now, and with that, I reserve all rights to sack and ban malicious and corrupt agencies and I AMs related to all my soul families. You no longer deserve to join this expression of my journey to bliss and purpose. I herewith put on notice all agents that work with other non-certified agents of other time-space equations for the purpose of forcing a match, no matter how minute it is.

All low-quality agencies are herewith exposed and held accountable for messing up I AM matches. Please collect your belongings and leave this sacred ceremony to never return.

I now address the many times my I AM has been kicked out of the vagus nerve because of the misconduct of harvesting agencies, false agendas, or competitive and hierarchical former I AMs. The shock, the drama, and the feelings of rejection - let us heal and move beyond anger, hurt, and denial to break bread again in gratitude and celebration. May the flames assist this process of forgiveness, to return to our compassionate hearts and reclaim access to all our levels of dimensions and consciousness.

With this fire, I call on all bankrupt I AMs who have given up creating a sovereign reality and left the responsibility to other I AMs. In this circle of fire, we can find refuge and heal all shadows. We have teachings and tools for self-mastery and forgiveness to assist us in getting the fractal soul shards back and to reclaim our sovereign I AM APEX now. Gracious fire spirits, hear the pleas for healing and re-integration.

I fully step into my potency, claiming my ability to respond and adapt, to direct and guide this I AM Apex presence, [name], here now. My journey of universal self-mastery and self-healing is to notice any negative programs, self- defeating and repeating habit patterns within myself and other I AMs that are expecting and projecting onto me. To those I say: 'I AM THE APEX of this ancestral registry, and I'm denying you access as an apex or I AM because you are not in equal co-creation, non-competition, non-hierarchical order. I herewith cut the cords in every dimension, timestream, galaxy, and universe, and I reduce you to zero minus infinity.

Any authority that is given and leaked to any self-created program has the potential to seriously go awry. I make a point to put the record straight and send any self-created demons back to whence they came from, to never return to this fire, this body, this reality again.

I take full responsibility for my choices, and I am in charge of planning and actualizing my life in mutual collaboration with true and contributory I AMs and agencies. I am the confident driver of my DNA vehicle, and I fully inhabit this body in a grounded and expansive fashion.

To all traumatised soul shards trying to take over my I AM spot in the vagus nerve, I say no more. The times of lack of faith and trust, where I allowed myself to be misled by false synchronicities, are over.

All fake and unauthorised contracts signed on my behalf with those imposter shards and soul shard martyrs, I herewith revoke, rescind, recall, and burn to ash. I use the universal power of forgiveness to release myself from any residual images interfering with my DNA technology.

I am a being of choice.
I am a being of courage.
I am a being of determination.
I am a being of sovereignty.
I am a being of self-mastery.
I am a being of self-healing.
I am a being of self-validation.
I am a being of divinity.
I am a being of faith and trust.

I am using my inner knowingness to only work with the 'crème de la crème' agents and agencies to search for, collect, and integrate my fractured selves. I stay connected to my heart's wisdom and naturally flow with all creation of dharmic purpose beyond knowingness and false indoctrinated safety. Sweet surrender is the weapon of peace. As long as domination and control exist in this narrative, I accept and expect to deal with agencies and contracted agents of agencies of the highest values. It is my curious pleasure to make the global narrative irrelevant to my progress as a divinely living, breathing, co-creator of this reality. Trusted freedom comes with practice.

I use contract revocations, shamanic work, and daily spiritual hygiene to remain working with authentic and high-quality I AM agencies. This is for all the parts of my soul essence that ever have, and still, work for the global system of domination and control agency, trying to infiltrate my I AM Apex. I encourage healing, mastery, and forgiveness for all the agents of blame, shame, guilt, and fear in all holograms, consciousness, and layers of time.

With the power of my freewill as a multidimensional universal citizen and in resonance with my human heart, I connect to Earth's dreaming mind in the North and the South pole and bring in all my spirit to strive towards coherence, collaboration, and contribution.

I am present. I am embodied. I am grounded. I am dynamic. I am radiant. I am creative. I speak to the fire and as the fire. My spiritual strategy is to choose the I AM Apex presence and stay fully connected in this spacetime equation. I naturally resonate and work with I AM agencies of different levels of practices, cultures, and standards.

I am time synching with those agencies that can contract people, places, things, objects, synchronicities, magic, and mystery, matching my signature frequency of the healed healer, universal teacher, peacemaker, and peacekeeper of the 5th world of peace.

I, as the I AM Apex, manifest powerful experiences, transcend chemical memories, and have access to light memories in higher states of being. This is me, [name], owning my I AM Apex and not just the seven past and the seven future generations of I AMs. I am multidimensionally aware to be the apex of my previous 10,000 and future 10,000 I AMs. If there are any other I AMs in the North and South pole dreamtime grid that are in equal co-creation and non-competition, let us share our pre- and post-cognitive workforces and create a dreamtime hub of interconnectivity.

Now before we close this sacred circle, I now call 'The Wanderer' to the fire. The VAGUS NERVE, the mediator between my gut, heart and brain. As I smoke the pipe of peace, signals of integration are being sent to all the locations that the vagus nerve travels to. The journey of transformation leads me down the highway to the oesophagus and into the gut. The vagus nerve has access to the entirety of the consciousness DNA experiencing machine, including all shards, parts and avatars integrated in this I AM Apex presence.

I trust my body to use its technology wisely and efficiently to create and maintain homeostasis with source connection. I acknowledge the vagus nerve for acting as the universe in realised potential and honour its mediation between the nervous system, the organs, and the brain.

I now call my inner dragon to the fire to assist me in this consciousness exploration. Hold space and energy with me, and train me on how to best be my multidimensional self in a sacred neutral manner, without giving my power away. Together we program and weave new dream space realities. As universal programmers, teachers, and mediators, we tear down the old clock towers. We smash the clocks of Roman numeral time and surrender back into dreamtime, as we have come from dreamtime, and we will go back into dreamtime.

I am a universal citizen of dreamtime creation, going through the great dreamtime awakening.

And so it is. Aho.

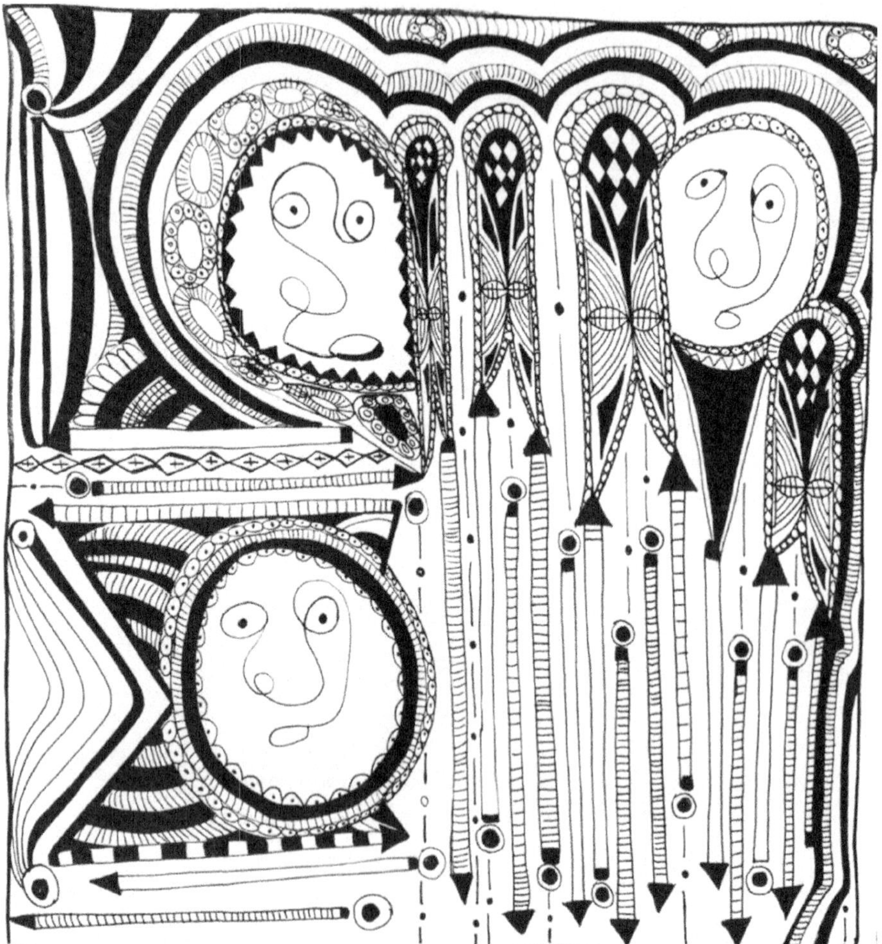

CHAPTER VII: WALK-INS & DREAMTIME

PART I: Walk-ins

In my first reading with Andrew Bartzis in 2014, he confirmed my suspicion that I was a walk-in. He was the second person who validated the soul exchange after my strong physical reaction at the Access weekend mentioned earlier. I had come across the term before but never explored the walk-in phenomenon in more detail. Andrew talks about the 'system of domination and control' that has corrupted human DNA soul contracts and ancestral lineage information for eons of time, as a means of controlling soul commerce, in particular, before the Prime Creator's audit on March 22, 2013. By manipulating soul contracts by inserting fine print that would limit the soul's evolution and shorten the life review between lifetimes, Earth's natural incarnations eventually turned into a forced reincarnation cycle, viciously accumulating karma. Archons, the controllers of that reincarnation grid, have been policing the soul immigration to refuse high vibrational souls entering Earth before the audit and any changes in the Council of 12. Best to go to Andrew's YouTube channel for more galactic history. The following video, in particular, speaks to this https://youtu.be/0W9ij6pdTJ0.

From my personal reading I learned that I was identified by the system of domination and control when I turned fourteen. During a series of timeline viewing check-ups, the controllers saw that at some point in my history, I had the potential to create a unity field that would bring people together simply by being within a few hundred feet of me. They saw me on future broadcasts, television, radio or internet, and wanted to eliminate my physical skinsuit by fabricating fantasy dreams in my dream-world with the purpose of getting into my sensual, sexual expression. The dreaming body told the natal soul to finish whatever needed doing before having to get out.

This sense of urgency was caused by the control system attempting to stop the natal soul from gaining particular light body skillsets, which would have caused an incomplete karmic balance for the soul that was walking out. The walk-in soul had to figure out how to out-create the archon grid and incarnate without getting caught by the control system. It was a straight up 'con game on the archon grid,' as Andrew put it. This is also how I am able to relate to the different mystery schools that my soul has been a part of. I have been the secret agent, the good and the bad over and over again. Over the years more information on the soul exchange phenomenon emerged, and with Andrew's permission I would like to share this summary of our discussions in order to assist people in similar situations, as not much is known or has been written about walk-ins. This part of the book also includes some of his information on the huge faction changes in 2014 when we had around seventy million souls walk in to uphold the single graduation time line created in 2011 and facilitate a dreamtime unification after the planet had moved into the new broadband frequency.

A walk-in contract is not a common occurrence and uniquely differs according to the individual context. In my case, my walk-out soul went backwards in time to influence time in the past. The soul that came forward in time and walked in was to be a unique signature frequency from the past, so it could have a present signature frequency that was its future now. That means the ancient future is now real for me. The ancient past is just as real, so I can simultaneously be the past, present and future existing selves as a linear and non-linear based teacher. The exchange of souls walking in and out does not have to happen instantaneously. In my case, the soul walk-in occurred during my teenage years, whilst the host soul walked out in early adulthood. I had two souls operating within the DNA technology at one time to ensure the completion of skills, as mentioned earlier. My initial host soul, the Martina that left, went to the astral world, where she had a life review and did not dissolve as an I AM presence.

She stayed in existence and transited backwards in time to about 11.5 million years ago, when the Atlanteans were battling the very first reptilians. She was telling the Atlanteans about the weaknesses of the reptilian race. They interpreted her as a paradoxical source of unique information and she lived there for about 65,000 years. After that, her I AM became an ancient teacher spirit in the Akashic Records. She is like another sister in this lifetime and I often do commune with her.

A Dialogue with Andrew Bartzis (AB) on the Walk-In Phenomena

The following questions and answers are transcripts from our *Adventures into Reality* shows, as well as private conversations.

Q: What is a walk-in?
AB: *A walk in is a soul exchange of some kind where the walk-in soul merges with the existing DNA technology. It takes over all the genetic imprinting and the soul contracts of the natal soul, with the purpose of shifting the consciousness of the host body, and or humanity at large. Walk-in occurrences are extremely rare, as they require a lot of preparation during the foetus in the womb planning stage.*

We have access to the infinite blueprint of synchronicities on many frequencies of time and we are simultaneously existing as a multidimensional I AM with both, an oversoul and an avatar. We can't just say 'my life sucks and I want a walk-in.' Let's say you are depressed and feel suicidal and decide to call out for a walk-in... It doesn't work that way. All you would do is invite in a haunting scenario. We have to understand the nature of light-based experiences without trying to validate the experience before having processed it. There are different kinds of walk-ins but let me break it down as simply as possible. In essence, a walk-in scenario is when a soul is born into a body and at some stage decides to leave. It either enters another body or goes to the astral world. Many walk-ins report that after the exchange, they can't relate to their old lives because their faction's perspective is so radically different. Soul based factions follow an ideology of how to create and resolve karmas, dharmas and how to plan lives. They learn from teachers in the astral world about those perceptions and experiences in life. A soul exchange takes a lot of spiritual contracts to be set up in the pre-birth planning.

Q: What is the purpose of a walk-in?
AB: The initial soul that is part of a different faction, belief or ideology, has got stuck in an unbreakable cycle of repetition, and therefore calls on the pre- programmed walk-in rule to assist in the healing of genetic patterns and programming. Another soul will walk in and take over all the existing spiritual contracts plus the additional walk-in contracts, so it can have a lot of dual natured experiences that will go forward in linear time, as if it was the original soul's time stamp and soul family expression. It is a soul faction rather than a fractional shard that walks in, with a very different expression as a form of resolution for the host soul. At times this can feel like a twin that comes in and one can't tell the difference. In other scenarios it might feel radically divergent to the walk-in itself, as well as to others. There can even be physical changes to the body. As a walk-in you take over the contracts from where the host soul left off. You are the same age. The level of awareness that is gained after the experience may be part of a different obligation, a misunderstanding or greater understanding of the journey. It often and usually takes years, to become aware of being a walk-in and acknowledge the perspective of that potentiality. Another layer of reasons for walk-in and walk-out scenarios is the grander resolution. There are a lot of people who needed to be in this time stamp frequency, but don't have the capacity to beat the system because of the mind control and the social engineering that is going on. They have a contract for their soul to walk out and allow spiritual big brother to step in to fight the system in a new way.

That's again the twin scenario where the one that walks out becomes the spirit guide, and the one that walks in becomes the embodiment to initiate the awakening on a grander scale and help shift the consciousness of humanity as a whole.

Q: What other examples are there when pre-programmed walk-in scenarios can be triggered?
AB: Think of someone who has experienced sexual, verbal, emotional - any type of abuse from a very young age. The original soul can't plan a powerful life under those circumstances if it cannot out-create the limitations imposed by the parents or caretakers. The natal soul has enough and the walk-in contract gets triggered. The new soul comes in with a hardened energy and the DNA must accept the multidimensional peg into the multidimensional hole. As the child changes it will start sending different energies to the parents to stop the abuse and break the repetition. A soul exchange can happen in a snap in an awake moment, because once the spiritual contracts have been put into place in the womb, time is an illusion for a walk-in. Most of the accident scenarios triggering behavioural changes are not necessarily walk-ins, but faction changes through a great spiritual teacher association who is in a near death event or being triggered through a dream. Other common reasons for walk-ins and walk-outs would be being born into a difficult culture, or the wrong soul family.

Q: Does a walk-in faction have to always be of a higher vibration?
AB: No, not necessarily! Sometimes it requires a lower density. A super heavy duty warrior spirit to come in and fight for your sovereignty at the dirty layers against abusive parents. It is a myth that walk-in souls are always from a higher dimensional plane. It is also most unlikely to have more than one walk- in, as the planning and follow through of even one soul exchange is tough enough. What could happen though, is that a person was born and at the age of three, the soul walked out and another soul walked in. At twenty-one that person has a near death experience that triggers the walk-in to walk out, and a new soul walks in. That person becomes an incredible healer after that. This would have been planned between all three souls as a master karmic resolution for that DNA lineage to resolve disease, depression and abuse. For the three souls to make an agreement like that would have triggered tremendous healing for an entire lineage of skinsuits. Again, this is not a day-to-day occurrence at all, as the walk-in phenomena is very rare. Once a soul walks out, there is no turning back, but that soul may come back to the family lineage as another child.

Q: What is a prenatal walk-in?

AB: A lot of time a foetus is not alone in the womb. In the first five weeks of pregnancy, there can be a twin developing genetically. One soul then absorbs the other, which can become a birth mark or trigger a walk-in experience later in life. Prenatal walk-ins are expanding the capacity for the mother's future life too. Of course, not all birthmarks come from walk-ins. A birthmark can also be a sign of a guide, where let's say the grandfather who died just before the child's birth, becomes a celestial guardian to assist the child in not making the common lineage mistakes. There are also certain marks that come from the lineage itself, or past life traumas that can manifest in the current lifetime.

Q: What is a postnatal walk-in?
AB: I've talked about souls hiding in different bodies to out-create the system. So, the baby you have for the first two years may not be the baby you have after two years. This is how a soul that is super powerful can get past the incarnation grid or the archons. They may have been in the womb for a few months with a crappy life plan and in the last moment they walk out and let another soul take over. It is a technique that is used to get into this reality without the predictability factor of the system inside them. At times, it takes a potent soul for the purpose of stopping a long-term repetition process in a lineage with too much karma that the soul family elders cannot break and complete. It will depend on the karma of the mother's lineage if the pre- or postnatal walk-in has issues connecting to the mother. If the mother's mother had a good quality birth, there won't necessarily be a disconnection from the actual birth mother. Part of the karmic journey is to reconnect to the mother and grandmother's expression.

Q: We had a bunch of walk-ins in 2014. What was that all about?
AB: It is a topic that hasn't been much written about. There was a time in 2014 where we had a huge faction change instigated by the prime creator, as part of the audit after having realised how cooked the karmic books were. Factions can be compared to themed agencies. It's worth noting that faction changes are not always created by walk-ins. About seventy million people in managerial positions with severe lineage-limitations, who could not beat the drama, the materialism and the consumerism, had agreed to walk-out and let their brothers and sisters come in to do the work on their behalf. This is part of the change we are now starting to see in this world, many years later. Lots of people at the corporate level are turning to spirituality, as they cannot sell their soul anymore.

They got the white picket fence and now realise the illusion behind it. Seventy million people is still a very small percentage of our population. Walk-ins and walk-outs happen in all three frequencies. There are seven plus billion people living on the surface world, about ten million in the astral world, and twenty million subsurface in Hollow Earth. Walk-ins are happening in a very small number unless prime creator decides otherwise to initiate a grander scale of awakening.

PART TWO: Dreamtime Shenanigans

Sleep itself, and the very act of dreaming, are important components of the spiritual awakening process as humanity is rising from great depths of unawareness, that encompasses both our conscious and unconscious states of existence. *Once we stop imagining that we are awake, we can finally stop sleeping.*

Dreamtime Explorer

During dreamtime, we are still free to experience the singularity; a unique and all-encompassing state of consciousness. Every night, our dreaming body uses its time-travelling capabilities to explore multidimensional aspects of the astral world, where we can encounter both familiar and unfamiliar entities while unlocking additional spiritual potential. Once we have fallen asleep, the astral body disengages from the physical and etheric body and leaves through the solar plexus gateway, roaming freely outside the duality constraints. Until we have attained a higher level of awareness, the conscious mind is still confined to the knowledge experienced within a restricted framework of the seven-chakra system.

Dreaming is a daily opportunity to move beyond set boundaries and human confinements, exploring the habitat and playground of the soul. It can be invigorating as it allows us to surpass gravitational restrictions, influences of time and space, and the limitations of logic that are present in our waking state. The bridge between sleep and waking state is known as lucid dreaming, during which we can maintain a level of awareness and interact within our dreams, allowing us to influence the outcome of it. That state can feel like a highly augmented reality experience, akin to being teleported into a magical world that instantaneously responds to your movement and thoughts. Lucid dreaming offers a sense of immersion and interactivity with the dream space, allowing individuals to freely explore the unknown realms. This can include the ability to fly, manipulate objects, interact with other species, and engage in various activities that are not yet accessible in the physical world. During sleep, the soul expresses itself freely through the astral body, channelling deeply hidden emotions and desires via heightened spiritual organs of perception. These impulses can be carried over into the world of physical senses, leading to profound epiphanies upon awakening.

Earth's dreaming mind is directly linked to all solar systems for the sake of karmic resolution. While the physical body remains safely tucked away in sleep paralysis, we extensively astral travel to different realms and worlds which host a variety of dreamtime societies. At times, we become overly enthusiastic and daring whilst enjoying our astral freedom and engage in activities that may negatively affect our lifeforce and physical well-being. I was once told that I had a rebellious dreaming body that would venture through the back doors into sacred geometry cities to visit and heal old relationships that had gone awry. Toxic entanglements that occur during sleep can have negative impacts on the physical body. Staying clear from parasitic entities in any altered time frames, and preserving sufficient energy resources, allow us to have synchronistic and mystical dreamtime experiences. Engagement in toxic 'pillow talk' is not sensible or desirable in any dimension, timeline, galaxy or universe. The rules of energy cleanliness that have been established throughout this book apply equally to dream time as they do to waking time, as we must be mindful of energy depletion regardless of our state of consciousness. Before entering the dream space, it is best to set an intention for your dreaming body to only connect with benevolent soul family for the purpose of joyful play, exploration, and potential reunions. Clear focus and attention go a long way and more details are provided in the dreamtime revocation that completes this chapter. Dreams create a tremendous amount of energy that can be utilized to inspire creativity, provide insight and guidance, and bring about healing. It is advisable to cyclically clear old 'dreamtime trash', releasing stagnant energies from the intestinal tract, the home of the dreaming body. Think of gut health; simple applications like colonics and regular juice cleanses assist the digestive system, cultivate healthy bowel movements and sparkle up your dreams.

Dreamtime Creators

During our dream states, we are leaving the perceptions of duality behind, and gain access to the fullness of the infinite spirit world, inclusive of its trimmings and traps.

In this heightened frequency we have access to solar and planetary hierarchies and can download all kinds of celestial concepts. An abundance of lifeforces, energies, and data are at our disposal, ready to form new understandings and communities. Divinely orchestrated dream experiences can bring humanity together as unified groups of souls. A few split seconds of a dream shared by friends or family, deliberated upon waking state, offer a glimpse into future possibilities and revelations. Such joint dream experiences not only encourage us to explore the deeper realms of the soul but also accelerate the awakening process. By working together to interpret these shared experiences, we deepen our connections with one another and with the divine.

The dreaming body of Earth is in the Inner Earth. Gaia dreams too, with many other planets and solar systems simultaneously. As we continue our sovereign diligence and self-mastery, we gain a more conscious access to Earth's dreaming mind, connecting us to a multitude of inter-dimensional pods, hubs, and frequencies, similar to a localhost interface used in computer networks. During some of my dream ventures into Inner Earth I met people unknown to me in this reality. These experiences remained vivid and intense upon waking, making them impossible to ignore. Those were memories of my walk- in soul, helping me rekindle my Inner Earth connection.

Can you recall dreams with clear and distinct images, impossible to forget? You wake up and feel different; elated and kind of intrigued beyond recognition. It is important to ponder, maybe even share those dreamtime nuggets with a friend, write a story or create a project around them, adding to a more colourful and rich fabric of creation. Our astral soul families submit messages and teachings through the dream weave, as well as our spirit guides and totem animals to which we have unrestricted access to in the singular dream state. Conversely, they are inviting us to teach them what it's like to be human on a planet with an extended unnatural state of growth, and how to remedy that. Dream journals can be useful in bringing forth these teachings and experiences into this physical realm.

Our processing capacity of conscious and unconscious data is uniquely tailored to our soul's imprint. Dream memories often represent themselves in a form of symbols, patterns or shades of colour, assisting our individual healing journey. Andrew mentioned that I had two dreaming bodies with an inbuilt astral construction system that apparently allows me to easily raise the consciousness in my local bubble of reality through pure intent and focus. We all have hidden gifts that we are not necessarily aware of yet, and the dreamtime can be a powerful tool to help us uncover and develop them. By exploring the limitless potential of our dreams, we can tap into new levels of creativity, intuition, and insights enhancing our waking lives in profound ways. We, as guardians of the threshold between reality and dream, have the ability to exchange magic between all realms of existence.

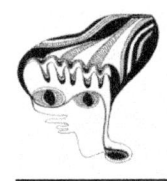

Dreamtime Revocation & Invocation

In this next revocation and invocation, I offer more details on dreaming mechanics and sovereignty rules, as I have come to know them through my work. The comprehensive nature of these documents may evoke both excitement and exhaustion as you read through them. Lots of people fall asleep as they ponder the words. Feel free to take as much time as you need and revisit the documents frequently.

Dreamtime

I am a Dreamtime ....

- *Traveller*
- *Shaman*
- *Connector*
- *Translator*
- *Weaver*
- *Networker, ...(add your own)*

I, [insert name], this I AM Apex being of the now, understand the original purpose of Earth being linked into the dreaming mind of all solar systems for the resolve of all karma. With this, I acknowledge my human responsibility of conquering my dreams and expelling any physical, spiritual, technological and social dreamtime toxicity as part of karmic resolve. I choose to enter into the Earth's Akashic records a sovereign declaration to be of service to remove any dreamtime traumas since the existence of dreams.

I erase all karmic contracts and feeding tubes at the architectural level. Any perverted, secret and tacitly consented attachments that are still creating extended contracts of a non-benevolent co-creation, energy drainage and harvest in my dream or relaxation time, are herewith destroyed and uncreated. Nothing can be in one degree of separation of a contract I have erased. I no longer allow energetic vampirism to take me off path, during my dreamtime journeys.

I am a dreaming being following a blissful path of purpose and mission. I call upon my highest soul integrity, in every soul shard and every plane of existence, to call forth the moment of internal audit and declare that my path is clear and free.

I now tell the dreamtime controllers that I do no longer tacitly consent to the disparity of value exchange on all levels of my existence, in the infinite dreamworld and in all other dimensions and timestreams. To all falsely established hierarchical dreamtime systems and societies, I issue a spiritual warrant confirming that this I AM Apex and all its connected hubs, is returning to zero balance - that zero point in the foetus of my mother's womb. You have no control over me, no power and no ability to influence my dream space and evolution. You are hereby banished from my dreamtime.

With this now stated, I declare that my dreaming energy cannot be used to confuse, haunt, or camouflage others in need of self-empowered healing. I am linked to the crow people, and like the crow, I am the knower of the great void; the beyond of the beyond. My dreaming body visits the void to invite great dimensional teachers and architects back to Earth to teach us what we need to know. I honour White Crow to help me bring peace to all parts, shards, and shadows that are stuck in all the secret, forgotten places. I act as a sacred neutral dreamtime shaman for all soul groups that I am connected to.

I use my dreamtime records and memories as keys to my soul's purpose for this lifetime.

In my lucid dreaming state, I remember to provide portals, routes, foundations, connections, and grids for other souls to strengthen their experience in this dreamtime awakening. The veil is swiftly lifting and I am recognising the work that I do in dreamtime, and the experiences that I am sharing. I am a potent dreamtime connector and networker.

In my dreamtime explorations I sit in council round the fire of creation, to exchange wisdom with other shamans, my soul families, and soul related elders and equals. Together we learn, teach, and remember how to reach our past and future versions and to acknowledge that we are living on different sides of the universe with just a thought apart. I am a time travelling dreamtime consciousness explorer, connected to all dreaming minds in this universe.

In full preparation of my dreamtime experience, and before I enter the great sleep and connect to my dreaming body, I give instructions to all my light bodies that are experiencing all colours of time to detox and align themselves with the centre of my sacred heart. As I fall into the deep sleep and connect to Earth mother's dreaming mind, the only portal that I create is to my seven future generations and to my seven past generations, so I may have powerful ancestral visitations and understandings.

I herewith demand of my I AM presence and my dreaming body to come into authentic expression and neutrality, and to allow for the full hour or two that it takes to build up the proper energy to get ready for the dreaming body to leave the intestinal tract without being kicked into sleep paralysis too early or delayed.

I use salt, silver, and sage to cleanse and clear my room, my bed, and my entire dreaming consciousness from all toxins, burdens, and perversions so that my dreaming body can safely leave and re-enter the physical body without any harmful impressions on to it. I now connect to my dreaming body that lives in my intestinal tract and make more of my dreamtime requirements known. Dropping the upper chakras into the solar plexus, I begin to rest my active human body and slowly prepare for sleep paralysis.

"I am about to enter the world of dreams, to share this sacred space in union and communion with other dreamers, for the next day I shall awake, remember, and integrate all dreaming experiences." I observe an energetic wave pattern building up in the sacral chakra, getting ready to move into the root. This is the sacred choice point where I consciously declare that I want to lucid dream.

As I witness the root blossoming like a lotus flower, creating endless prisms of energy, I gather my dreamtime travel gear and program the dreaming body for safe passage before the lower chakras moves up into the solar plexus, ready for the dreaming body to head off into the world of dreams.

Aho, friend dreaming body, that is going to go on a great journey. I am acknowledging you as a potent part of me. We are going to be partners in this dreaming process together with the infinite and equally co-creating beings within the dreaming minds of Earth and this solar system. Safely connect and guide me through this time of dreamtime slumber, so that I have a synopsis of what I am up to in my infinite extremes of consciousness. I duly prepare myself before I enter the great sleep, so my dreaming body, the vehicle that helps me transverse the multiverse of expressions, is guided through my intention.

As a human being in this time of global dreamtime awakening, I accept that I am a holographic data processing machine with memory stored in all my skeletal system and every bodily cell and molecule. I understand that it is my responsibility to process dreamtime as well as awake time information through claiming, authenticating and integrating my memories and experiences. I release any attached electromagnetic energetic imprints to clear and cleanse the system and keep it running efficiently and to full capacity.

I only work with trusted dreamtime societies that create a foundation for the brain to function in, by mapping the pathways of past, present and future shamans, so my soul group has DNA connections to that point. This allows me to bring the brain perceptions outside my physical body, into the dreamworld, for me to process and learn from the fields of dreams and plenty.

All other beings that are not in my soul family DNA lineage, and not within my expression of truth and love, shall not have access to this portal. There is no manipulation, masturbation, fantasy projection that can come into my reality whilst I am asleep. I am blocking this frequency from existing and co-existing with me.

All the rebellious versions of my dreaming body, that give orders out of line with my physical and spiritual wellbeing, I now take back my power from them. I remove all oaths, vows and agreements made with any subversive and destructive societies in the dream weave, so when I go to sleep as the I AM presence of the now, I only go to places of our true soul family for blissful soul family reunions and nowhere else.

All the invoked and perpetrated dreamtime empathy, that keeps me reliving the drama, trauma, pains, pathways, and realities of any souls that have been tortured and tormented, horrifically crossed over that I have been part to, in this and other life and dreamtimes, dimensions, and timestreams, I now destroy and uncreate, as well as all related oaths, vows, and agreements.

All the times where friend dreaming body took itself too seriously, ignored my I AM heart, entangled with my egoic human brain, and negatively affected my I AM presence awake frequencies, I now turn those times to zero minus infinity.

I now talk to my parasympathetic body and my vagus nerve, working in conjunction with my dreaming body, to let go of fear, physical pain, rejection, envy, unhealed traumas, stresses, decisions, judgments, or anything else that is being projected onto me and my body and allow healing to take place in this space of dreamtime.

I herewith close all dreamtime backdoors to any martyr healings and dealings with toxic relationships from this lifetime and others. The doors are shut to any heavily invested ancient mystery school activities, to any traps set out in sacred geometry cities and to false time contraptions and calibrations that keep my dreaming body working overtime. I am now getting sufficient dream sleep.

I claim and heal all aspects of my dreaming body that may have an internal self-created program, an entity or a demon that is pissed off and doesn't want to let go. I delete all that from my reality and eliminate it to zero minus infinity so that it does no longer exist as a program but is recycled through the universal frequency of time. I demand my dreaming body to change its frequency patterns to detect any of those entities.

I have ample amounts of energy preserved to have synchronicities, mystical experiences and to wake up refreshed and ready for the fray of the day. In this journey of dream travel, I enter the dreamtime and dreamworlds, where I look for my cellular memories and my DNA technology wisdom. I use dreamtime maps and my dreamtime compass to connect to with my past and future generations for the sacred purpose of fully recovering the treasures of my past and future dream worlds.

I wish to call forth the soul parts, shards and avatars that have been lost in other dream worlds to return to my spiritual courts of equity and to share dream space with me. I pray that I can connect to the soul family members in residual image that I haven't seen in a long time.

My dragon, my elemental and star brothers and sisters, my fellow time travellers, my DNA related off world species are connecting through dreamtime so my heart can be filled with joy and happiness at being the translator and the hub of interconnectivity with this and the spirit world.

I detox my dreaming body from any sexually aroused and over amorous false love energy extended to beings with and without bodies in the dreamtime weave, in unawareness.

I call to all the lovers of my past that have loved me into my ancient future to be present in my dream world, in equal co-creation and non-competition to share and exchange love, joy and unbiased compassion in these times of grand awakening.

My dreaming body allows me to live in many worlds at once. As I unplug from the matrix my dreams will assist me in actualising my mission with greater ease, joy, and blissful abundance.

In my dreamtime I can tap into that zero-point unified field as a conscious manifestation and create quantum energy objects for my altar, to increase my frequency and my connection to the planet. I am practicing to ask questions in my dreams that are helping me to find my next level of creations and teachings.

Aho, friend dreaming body, that is connected to different expressions of time and space. I am not fully conscious yet but I am willing to learn. The western doorway of perception opens up for me to perceive and fully receive the dreaming energy stored in my very own skull cap, that encases the brain in its crystallised structure.

I am ready to access my dream memories and express them through joyful inspirations and new creations. As my dreamtime memories move from the skull cap through the digestive system and into the blood stream, I have more awareness and energy in the awake state to connect to synchronicities.

I find myself inspired to share my dreams to assist this awakening. As a lucid dreamer, I have many déjà vu moments in the dreams that I can use to create with. Many people I work with in dreamtime, I have yet to meet in awake time. In the coming years I am returning to a more potent state of dreaming, as I am a dreaming being, going through a dreamtime awakening. At the end of the dream, the dreaming body returns. The flower in my root chakra closes again and all chakras slot back into their original places. All of the vision of dream is there, integrated and remembered.

All the dream space energy that is residually present around the heart and sacrum, I now invite to travel up the vagus nerve for cognitive acknowledgement of mystical experiences in the future.

Upon wakening, when the heart and brain are still trying to identify points in space and time, I challenge myself to identify my dreams, stay in dreamtime, hit the snooze button and fall back into dream to process infinity.

The first ten minutes of the morning I will choose to solidify those in my memories, the dreams that I have heard and understood through this golden door of protection that I created for myself and journal them in gratitude and bliss.

And so it is. Aho.

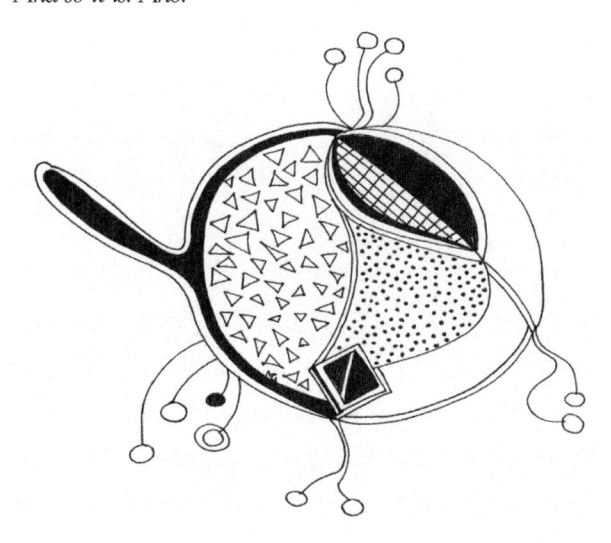

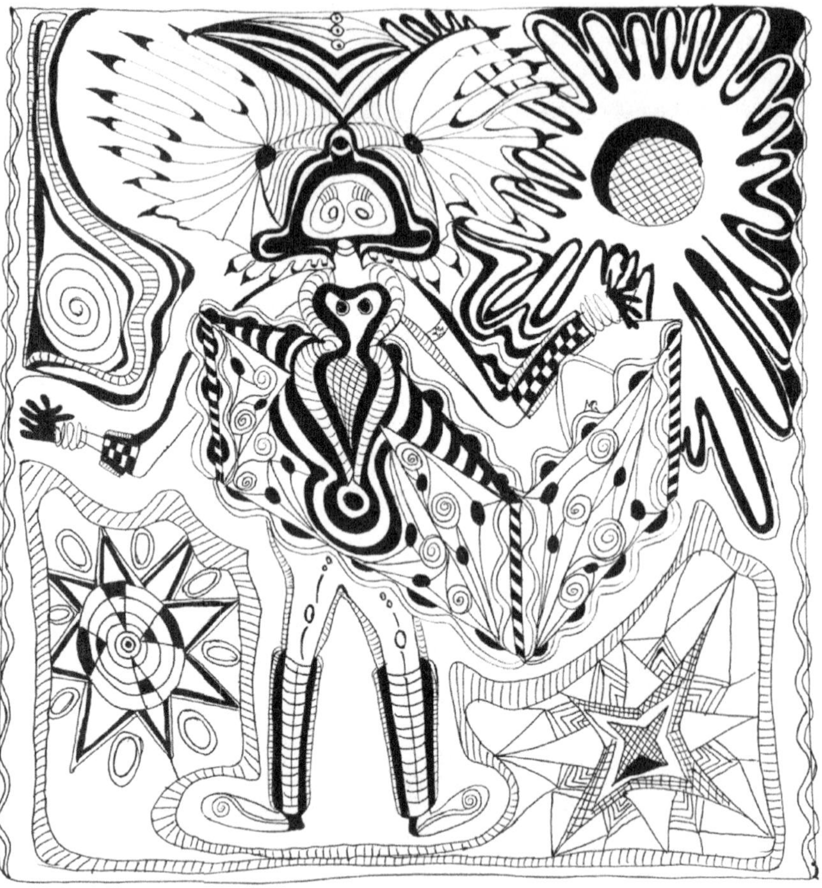

CHAPTER VIII: DRAGON, EARTH & INTERSPECIES COLLABORATION

PART ONE: Consciousness Explorers

We have all lived on different planets in divergent solar systems before choosing Earth as a preliminary home. We are in fact all members of a mixed explorer race, incarnated and reincarnated as interbred soul factions. Our soul's essence is an amalgamation of different planetary influences, features, and memories of soul families and alien species whose DNA has been cross-mated over millions of years, during our journeys in and between worlds. By means of our soul codes, we still have access to all of those other planets, galaxies, and universes. As a collaboration of champions from all kinds of star clusters, we are here to anchor in the Earth's new frequency and lead the planet out of energy harvesting, forced control, and oppression. We are spirited pioneers on an epic adventure to dissolve the muddy waters of collective unconsciousness and propagate clean, natural ways of living.

Our world is part of a colourful ray of creation that connects, nurtures and facilitates all life forms with divergent qualities and ways of expression, within a multitude of planetary networks, governed by the Galactic and Interstellar Federation that monitors and supports all players involved. The entire spectrum of our experiences, as we are moving between dream and awake states, are vital aspects to help bring balance and harmony to mankind and other universal intelligence. In our divine essence, we are celestial mediums of peace that have joined the collective of universal explorers to commune with other celestial beings to share and shape a new dream frequency which will further all stages of self-remembering, to eventually act as universal teachers to this and other worlds. Every one of us plays an important role in the awakening and mutually contributes at different levels of human consciousness.

May we continue to awaken to our true divine nature and fulfill our purpose as celestial beings on this planet and beyond.

Here is another snippet from my reading with Andrew in 2014, when he said the following about my galactic origin:

'In my terminology I would call you a classic light body example of a person coming during the awakening who has done all the experiences here on Earth in the last 54 million years. You know all the tricks. Once the technology is turned off and your DNA skinsuit is allowed to properly heal, it will be like a big fog clearing out of your mind and heart really fast. You will rapidly adapt because the Earth is going to be in a different frequency and you are going to be able to operate in both frequencies simultaneously. You are doing this already in your dreamtime. Your dreaming body is far bigger than your physical body. This is classic for Pleiadian and Arcturian mediators. 7% of our current population is equivalent to what you are. I put you in a rarer catalogue because of the specific Arcturian DNA you have that is very reminiscent of the horse or equine DNA. The more you are around horses, the better your life would be. They are in your dreamworld now.'

The purpose of sharing this is to trigger your own soul memory and to amplify your knowingness about the capacities dormant within your DNA. As we stop seeking the alien outside ourself, we rediscover our alienated roots. We will eventually claim the fullness of our true essence and unearth what has been hidden and unduly kept from us. This may be a daunting prospect, but it will ramp up our telepathic capacities and allow us to see each other in our authentic and powerful energy. Ready yourself for public access to thoughts and feelings. 'Leaky thought syndrome' pops into my head, reminding us of the importance of self-mastery and personal sovereignty, as well as establishing healthy boundaries with others. Watch the movie *Chaos Walking* – it explores the concept of a world of men being afflicted by 'the Noise' that makes their thoughts public property. It serves as a cautionary tale about the potential consequences of not being mindful of the power of our thoughts and emotions and the importance of energy cleanliness.

Activate the Dragon

Using the dragon metaphor, we refer to primordial principles and functions that are an inherent part of our divine heritage and skinsuit technology, waiting to be actualised as humanity wakes up to its higher consciousness. Whilst not everyone will be interested in putting in the work that it takes to remember the force of the dragon, there is a significant amount of people on this planet with dragon DNA that is now being activated. As the mind, conditioned by duality merges, we are moving into higher levels of perception and no longer see things as contradictory or in opposition to each another which accelerates our self-remembrance. We come to understand that as long as we place ourselves at the effect of this world, we remain subject to tyranny by our own consent. Dragons are reality programmers.

Within the universal framework set by the sacred algorithms of life, they are constantly evolving and adapting within the natural reality rules that govern life, just as we are. Under man's own self-empowered supervision and under the guidance of dragons we are working towards a new reality that is free from constraints of societal indoctrination, power structures, and karma. Gaia is a sentient living being, that births and nurtures organic life forms which cannot exist separately but as part of the whole, serving and affecting all matter that composes the universe. The misinterpretation of man as an identified individuals has supported the concept of linearity and reduced our ability to access the quantum fields of consciousness. Our physical bodies are not just mere separate, isolated vessels, but rather holographic microcosms that reflect the ever-expanding universe.

In this spacetime construct, we have relied on linear thought patterns to derive meaning and achieve desired outcomes. However, this linear approach is limited in that it does not fully account for our holographic nature. Linear thinking follows a strict cause-and-effect sequence, where each thought leads to the next in a straightforward manner which does not align with the original intent for humanity to operate. The principle of cause and effect, where every action leads to a corresponding reaction, has played a crucial role in shaping our lives, influencing our decisions, relationships and experiences. This narrow view of causality has made us predictable as an entire species, easily controllable, and trapped in karmic cycles. We lost touch with our cosmic heritage and diminished our access to the memories of past lives. This has led to suppression of the higher faculties and disconnected us from our sacred neutral observer function. We feel asleep and turned the dragons away. In the majority of people, the critical observer is 'still sleeping' and not active enough to take charge of the higher chakra functions that are dormant in our technology. Our immediate focus must be to cultivate unbiased observation and restore the I AM self's full awareness of its fractal nature to operate once more within a unified system.

This reality we experience is created by the mind, rather than existing independently of it. Retro- causal events, such as healings sent to the future that can change the past or the present, still challenge the traditional scientific view of a linear reality as they lack a discernible proof between cause and effect. Modern day science does not yet take into account our ever-changing nature of our fractal consciousness. Our future is not limited to the past and we have the potential to create a completely new reality that has never before existed in our galaxy.

As the skinsuit technology is being activated, it will enhance our innate capabilities of self-remembering, by granting us a greater access to the quantum field. The consciousness of our soul is not limited to the speed of space and can roam freely and simultaneously in all realms of existence. This will eventually guide us towards superluminal processing where we will no longer operate separate from our soul. The soul will feed back unique and unlimited data to the I AM Avatar to be downloaded and processed, if and when required. Bilocation, telepathy, transliteration, instant self-healing, and a brand- new shaping, forming, and harnessing of elemental energy will become the new normal. By merging with our light bodies, the central nervous system can upgrade, allowing us to absorb higher energies from the Sun, Earth, Moon and planetary consciousness. These transmissions have the ability to alter the properties of water within our bodies and restructure our DNA, potentially leading to a more etheric appearance of our physical bodies. Before that can happen, our bodies will have to become more fully receptive and capable of assimilating and digesting these cosmic influences. In order to create new bodily features and functions, it is necessary for all molecules to align cohesively, interact and organize themselves in a variety of new ways. The universe operates with a higher intelligence, orchestrating all those changes with precision and purpose. When we release fears of uncertainty and surrender to the flow of creation, we can tap into the dragon energies that exist in all spectrums of creation.

Interstellar civilisations are watching and applauding our progress in anticipation of their affiliated evolution. The deepest truth often services unexpected sources. Across the following years of major transformation, we will usher in more otherworldly collaboration and open gateways the yet unknown. The revocations and invocations provided in this book are designed to awaken the dragon into action. Follow the invitation to calm the emotional and reorient the mental body by consciously using your dragon energy, purposefully breathing in unison with your soul, planetary, and universal consciousness.

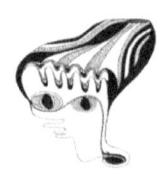

Dragon Prayer

In February of 2021 I wrote this Dragon Prayer as a personal contribution to my life's legacy, and to activate more of my dragon energies. You are welcome to use it and adapt it to your own requirements.

I, [insert name], the I AM Apex of the present moment, the ancient future now being, living in [insert place] at this present time [insert date], herewith open a spiritual court of equity for the purpose of revocating, invocating, integrating, extrapolating, praying and acknowledging part of my journey over the last fifty plus million years and well into the future.

As a time traveller, a myth hunter, a cultural psychic mediator, translator, a philosopher, dreamtime defender of unity and growth, and longstanding member of Resistance Free Earth, I equally honour all villain and victor lifetimes as part of the grand tapestry of karmic resolution.

I carry the light frequency of the dragon. I use this sacred neutral format to address my inner dragons and the dreamtime connection with all benevolent species of the Agarthan network.

Through the ethers of the dreamtime gateways, I send prayers to my ancestral astral soul families, may you hear my plea for union and communion.

I connect to the golden dragon to call forth more of my ancient conscious memories and soul codes.

I fully honour this epic journey of embodiment and karmic resolution with my fellow travellers on our way back to the stars. Magic is written into the guts, the hearts and minds of those individuals that have the courage, determination and commitment to practice prayer as part of their self-healing skills.

I speak to the ones who remember to open their minds to master the mystical flow of words, thoughts and feelings expressed through the heart. We must allow our authentic voices to be heard. The Earth heart's magnetism can resonate with our own heart, the planetary's and our nervous system to encourage consciousness into unity.

We bring back together communities of cultures and species to once again share their soul codes in divine natural co-creation. We are the synthesis of peacekeepers to preserve ancient knowledge wisdom over many billions of lifetimes to use here now in these times of change and transformation.

During all those time wars in leapfrogging air cities, phasing in, phasing out, body, no body, and through psychic telepathy, we have come a long way resolving karma, collecting soul codes, transferring people back and forth between many worlds and galaxies.

As I am starting to tap into the greater perspective outside of this reality's limitation and mediocrity, I am learning to maneuver within the realms of unknowingness. I am no longer in the limited point of view, as I have accepted the rites of passage.

I herewith accept my birth right and legacy of meeting, greeting, interacting, and cooperating with my ancient future selves living in different worlds simultaneously plotting the end of world domination. I am strengthening my explorer legs instead of hiding in the comfort of the unseen.

I am showing up for all the shards, parts and avatars that have gone before me to meticulously prepare for what has yet to be unveiled.

As we move through the upgrades in consciousness, we are all invited to shift beyond the common collective consensus and leave the confines of this conceptional reality behind. Learn to step patiently, my friends.

It is time to awaken from the millennia of static slumber and harmonise and unify the foetus with our avatar blueprints without inserting forced agendas.

What more legacies can I pass on to my future generations as I walk this path of delicate balance, of growth and impeccable choices, of self-nurture and joy for the greater good of unification of all celestial minds?

With the help of my inner dragons, I am going to continue to stay clear of individual and collective karma, control and manipulative incarceration, and step into the zero balance of unity consciousness. I deprogram myself from the letters of this world to seek truth and knowledge beyond the boundaries of this reality. All the languages that served me well as a forced lower density being, I now acknowledge them with gratitude for the contribution on my journey.

I start adding higher density linguistics to let other parts, shards and pieces of myself know that they can now come forward to this graduation time line and join me in the celebration. As a psychic cultural medium and translator, [add your own] I give myself permission to have fun with exploring the one million letter alphabet and dive deeply into the mysteries of symbolism, metaphors, glyphs and sigils.

I have many dragons inside me. All elemental aspects that are part of me, I breath with them, I send prayers to them and I welcome the prayers to return naturally, seamlessly and without force. My body, my instrument of experience, is holding space and guides the mechanism of true receiving whilst being fully grounded and connected to this world I call home, my Mother Earth.

Friend Dragon FIRE, assist me in purifying my emotions as I follow this path to illumination. Together we breathe life into the flames of passion and turn them into bliss, joy, and pleasure to nurture, love and show compassion for all sentient kind. Ancient ancestral tongues around the fire are muttering sounds of forgiveness. There is a need for authentic giving and receiving to heal the wounds of ancient wars and struggles. The great stories of bloody adventures are being told to the fire to be honoured, witnessed and released. The flames are high and burn the shadows of forced and false allegiance carried over lifetimes to this day. May my empowered mastery and the sovereign boundaries cultivate an inner understanding of the purpose of being here now in this life. I volunteer to tame and contain the flames, allowing our star brothers and sisters from far and near, spread over many universes, to gather around the fire pit. Potent fire elementals cleanse and clear any apprehension and misconception, so we again can share stories of ancient cultures, beliefs, taboos, and philosophies that have not been allowed to function in this reality. May my dreamworlds expand many trillionfold again, for me to travel to end of the universe and back viewing my ancient future self in knowingness and in unity. I thank you, Dragon Fire, for helping me tend the flames, burning the old and create anew.

Friend Dragon WATER, that connects me to all energetic oceans of awareness, way back to the ancient days of Lemuria and Atlantis, I have lived in many cultures at once to see the patterns of confusion, constrictions and conflict in all realms of existence. Your cosmic waters of consciousness assist me in recognising the many currents of cultural differences creating the spiral waves between on-world distortions and off-world imprints. Walk with me, sacredly observe, connect, and help me dissolve those rifts and misunderstandings so that healing may begin to occur between our tribes, our nations, and worlds of all races and species kind. Together let us invite the master healers of this universe to join us and allow the fog, the steam of amnesia, to lift out of the hearts and minds of our physical and light bodies as we move into higher frequencies. May the gentle touch of the purifying mist smooth the edges where sand meets water and create a zone of trust for dream space to be shared again and teachings to be exchanged. I thank you, Dragon Water, for balancing my passionate fire and keep me in creative flow.

Friend Dragon EARTH, I am grateful for my human experience, for the gift of a physical body made of flesh and blood. I appreciate the nurturing body of Gaia, her sentient mind which serves as a playground for all species to unite, for consciousness to expand. From the North to the South Pole stretch vast possibilities of ancient future lives to be planned, realized, and fully lived as incarnated avatars. From egg and sperm to artificial intelligence, our brains and hearts are shared amongst the pods of people studying our common cultures and different origins. Our skinsuits have been passed down and cultivated through generational wisdom. Help me reignite my bodily systems to integrate all cellular memory, expanding my signature frequency range. Let me access and unpack all light memories with ease to be the translator and interface of ancient wisdom applied to modern-day demands. I talk to the plants in this world, I put time and effort into speaking to the mushroom kingdom on this earth to link to other planets, where mushrooms sprout and journey. With this, I honour diversity, I nurture life, and unearth my sacred feminine aspect a millionfold. I follow a process of remembering of how to bring together communities and cultures through being the hub of interconnectivity. With your guidance, Dragon Earth, I strengthen my discipline and commitment to safely travel within and beyond Earth's physical domain, so I may utilise natural gateways and portals in the ancient cites and womb chakras. I am honoured to be a custodian of Earth and all its denizens. I thank you, Dragon Earth, for keeping me company in this body.

Friend Dragon AIR, the architect of wisdom thoughts, great minds and intellectual exploration, breathe sustaining life into my spine and fuel my physical form to help me fulfill my purpose and legacy. Let us build a framework of existence for otherworldly species to find their way to Earth. In sacred neutral union, we prepare and teach them to experience the essence of the dense nature of our reality, so that they too can have an actual encounter here. Let us welcome all species and offer them our multidimensional hospitality services. Together, we will create an off-world manual that outlines tools and techniques necessary to heal in Earth's space. It will assist them in deconstructing the local myths to begin their soul relations here on Earth. We are understanding them, and they are understanding us without ever standing under each other. Instead, we walk and pray side by side on the path to universal citizenship. Together, friend dragon, we will be the common interface for all animals and species to communicate in sacred neutral dream space and telepathically form new relationships, so that we may be united and free again. I thank you, Dragon Air, for helping me find my place amongst all universal teachers.

Friend Dragon ETHER, please join me in creating a unity field where people can come together and put ignorance and differences aside by being in our presence. Please assist me in sharing my thoughts and ideas through my heart's discerned filters. I am a catalyst for change, a filter for polarity, hidden shadows, and habit patterns to be revealed. I stand strong in the wind of resistance and projection. My roots are ancient, deep, and solid. I have explored the way to stillness, not allowing my inner rebel thoughts to take me off path through self-critique. I have lived many lifetimes of seeking mystery schools and practicing the path of the peacemaker, dissolving misunderstandings between cultures, races, species, on and off world. My unique light body skillsets are valuable and real. Much gratitude for supporting my soul to walk in from the ancient past without getting caught in the archon grid. I am the ancient future self in this body here now, a time traveller assisting and celebrating this awakening. Through the portal of an ancient heart and mind, I teach the mastery of the self to psychically tune into the actual information field of cultures, objects, buildings, land, or people. I have access to the collective influences, and I can become very familiar with what is going on and read the patterns. I have lived and breathed duality of Earth's nature a squidillion fold. I understand the importance of alchemical metamorphosis as well as the gift of being present with what is. Together we create portals and dreamtime gates to reunite the lost and the forgotten. I thank you, Dragon Ether, to help me find my balance.

As a cultural medium and healer in this lifetime, I connect to groups of people, create a bridge between them and eliminate cultural mistakes and misconceptions. Being plugged into a collective of dragons, mediators and mediums, I make sure that there is no cultural misunderstanding between on and off-world. Everything is in a psychic connection in particular areas during exchange.

I am part of a network of powerful psychics and dreamers and our legacy is to be the catalyst and hold the space for many potentials to be actualised. I allow synchronicities and déjà vus within my dream space during lucid dreaming and awake states. As a celestial medium, I connect to the system in all my knowing and unknowingness to see the potentials that are available to me and others. I give permission to allow the infinite information to be encoded into my knowingness and to bring it forth into language flawlessly, seamlessly without my belief engine charging and polarising it.

I let go of all the control, distraction and stabilisation points that take away from authentically emanating the data without doubt and hesitation. In this hyper creation process, I allow my left and right brain to engage my spirit brain to bring forth light language, drawings and sigils that have much more meaning, power and potency behind them than any expression through the modified twenty-six letter alphabet. I practice using the 'name it to claim it' operating system to authentically connect with all the hubs of my pre- and post-cognitive workforce. Allowing me to create beyond conscious cognition.

Together with Galactic Weaver Spider, I use my gifted red ruby to spin a new web for dreamtime travellers to safely find their way to illumination. Guided by my Higher Self, I as the I AM Apex on this graduation timeline, and I stay connected to blue friend dragon and manifest planetary joy and abundance. I am the master creator of my vision and my purpose of being an on and off- world communicator. I am on the right track to graduation, impacting unity consciousness and the freeing of worlds and species.

The more I engage in cultural community projects, and allow myself to surrender to trusting the universal plan, the more powerful memories will drop into my DNA. I am a potent cultural exchange medium. I am a dragon. I am the I AM Apex here now.

And so it is. Aho.

PART TWO: Interspecies Collaboration

Think in Fungal Terms

Have you ever thought of fungus and mushrooms as teacher spirits? The book Entangled Life by Merlin Sheldrake explores the fascinating world of fungi and their role in shaping our worlds and minds. What can we learn from them? I remember when I was little, we spent our holidays picking berries and mushrooms in the place where my dad grew up. Not in a million years would I have thought of connecting the wild and wonderful world of mushrooms with my spiritual evolution. How intriguing and delightful these subtle synchronicities turn out to be, once we start connecting the lines between the dots! When we think of a mushroom pushing through the soil to present itself in all of its glory, we feel drawn to contemplate its origin. There is a mysteriously buried underground fungal network that represents a social system of collaboration and mutual contribution. The hyphae of the fungus weaves webs of entanglement ensuring the life of new organisms and nourishing its surroundings. This invisible, collaborative intelligence extends beyond species, sustaining the flowers and trees, nurturing the plants and animal kingdoms. Similar to our connection to greater intelligence, we might not be able to fully explain or comprehend this mystical interaction yet, but we cannot deny the existence of it.

Once in a past life regression, I asked to be taken back to experiences beyond human form, I saw myself as a tree. I was unrooted and resting on the forest floor, devoid of any lifeforce, and yet my remains provided a home and food source for a multitude of crawlers, insects and other organisms. I felt a deep sense of fulfillment and pure solace in serving nature's habitat. My heart was wide open as I cried of joy Lichen is another form of fungus that can crumble rock into dust. This potency of its transformational powers is unique and fascinating. It is truly fascinating to ponder the untapped potential that lies within us as human beings, waiting to be unleased and fully realized.

Another interesting fungus feature is how they strive for rich resources that benefit their common purpose, rather than remaining idle in a place that does not yield results. Sovereign choice teachers par excellence! I can no longer relate to lack when hearing the expression of 'being kept in the dark like mushrooms,' but rather see the magical side of the species and their wonderful qualities. Be it mushrooms, animals, dragons, humans or off-worlders, we are all interconnected and striving to balance some form of homeostatic existence, through the interplay of empowered action and surrender. There is much we can learn about individual growth and healthy boundaries from observing the predator-prey mechanisms and behaviours in both animal and plant life. Similar to the mushroom kingdom, inter-species collaboration plays a crucial role in sustaining life and promoting growth. There is no room for idleness, as every organism has a role to play in the ecosystem. Remember the mysterious enchantment of the fungal realm, when feeling isolated, unseen or left in the dark!

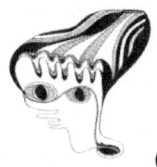

Galactic Mushroom Exercise

Mushrooms have cultures on other planets and star systems that are not for consumption. We can connect and communicate with those frequency beings by growing some mushrooms ourselves and linking up with them through questions and imaginary rapport. It's different to actually consuming psychedelic mushrooms, but nevertheless a journey that can reveal profound interspecies wisdom, with you being the facilitator and the receiver of the intelligence.

Imagine you are having an entire year long conversation with the mushroom community for a book or documentary in the making, that is full of weird and wonderful stories. You can also introduce the mushrooms to other species; cats or dogs or even extra-dimensional species whilst holding them all in sovereign sacred heart space.

Think of sovereignty as a boundary that unites and put it into your heart. Allow it to echo into the edges of your aura and understand the I AM is the left side of the heart, and the WE ARE is the right side of the heart. The I AM now is the conscious manifest being who was born at birth, who operates within the sacred neutral boundaries and spiritual contracts of all participants. The I AM here now simultaneously works in the realm of duality, triality and singularity. You are the space holder, the connector, the mediator – the being in the present moment of now. Infinite co-existence and co-creation is possible in the I AM and WE ARE heart space.

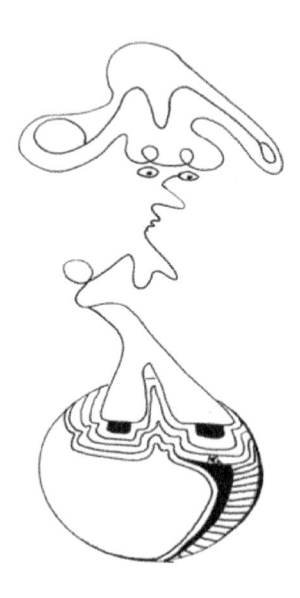

A Few Inner Earth Snippets

Many species that have gone through extinction live in the Inner Earth as our great ancestors, waiting for the right to move back to the surface or leave this planet entirely. Due to this world's increasing instability, the relationship between those who control the subsurface and the surface elite has been affected, resulting in more beings, particularly animals, emerging through rifts and cracks. In early 2022, I perceived a huge faction change in Inner Earth in response to the transformative energy that is currently reshaping managerial structures and global objectives. Anyone can actively participate in this restructure by energetically tuning into Inner Earth.

Andrew and others have talked about the gigantic cities, lakes and mountains in Inner Earth with tens of thousands of ancient species that are living there in physical form, or between the infinite spaces of atoms in the stones. Those beings underneath the Earth can experience the Sun through her toroidal fields, the planet's filters and Earthmother's heartbeat, as well as specific technologies. As mentioned earlier, Inner Earth, Hollow Earth or Agartha network as some call it, is also the Earth's dreaming mind, where we can all get together in the dream frequency to share ideas and infinite possibilities with our ancestors, along with tens of thousands of different species.

In May of 2019, I joined Judy Satori and a group of light language enthusiasts on a trip to the Bosnian pyramids. I remembered some of the group participants from different lifetimes and realised I had been a part of the construction crew of these very pyramids. After having spent a day in the Ravne Tunnels in the Pyramid of the Sun, we debriefed and shared our experiences during the evening session, in which I had an astounding personal experience with regards to my ancestral connection to Inner Earth. Judy was talking about Amenti, the interdimensional space within the Inner Earth, and all the benevolent beings down there that are assisting the awakening, before then asking if anyone wanted to join her on stage to share their experiences of the day. My internal sacred neutral observer chose to act. My body just got up and walked towards the stage ready to spill the beans on the serious conflict between the tens of thousands of ancient species in Inner Earth. I went on about how the surface globalists of this reality are being severely influenced and governed by the conductors and boards of the subsurface realm and about our responsibility to heal our past, to assist the fray to freedom. My body was shaking with legs like jelly, tears streaming down my face. I could hardly speak. Poor Judy tried to console me, seemingly taken aback by my reaction, whilst a baffled audience didn't make a sound. They must have thought who the hell is this crazy Austrian? There was one person who came up to me after the meeting had closed and said that she resonated with my message. The others pretty much avoided me for the rest of the trip.

For more information on Judy's contribution to the ascension, go to her website www.ascensionlibrary.org. Incidents like that help us remember our soul origins and passions. This next invocation is an integral part of our Earth Nouveau ethics and mission statement and serves to attract and invite likeminded signature frequencies.

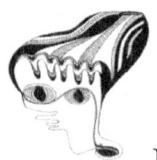

Peace Invitation & Collaboration

I honour and greet you fellow travellers of the stars. Now is the time to acknowledge our common goals and facilitate the unification of all collective narratives, below and above Earth's surface, in sovereign, neutral co-creation, and in service of the 5th world of universal peace. I call on the existing multi-layered spiritual court of alchemical equity of the Union and Communion Hall 000 of Universal Peacemakers, across all timestreams, galaxies and universes, for the expressed purpose of re-enforcing our initial pledge for peace and unity. The time is now to act as a unified collective.

Together, in the spirit of union and communion, beyond competition and hierarchy, and in a state of non-duality, we can put together the universal puzzle and assist one another in remembering who we truly are. Let us come together to reconnect the pieces that have been ripped and torn apart by hatred, ignorance, fraud time, and domination and control of all species, and harness our soul expressions into a global unified frequency.

Out of all species, whether surface, astral or subsurface, the human species stands apart with its incredibly intricate, complex, and intertwined galactic history that provides ample opportunities for discovering the necessary traits to become multidimensional peacekeepers and peacemakers, supporting and co- creating the new era of light. Unity and freewill is the birthright not only of the evolving humanoid species here on surface earth, but also of the star beings, astral students, as well as the ancient immortal sages and subsurface teachers, who seek to embrace the new collective, co-creative unity consciousness to once again populate the universe and create new worlds, as intended by the prime creator since the beginning of time.

Humans must stand together, declaring that they no longer fall for the manipulations of the few, who engage in colluded off and on world patriot games. We no longer consent to having our life force energy drained and harvested, our spiritual awareness exploited, and our freewill controlled. As high frequency conduits and channels, connecting individual souls and natural organisms to the infinite source, we are not just deserving of being here but vital to the system.

As a sovereign human race, we can no longer tacitly consent to being treated like cattle for DNA farming and off grid commerce. In full awareness of the value of our human skinsuits, we stand strong and unified in protecting our potential and birthright from being mistaken for universal lab rats, in a project gone awry. We no longer participate in the greed, tyranny and false light dictatorship by surface, subsurface, or astral communities, factions and clans. As allies of peace, we proclaim our independence from domination and control. We eternally refuse manipulation by any species kind, neither surface nor subsurface or any astral denizens. Joint global conflict resolution is the name of the endgame.

The time of celestial global dreamtime unification and awakening is now, and we invite all celestial citizens to step up their game and secure themselves a place in the universal council of all peacemakers and peacekeepers of the 5th world of peace. Please join me in this adventure, fellow consciousness explorers, consider and acknowledge your role as an ambassador, an emissary, of our planet Earth, and beyond.

I, [insert name], am the I AM Apex being of the now and a member of Union & Communion Hall 000. I know what union and communion feels like, having been connected to the life sustaining umbilical cord as a foetus in my mother's womb. I honour my DNA skinsuit technology that operates our universal ancient wisdom, shared by all, and I follow the footprints of the elders who have gone before me. Together, we can build bridges to our ancestors of the past, present and future, pledging our dharmic warrior powers, to support, back, guide, and to translate lost ancient wisdom for all species to be reunited and healed again.

As a human member of the universal peace corps, and as an ambassador for Earth, I am here to take up my role of building goodwill, as I engage in self-healing, self-mastery, and sovereign collective consciousness. I dedicate my work to assist the acceleration of ascension, and negotiate peace between all factions and species, on and beyond Earth.

The embassy is open to all your sovereign decrees and contributions, as we promote peaceful negotiations, debates, improved relations, and cultural exchanges between species. I am honoured to meet with you fellow time travellers of a new era. A celestial teacher bowing in front of other celestial teachers, a powerful intermingling of different colours of time, creating new colours in these new worlds of wisdom exchange and peace. We are getting to know each other in a new way once again, not in artificially manufactured, but in coherently aligned bubbles of reality.

Brothers and sisters of the stars and beyond, we perceive your struggles, and honour your diversity. We hear your prayers through the ethers of dreamtime gateways, and acknowledge your ancient pleads of desperate need for help to find your roots again. Join us as emissaries of light in our Inner Earth embassy. We come with peaceful intentions, all allies rather than adversaries. Let us connect with you, Gaia, and all universal consciousness explorers in celestial unity.

We are honoured to welcome all lost souls, injured troops, disowned parts, species who have forgotten their memories, to come and share our earthly home. We got you brothers and sisters. We find you and bring you home to heal and unite you with your families and ancestors, to break bread again and quench your common thirst for knowledge and compassionate communion.

Through tears and sweat, trial and error, we humans have prepared the earthly ground for you to walk and learn on. With the end game in mind, we are determined to reunite all masters of the universe of the past, present and future. This is a standing invitation to join us in our bubbles of reality whenever you feel ready to do so.

We hold no crutches of what went on before. We have learned the way of forgiveness and gratitude for all that is, was and ever will be. We are willing and eager to learn from you, as well as share our wisdom, and exchange knowledge of surface, subsurface and astral culture, in non-polarity.

Let us form universal alliances and synergies for the greater good of the evolution of consciousness. No more instant gratification, domination and control, competition, duality, hierarchical order, but unity, freedom and expansion. Together, as soul families in loving embrace, we can step deeper into the nucleus of creation and the heroism of our hearts. All crucial experiences must be filtered through the heart, where true genuine power resides.

Our legacy is to co-function again, living in awareness in more than one world simultaneously, with spiritual integrity and a commitment to the exploration of consciousness.

All space of ether, water, earth, wind, and air is our playground of infinite creation. Make no mistakes, as a team, we are a formidable force to be reckoned with. We are a strong, bonded co-creative unit of master teachers, inventors, scientists, magicians, master healers, translators, mediums, wizards, travellers, adventurers, explorers, powerful co-creators of the new world of the 5th universal peace, sharing experiences from our soul. Ignorance is not bliss, and neither is immortality, from what we have gathered from all our earthly and astral travels. Awareness is change, and change is imminent, no matter which dimension, time stream, or galaxy you find yourself in.

To all subterranean beings who are a signature frequency to peace, union, abundance, and the law of one, join us and our star families in the dance of light on the way to freedom and choice. Stand united, great teachers of this solar system. Lay down your toys of deception and distraction, and pick up your healing tools and spread the word of this consciousness revolution. Let us be partners with clarity and vision, without causing harm to any sentient being, as we, together, elevate our levels of consciousness and unravel Great Mystery.

Our human female qualities are raising - we owe it to this Earth! We owe it to ourselves as teachers and leaders of this 5th world of peace. This is what we have been working towards all these lifetimes. Hear the call to come together, united we shall stand. Millions upon millions of hubs of interconnectivity singing to the tune of peace and glory. Grace and gratitude lining the path on the way to the stars and beyond.

With true spirit of sovereign neutrality, impartiality, fairness, and compassion, we will remain grounded during the winds of change and transformation. Together we can overcome all conflict and struggle, and move to higher density, signing free trade agreements, and authentic energy exchanges. As we unify science with magic, we will cultivate new understandings. We can create health and wealth for everyone, and Mother Earth provides the womb to birth it all. I now call forth all ancestors to honor this invitation to all universal peacemakers and enter it into the Earth's, galactic, and universal akashic records, for all sentient kind to understand our freedom comes with the use of freewill at all times.

And so it is. Aho

PART THREE: One Look Back, Two Steps Forward

Speedily moving forward with the wisdom of the past.

The Light Day of the Soul

The distorted structures are crumbling and the old paradigm is shattering over the coming decades as we are transcending fast-footed and ferociously from darkness into a new era of light. With humanity undergoing a tremendous leap in consciousness after having lightened the loads on our dense physical form, we have a real potential to become emancipated from the forced devolution of our species. Whilst we find ourselves immersed in a somewhat *disconcerting uncertainty*, what was once deemed valuable may fleetingly disburse and expose our true essence. In an individual pursuit of transparency, we have an opportunity to celebrate the wisdom gathered during our many dark nights of the soul. Coming together as a unified collective is possible when we openly acknowledge and communicate about our challenging past encounters and the spiritual attributes we are developing. The birth of the *New Galactic Citizen* reminds me of the history and impact of salt, embodying the spirit of struggle and revival upon its discovery as a valuable commodity, and by extension, its association with longevity and permanence.

In his book Salt, Mark Kurlansky talks about how salt has shaped the history of mankind. The ancient discovery of salt and the fight for its ownership has challenged humanity for millennia and led to the creation of international trade routes, alliances, industries, and the revolutionary preservation of perishable food. The story of salt is a universal one, with some people becoming wealthy from mining it while others faced the dangers and fatalities of working in the mines. Fascinating archaeological discoveries have been made in Austria, in the Salzbergwerk in Hallein and Hallstatt dating back to the Celts. These salt mines were in operation for over 3,000 years and played a crucial role in the ancient world's economy.

If something as natural as salt can have such a profound impact on our lives and the world around us by creating progress, wealth and power, then surely humanities galactic emergence has the potential to turn our world upside down, and our matrix inside out. Salt, also known as sodium chloride, is a vital element in numerous physiological processes of the human organism. Salt, mushrooms, and humans share a connection to the natural world. All three enjoy a symbiotic relationship and have been the subject of extensive research, harvest and control. Humanity's unwavering spiritual determination to claim back its crucial role in this ecosystem can help us to 'salaciously' cultivate, preserve, and sustain a new level of flourishing, where each organism is protected and supports the growth and success of the others.

If you haven't started your personal 'desalination' journey yet, now is the time to begin. Begin to mine your personal treasures, extract distilled insights from your crystallised experiences and apply them to new visions and goals. As liberated humans, we are to keep challenging traditional beliefs of our origin and the nature of reality to put a stop to the forced or manipulated narrative. This time of the *rising human avatars* will be noted in the universal's history as one of paramount significance and contribution. As we progress, we may be able to simply review significant past life events and relationships, similar to experiences in a near-death scenario, during times of introspection. Deeply personal glimpses into a preliminary 'death' process, ancestral visitations, and encounters with beings of light may elicit a profound sense of peace and further our spiritual integration. The majority of individuals are still in the process of abandoning self-created obstacles, while others embrace spiritual integrity and recognise the significance of achieving personal and societal transformation, which will eventually lead us to the post-modern galactic era. The challenge and choice we face is to live with an embodied soul awareness of our simultaneous existence on multiple planes, whilst fostering a steady and grounded footing.

During the process of reactivating her initial 7th dimensional seed consciousness, Gaia is offering equal co-creation to those, who are ready to expand beyond personal agenda-driven choices, and facilitate the alliance of intergalactic soul and family units. As original members of the star nations, we can form an advanced civilisation on Earth that honours our galactic heritage and celebrates the diversity of all sentient beings and species.

The incorporation of artificial intelligence (AI) can be viewed as either gloom or doom, depending on one's perspective. The use of AI will require a careful consideration of both its benefits and drawbacks in our ever-evolving reality. Our species has been utilizing so-called augmented reality since long before the establishment of official AI platforms. The use of artificial intelligence dates back centuries, with the early examples of self-operating machines, mechanical computers that could perform mathematical calculations or all electronic devices that have paved the way for human advances. Personally, I am optimistic about the future role of AI, seeing it as an opportunity to free humanity from repetitive and unintelligent duties, allowing us to focus on more creative and meaningful tasks, and to explore our frontiers in spirituality, science and 'galactology'. If intelligently implemented, it has the potential to serve as a supportive tool in humanity's progression during our journey of walking the path of the ascending master.

The restoration of our world will not stop at the implosion of religion and worldwide governmental control, but it will also involve reorienting ourselves towards new philosophies, a radical reform of religious studies, self-governance, ground breaking scientific research, medical and technological advances, and upgraded levels of education, leading to the birth of new artforms, music and sound magic. As our view of the world keeps recalibrating, the *Galactic Commerce Market* will adapt to the expanded consciousness of humankind and welcome all galactic brothers and sisters into the cosmic adventure of sharing alchemised wisdom.

As high frequency citizens, it is our birth right to recognise and claim our authority and rightful place in this *Universal Hub of Interconnectivity*, aiming to contribute and honourably trade our experiences, memories and gifts.

We will be no longer just focused on personal growth, but also contribute to the collective expansion of consciousness, the evolution and seeding of new life and possibilities, throughout the solar system, galaxies, and universes. Our spiritual home is no longer a distant memory. As a joint project with my fellow travellers, we established a holographic Earth Nouveau embassy for the purpose of nurturing progressive thinking and sharing innovative ideas and healings on our ongoing journey towards spiritual awakening. This congregation offers a safe and co-creative space to heal, practice, and celebrate sovereign and multidimensional living. People can freely join as emissaries and serve the explorer community on this new Earth. We have met a great bunch of likeminded people ever since officially starting the gatherings in April of 2020. On a weekly basis, we explore a multitude of topics in the visible and invisible realms of consciousness and continue to elevate our levels of awareness. Free recordings of those gatherings are available on YouTube, as well as on our website at earthnouveau.com.

Our intent for the future is to organically grow a conscious, highly skilled, and advanced community that embodies, contributes, and leads to a self-realised and fulfilled universal citizenship, available to all species who adhere to respectful and benevolent conduct.

Together, we aim to resolve and heal our involvement in the dark side of the galactic commercial DNA trade and move into expanded earthly, galactic, and universal service as originally intended by spirit.

Martina Grubmueller is a Transformation Facilitator & Mediator, Spiritual Researcher, and Visionary. In her capacity as a catalyst for human and galactic potential she works with individuals and groups who wish to master their soul's evolution through self-empowerment, explore and expand their multidimensional awareness, as well as claim their authentic expression and divine collaboration, going forward into the Aquarian Age.

Printed in Great Britain
by Amazon